Macintosh

WEST'S COMPUTER LITERACY
SYSTEM INTEGRATOR

Linda A. Hardman
Tomball Independent School District
Tomball, Texas

Carroll K. Melnyk
Lubbock Independent School District
Lubbock, Texas

Steven L. Mandell
Bowling Green State University
Bowling Green, Ohio

Gary Bitter
Arizona State University
Tempe, Arizona

West Publishing Company
St. Paul   New York   Los Angeles   San Francisco

Production, Prepress, Printing and Binding by West Publishing Company.

COPYRIGHT © 1993 by   WEST PUBLISHING CO.
610 Opperman Drive
P.O. Box 64526
St. Paul, MN 55164–0526

ISBN 0–314–00824–1

CONTENTS

Appendices:

Preface

Learning System

The *Learning System* is an electronic multimedia instructional system employing interactive software. The system will provide comprehensive training in:
- the use of commercial word processing software.
- the use of commercial database management software.
- the use of commercial spreadsheet software.
- the use of telecommunications, desktop publishing and graphic design.
- history and development of computers.
- problems and issues of computer usage in society.
- communicating instructions to the computer.

The Learning System, available on three different computer platforms, utilizes *West's Computer Literacy System* text, exercises and activities, assessment tools and videodisc. For a more detailed description of the *Learning System* see Appendix D.

Introduction to the Text - Computers: Tools for Today

Computers are everywhere today. In fact, personal computers are almost taken for granted, similar to television and microwave ovens. The key is for people to make use of them. That is the intent of the book *Computers: Tools for Today*.

Organization of the Text

Students learn more when they work with computers than when they just read about them. Therefore, *West's Computer Literacy System* has been organized so that they are alternately reading the book, doing Practicing Computer Skills, using HyperCard for computer instruction, and actively participating with the videodisc in discovering how computers are used as tools today. Some of the exercises are based on Microsoft Works, and others help them learn how to problem solve with the HyperTalk programming language. In addition, exercises, based on the WestSoft programs, are designed to simulate real-life experiences with computers: home banking, ticket office management, and on-line information services.

The book contains three sections that help students use computers to do a job, learn about computers in general, and, using problem solving strategies, make computers do new jobs.

Part I, "Computer Applications," demonstrates the Microsoft Works word processor, database, and spreadsheet programs for Macintosh computers. Part I discusses how to use telecommunications and desktop publishing, both important applications in our ever-changing world.

Part II, "Computer Concepts," discusses the history of computers, examines computer hardware, discusses using computers responsibly, finds computers in the world around us, and investigates computer careers.

Part III, "Computer Programming," explores various programming languages, investigates problem solving with computers, and introduces the HyperTalk programming language. This section shows students how the computer can be made to do what they want it to do and helps them develop strategies for solving a specific problem using the HyperTalk programming language.

Each chapter of the book component of the *Computer Literacy System* has several study aids:

1. Projected learning outcomes give students an idea of what is coming in the chapter.
2. Chapter outlines show the major topics in a chapter, and also helps students prepare for the material they are expected to learn.
3. Margin definitions provide conveniently located meanings for terms used in the chapter and offer a form of summary or review for material in the chapter.
4. Learning checks enable students to test their knowledge of the facts and concepts in the chapter.
5. Summary points provide a short review.
6. Chapter highlights offer interesting material in an informal manner. They are planned to correspond with the material in a given chapter.
7. Discussion questions provide the challenging opportunity for in-depth thinking about the material in the chapter. They can be used in an actual class discussion or for relevant homework.
8. Activities and Enrichment Activities challenge the student's ability to use and understand computers as tools beyond the structure of the book. These can also be used for class activities or individual work.
9. The Chapter Review offers a self test before students take the chapter tests.
10. In Part III, programming hints list some new material about HyperTalk and some things to watch for while writing programs.
11. A glossary and an index complete the book.

The book includes several appendices, listed here:

1. Appendix A: Microsoft Works Complete Command Summary
2. Appendix B: Microsoft Works Advanced Features
3. Appendix C: HyperTalk Commands and Statements
4. Appendix D: Keyboarding
5. Appendix E: ASCII Table

Software

Computers: Tools for Today is designed to incorporate the commercial software Microsoft Works as the application tool for students to use. Any version of Microsoft Works may be used with the text. Chapters one through six cover the word processing, database, and spreadsheet programs thoroughly. Some of the later chapters use Microsoft Works in the Practicing Computer Skills exercises and/or the end of chapter exercises. For example, Chapter 7, Looking Back, has students use a History database and gather information from the chapter to complete it.

Included with the textbook is a student disk which contains Microsoft Works files for the students to use along with the Practicing Computer Skills exercises and the end of chapter exercises. The disk is designed to use with any version of Microsoft Works. Another disk for students contains the WestSoft simulation programs and data files for the appropriate Practicing Computer Skills exercises.

Also included with the text is a teacher's disk which contains hands-on tests for assessing mastery of the computer.

Practicing Computer Skills

Practicing Computer Skills are hands-on activities provided in blackline master form for reproduction. They can be used as transparency masters or duplicated for each student's individual workstation. The authors have organized the book so that teachers may integrate the reading of the text and doing the Practicing Computer Skills exercises at the computer. Some of the exercises are based on Microsoft Works and others help the student with HyperTalk programming. In addition, three chapters have exercises based on the WestSoft programs that are designed to simulate three real-life experiences with computers: home banking, ticket office management, and on-line information services.

The Practicing Computer Skills exercises can be used either to introduce computer skills or provide practice after the text explains a procedure. Items that students see on the screen are printed in a different type and items that students should enter into the computer are printed in still a different type. The keys to be pressed appear between brackets. For example, "Press [Return]."

Computer systems and procedures vary from school to school. For this reason, most of the Practicing Computer Skills exercises ask students only to access or load a piece of software or a file. Only the first time the software is loaded or HyperTalk is accessed are students told exactly what to do. This practice enables teachers to use the text without having to change instructions to fit their computer laboratories.

Videodisc

The videodisc vividly illustrates the computer used as a tool with real-life examples of computers at work and play. Short film clips can be used as "attention-getters" to introduce each chapter. Stills can be used instead of transparencies to unfold an idea and enhance vocabulary review. Unlike transparencies, the stills can bring the material to life with beautiful colors and graphics along with actual computer screens. The figures contained in the text are also contained on the videodisc. The videodisc contains a vast amount of electronic information that is current, graphic, and interesting. For further information about using the videodisc, see Appendix A: West Computer Literacy System Videodisc Index and User's Guide.

The Learning System also has authoring software available. Lecture Builder software is a user friendly authoring package developed specifically for use with West videodiscs. It allows teachers to customize the videodisc presentations prior to class and to deliver the presentation without the use of a hand held remote control. Customizing allows the teacher to select and order items from any section on the disc. You can also edit video clips and still frame sequences.

To deliver the presentation stored on the computer, the teacher simply presses the [Return] key on the computer and advances to the next image. This process eliminates the need to enter codes with the remote control while presenting the lesson. Available for IBM PC/ compatibles and Macintosh computers.

Electronic Media

The HyperCard lessons lead the student through concepts on the computer. Each lesson consists of a HyperCard stack and a worksheet. They may be used to introduce, review, or assess concepts.The lesson is given by the computer but allows individualized instruction through interaction between the computer and the student. Material that students did not understand the first time can be repeated. Thus students can work at their own pace. Answers to the HyperCard worksheets are in Appendix C.

Transparency Masters

Transparency masters are included for every chapter to be used at the teacher's discretion. These may include specific examples from the text, pictures of the computer screen, discussion items, and other useful items to help in preparing a successful lesson.

Authentic Assessment

Several forms of assessment are available with *West's Computer Literacy System*. Paper and pencil tests, skills tests, portfolio assessment and computerized testing are included. Also, the HyperCard stacks and worksheets could be used as assessment. Each chapter has two paper and pencil tests (Form A and Form B). The two tests are very similar and can be used as a test and a re-test or could be used as a review and a test.

Each chapter also has a Skills Test accompanying it. This test uses knowledge gained from the chapter, the Practicing Computer Skills exercises and the end of chapter exercises in a hands-on test on the computer. Students either create a file or alter a file following directions on the Skills Test sheet. These tests are brief so that several students could use the same computer for testing during one class period.

A third assessment tool is the portfolio sheets accompanying each chapter. The use of open-ended questioning, mappings, and activity-oriented exercises allows a different type of assessment of student understanding.

Computerized testing is available through Westest 2.0 which allows the teacher to create, edit, store and print exams. The system is menu driven with a desktop format and offers the options of using keystrokes or a mouse, accelerator keys and function keys. All of this makes the program quick and easy to use. Westest 2.0 users can randomly generate or selectively choose questions, add new or edit existing questions, use summaries of the tests, set up and preview their pages and print (the test, answer sheet, answer key, or the entire test bank). This software also makes it possible for users to import graphics. Available for IBM PC/compatibles and Macintosh computers.

Introduction to the Teacher's System Integrator

The *System Integrator* pulls together all of the components of the *Computer Literacy System* : printed materials (including the text, worksheets, and Practicing Computer Skills), videodisc, and instructional software. This conveniently brings together all of the components of the package to reduce teacher preparation time. It also allows for a teacher to use the various components in a way that is best suited to his or her own teaching style with complete flexibility. Each chapter of the *System Integrator* contains these elements:

Chapter Overview:

The Chapter Overview begins each chapter. It contains information about the videodisc, suggested additional resources, projected learning outcomes, vocabulary terms, chapter overview, teaching resources, and teaching strategies.

• Videodisc - The title, length, and description for the videodisc clip for use with the chapter is given. A bar code is provided so that if a scanner or wand is available, the teacher can automatically move to the particular video clip section on the disc.

• Suggested Additional Resources - A list of suggested additional resources such as reference materials, magazine articles, telecommunications networks, and software is provided to further aid the teacher to enhance the presentation of the lesson.

• Projected Learning Outcomes - Each projected learning outcome for the chapter is listed to help the teacher sense the overall objectives for the chapter. The outcomes are designed to be knowledge-based, as well as skills-based.

• Vocabulary Terms - A list of all vocabulary words are given in the order they are presented in the chapter. These words are used in the reading and defined in the margins of the student's textbook.

• Chapter Overview - The chapter overview summarizes the key points of the entire chapter. This helps the teacher understand the focus of the chapter and what key material will be covered.

• Teaching Resources - All resources for the entire chapter are included to give an overall sense of possible student exercises. These resources include the Practicing Computer Skills; Worksheets for Activities, Vocabulary, and Reteaching; Transparencies; and HyperCard lessons.

• Teaching Strategies - Suggested teaching strategies are included to aid the teacher, give new ideas, and reduce teacher preparation time. The following types of strategies are included:

- Opening - ideas, discussion questions, activities for introducing the chapter
- Teaching tips - suggestions and activities for enhancing instruction
- When and how - indicates a suggested order for presentation of material through the chapter
- Observation - suggestions of things to look for as students work on activities or on the computers
- Computer demonstration - ideas to help instruction of difficult commands or sequences of steps by using the computer to demonstrate
- Classroom management - suggestions concerning ways to organize the classroom and student materials
- Cooperative learning - activities that lend themselves to cooperative learning are suggested
- Writing activities - suggestions for writing assignments that align with the material in the chapter
- Trouble shooting - indicates potential spots in the chapter where students may have difficulty
- Reteaching - suggestions for further activities, presentation, or demonstrations to help students having difficulty
- Interdisciplinary learning - activities that incorporate other curriculum areas are suggested
- Closing - ideas, discussion questions, activities for closing the chapter

Assessment - Several forms of assessment are available for use:
- Chapter test (Form A and Form B)
- Skills test - a hands-on test on the computer to indicate the student's skill at working with the word processor, the database, the spreadsheet or programming.
- Portfolio exercises - open-ended questioning, mappings, and activity-oriented exercises allows a different type of assessment of student understanding.

Lesson Overviews:

Each chapter is divided into lessons ending with a Learning Check exercise. Each lesson contains the projected learning outcomes, vocabulary terms, overview, and resources for that particular lesson. Answers to the Practicing Computer Skills, worksheets, and learning check are included. Where needed, the computer screen display is provided for the Practicing Computer Skills exercises. The last lesson overview for each chapter also contains the answers and/or computer screen display for the Computer Skills test for the chapter.

Chapter Summary:

Each chapter ends with summary points and answers to the discussion questions, activities, onrichment activities, and chapter review. When appropriate, computer screen displays are shown.

Appendices:

Appendix A: West Computer Literacy System Video Disk

Appendix B: Chapter Tests Answers (Form A and B)

Appendix C: HyperCard Answers

Appendix D: Learning System

WEST'S COMPUTER LITERACY
SYSTEM INTEGRATOR

● Chapter 1

 EXPLORING YOUR COMPUTER

DESCRIPTION: Length 2:57. An animated program shows the basics of how computers work. Computers and components including CPU units, disk drives, monitors, keyboards, and printers are shown.

Search to Chapter 1........Play

Suggested Additional Resources

● <u>Understanding Computers</u>, Third Edition, by Grace Murray Hopper and Steven L. Mandell, West Publishing Co.
● Telecommunications networks and bulletin boards - CREN, TENET, DIALOG, PRODIGY, or a local bulletin board for your city, state.
● Computer magazines

 PROJECTED LEARNING OUTCOMES

After studying the concepts and practicing the skills in this chapter, students should be able to:

● Distinguish between what a computer can do and what it cannot do.
● Describe the three steps of data processing.
● Tell the meaning of computer terms such as data, information, hardware, software, peripheral device, read, and so on.
● Name the parts of a microcomputer system and tell the purpose of each.
● Explain the purpose and the two types of software.
● Show the ability to use and care for computer equipment and disks.

 VOCABULARY TERMS

Computer	Information
Program	Hardware
Keyboard	Peripheral device
Monitor	Software
Disk	System software
Disk drive	Application software
Read	Programming language
Microcomputer	Compatible
Primary memory	Printer
Secondary memory	Kilobyte (K)
Data processing	Character
Input	Cursor
Processing	Command
Calculate	Floppy disk
Output	Access
Soft copy	Load
Hard copy	Simulation
Data	Menu

Exploring Your Computer

CHAPTER OVERVIEW

● Computers process data electronically. Data processing follows a basic flow: input, processing, and output. Data—the input—are symbols for events, things, and facts. The computer acts on the data—that is, processes it. The output, or result, of processing is information, which is the meaning given to a set of data.

● Computers cannot act like people, but they can do many different tasks very quickly. They can calculate, make comparisons, and store data and return it to you.

● The physical parts of a computer system are called hardware. Hardware includes the computer itself and peripheral devices such as monitors, keyboards, disk drives, and printers. Some hardware—such as the keyboard—is used for input, and some—such as monitors and printers—is used for output. The disk drives are used for both input and output because they can get data and programs from disks and can record data and programs onto disks.

● Software is the program or set of programs that make the computer do its work. Software must be compatible with the computer in order to run.

● Treat equipment and disks carefully to avoid damaging parts or losing data. Keep food, dust, and dirt away from equipment, and avoid creating static electricity around the equipment.

● A program that imitates an event that happens in real life is called a simulation. The purpose of a simulated program is to teach the user how to do a certain task or to find out what might happen in a situation where particular conditions are present. The WestSoft program lets you try some simulations.

TEACHING RESOURCES

Practicing Computer Skills 1-1: Loading the WestSoft Software
The student is working in a ticket office that handles ticket sales for several theaters and arenas. The customers want tickets for concerts, plays, and sports events. The exercise guides the student through the loading of the ticket office software.

Practicing Computer Skills 1-2: Using the Ticket Office Simulation
The first customer would like four tickets to the September 15 matinee showing of the play *Annie*. The exercise lets the student choose seats and print out the tickets.

Practicing Computer Skills 1-3: Doing More Ticket Office Work
For this exercise, the student must use the simulation to perform prescribed tasks and answer questions regarding the steps taken and the results obtained.

Worksheet 1-1 VOCABULARY. Computer Terms: Write in computer terms in sentences describing computer operations.

Worksheet 1-2 VOCABULARY. Computer Vocabulary: Match up terms of physical components with categories such as software.

Worksheet 1-3 RETEACHING. Data Processing: Fill in the blanks in a table showing the input, processing and output elements of data processing.

Worksheet 1-4 RETEACHING. Working with a Computer: Write in computer terms in phrases on computer operations.

Worksheet 1-5 ENRICHMENT. Computer Resources: List resources to help in the study of computers.

Transparency Master 1A. The Human Edge: Lists things that humans can do and computers cannot.

Transparency Master 1B. Processing Functions: Lists examples of jobs that can be done with a computer and examples of their applications.

TEACHING RESOURCES
(continued)

Transparency Master 1C. Computer Room Guidelines: Basic guidelines for student behavior in the computer room.

Assessment:
HyperCard Stack. Parts of a Computer: Provides an introduction to what a computer is and does. Includes the terms input, output, processing & storage, hardware, and software. This is covered in more detail in Chapter 8, and may be covered then.
HyperCard Stack. Disk Anatomy: Introduces the parts of a 3.5 inch floppy disk (picture, explanation of its function, and how it works.)
HyperCard Worksheet. Disk Anatomy: Students will describe the use for the parts of a disk.

Test 1-A

Test 1-B

Portfolio 1. Learning About Your Computer: This portfolio will ask students to write answers to "thought provoking" questions, and to create and draw a concept map about data processing.

Skills Test 1. Students use the WestSoft disk and answer questions about the Ticket Office program.

TEACHING STRATEGIES

Opening. Several introductions exist to create interest in computers. The ideas include the following:
● Show a film.
● Draw out information from students who already use a computer.
● Compile a list of computer jargon--such as *byte, bus, boot, chip, menu, bug*--for discussion or for a student-prepared bulletin board.
● Plan a bulletin board with students about uses of computers.
● Do some computer demonstrations of games, graphics, or engineering.
● Discuss what students believe about the capabilities of computers.
● Prepare a display of computer equipment, books, and magazines.
● If students seem intimidated by the actual mechanical parts of the machine, show them the computers they will be using. Discuss the components, memory capacity, the keys, and so on.
● Make sure students know about responsible behavior in the computer room.

Teaching Tips. Students may offer information about computers at home and about ways computers affect them and their families in daily transactions. They may also discuss what happens when mistakes are made on a computer. Another important concept involves the power and limitations of computers. The section, *A Brief Look at Computers*, implies that the power of computers is attributed to speed and memory-- that is, the ability to handle huge amounts of data- -in a tireless fashion.
Scientists are trying to develop systems that are more human-like. Discuss how they have not yet designed computers that act like humans, or even the robots of science fiction. They cannot make decisions or judgments or give themselves instructions other than those directed by humans.

When & How.
1. Use ideas from the Opening strategy and the videodisc clip to begin the chapter.
2. To allow students quick access to using the computer, give students some time each day to practice keyboarding. Use Appendix D and the Practicing Computer Skills exercises as needed.

3. Often the term *feedback* is included among the steps of data processing. Discuss what the term means and how it might help insure the usefulness of output.

4. Use a variety of activities from the Teaching Strategies to maintain the students' initial enthusiasm about computers.

5. Use the HyperCard stacks, "Parts of a Computer," and "Disk Anatomy," and its worksheet for assessment, review, or to introduce terms and ideas.

Computer Demonstration. Use the WestSoft Ticket Office simulation to get students comfortable with using the equipment, pressing the keys, and using menus. Be sure they know where the special keys are, such as the [Delete] key if they make a mistake, and the [Return] key to register an entry.

Classroom Management. Students may begin individual notebooks that contain pictures and advertisements from magazines, newspaper and magazine articles, reports, tests, answers to learning checks, class notes, notes on the Practicing Computer Skills exercises, want ads for computer-related jobs, and other flat items. Photocopies are acceptable for magazine and newspaper articles.

Discuss with students the guidelines for computer use. Consider printer usage, storage of diskettes, and whether equipment will be left off or on after usage.

Cooperative Learning. Working in groups, students may prepare a questionnaire for their parents about computers. The questionnaire should have one chief focus--attitudes about computers, diversity of computer usage within families, or projections for the future, for example. If the questionnaires are used, data can be saved for the database module in Chapters 4 and 5.

Writing Activity. Before reading about computer care, have the students list their own ideas about good care of computer equipment. Then compare their ideas with the guidelines in this chapter. Students can also write three to five things that they believe about computers. After reading them, compile data on similar responses and pick several for discussion.

Trouble shooting. If the students have difficulty getting the computer to operate, check the plug and all cables to make sure that all connections are firm. If the disks are not being read, check the orientation of the disks in the drive, and make sure the actual disks are not scratched or dented.

Reteaching. After learning about data processing, have the students explain the sequence of activities used in data processing, such as input, processing, and output.

Interdisciplinary Learning. A scavenger hunt can be the starting point for computer items or pictures of computer items that students may not even have associated with computers. Display the items on a table and bulletin board. Items could include adding machines, an abacus, microwave ovens, self-adjusting thermostats, and so on.

Closing. Students can collect newspaper and magazine articles (or photocopies) for discussion about the things computers can do and about problems with computer equipment and operations.

Lesson 1 - 1

p.2 - p.9

 PROJECTED LEARNING OUTCOMES

After studying the concepts and practicing the skills in this lesson, students should be able to:

● Distinguish between what a computer can do and what it cannot do.
● Describe the three steps of data processing.
● Tell the meaning of computer terms such as data, information, hardware, software, peripheral device, read, and so on.

 VOCABULARY TERMS

Computer	Calculate
Program	Output
Keyboard	Soft copy
Monitor	Hard copy
Disk	Data
Disk drive	Information
Read	Hardware
Microcomputer	Peripheral device
Primary memory	Software
Secondary memory	System software
Data processing	Application software
Input	Programming language
Processing	Compatible

 **LESSON OVERVIEW**

● Computers process data electronically. Data processing follows a basic flow: input, processing, and output.
● Computers cannot act like people, but they can do many different tasks very quickly. They can calculate, make comparisons, and store data and return it to you.
● The physical parts of a computer system are called hardware. Hardware includes the computer itself and peripheral devices such as monitors, keyboards, disk drives, and printers.
● Software is the program or set of programs that make the computer do its work. Software must be compatible with the computer in order to run.

 **TEACHING RESOURCES**

Worksheet 1-1   VOCABULARY. Computer Terms: Write in computer terms in sentences describing computer operations. Use for a chapter review or as an introduction to find out what students already know about computers.
Answers:
programs
programmers
software
hardware
peripheral
system programs
compatible
command
menu
disk
primary
input
monitor
output
soft copy
hard copy
processing
information

Worksheet 1-3 RETEACHING. Data Processing: Fill in the blanks in a table showing the input, processing and output elements of data processing. Can be used to review or to introduce the data processing stages.
Answers:

Input:	typing on a keyboard
	loading from a disk
	data
Processing:	Calculate
	Compare
	command, or program
Output:	monitor; soft copy
	hard copy
	information

Transparency Master 1A. The Human Edge: Lists things that humans can do and computers cannot. Discuss what humans and computers can do. Give examples of each, also, using the three tasks (arithmetic, comparisons, storage) under the section *The Computer's Capabilities.*

TEACHING RESOURCES
(continued)

Transparency Master 1B. Processing Functions: Lists examples of jobs that can be done with a computer and examples of their applications. Discuss examples of the things computers do during processing.

☑ LEARNING CHECK 1-1
ANSWERS

1. arithmetic (adding), comparisons, storage and retrieval
2. Data processing came before computers; people have processed data ever since they have had things to count.
3. correct; complete
4. hard copy
5. to tell the computer what to do
6. c
7. buy a program, copy a program from a magazine or book, write your own program.
8. Owning different software allows for flexibility and choices for the best software for a particular situation.

Lesson 1 - 2

p.9 - p.19

 PROJECTED LEARNING OUTCOMES

After studying the concepts and practicing the skills in this lesson, students should be able to:

● Name the parts of a microcomputer system and tell the purpose of each.
● Explain the purpose and the two types of software.
● Show your ability to use and care for computer equipment and disks.

 VOCABULARY TERMS

Printer	Command
Kilobyte (K)	Floppy disk
Character	Access
Cursor	Load

LESSON OVERVIEW

● Some hardware—such as the keyboard—is used for input, and some—such as monitors and printers—is used for output. The disk drives are used for both input and output because they can get data and programs from disks and can record data and programs onto disks.
● Treat equipment and disks carefully to avoid damaging parts or losing data. Keep food, dust, and dirt away from equipment, and avoid creating static electricity around the equipment.
● Students should show responsible behavior around computers and show careful use of materials.
● While discussing the computer components, memory capacity, keys, and so on, show students the inside of the computer: main system board, add-on cards, chips, connections.
● A more detailed discussion of hardware is in Chapter 8.

 **TEACHING RESOURCES**

Worksheet 1-2 VOCABULARY. Computer Vocabulary: Match terms of physical components with categories such as software. Use as a worksheet now, or later as part of the chapter review.
Answers:
   1. b, h, p (r, d, f)
   2. i, j, q (e)
   3. d ,m, (k)
   4. f, h, l (d, q)
   5. e (h)
   6. f (d, q)
   7. a, k, (h ,l)
   8. o
   9. c, f, g, i
   10. e, i, q
   11. c, g, q
   12. q
   13. g, n (i)
   14. d, k

Worksheet 1-4 RETEACHING. Working with a Computer: Write in computer terms in phrases on computer operations. Use to review terms and rules for care.
Answers:

Top	Bottom
1. printer	1. c
2. keyboard	2. d
3. commands	3. c
4. menus	4. c
5. monitor	5. d
6. load	6. d
7. kilobytes	7. c, d
8. cursor	8. d
	9. c, d
	10. c, d

Worksheet 1-5 ENRICHMENT. Computer Resources: List resources to help in the study of computers. Useful for students interested in the first steps toward evaluating and studying computer equipment and other computer related items. Answers will vary depending on student's age and knowledge of computers and software.

Transparency Master 1C. Computer Room Guidelines: Basic guidelines for student behavior in the computer room. Other guidelines may need to be established depending on special classroom situations. Discussion question #7 could be used also.

LEARNING CHECK 1-2
ANSWERS —————————

1. c
2. before
3. floppy disk drives, hard disk drives
4. keyboard, disk drive
5. magnets, dust, food
6. It is important in using software, because different software packages have different memory requirements and also may come on a choice of 5.25-inch or 3.5-inch disks.

 **Lesson 1 - 3**

p.19 - p. 21

 PROJECTED LEARNING OUTCOMES

After studying the concepts and practicing the skills in this lesson, students should be able to:

● Learn the use of computer hardware and software by using a simulation.

 VOCABULARY TERMS

Simulation
Menu

LESSON OVERVIEW

● A program that imitates an event that happens in real life is called a simulation. The purpose of a simulated program is to teach the user how to do a certain task or to find out what might happen in a situation where particular conditions are present. The WestSoft program lets students try some simulations.
● Magazine and newspaper articles describing simulation software are useful. Simulations such as "Oregon Trail" from MECC and "SimCity" and "SimAnt" from Maxis Software are excellent examples for education.

 TEACHING RESOURCES

Practicing Computer Skills 1-1: Loading the WestSoft Software
The student is working in a ticket office that handles ticket sales for several theaters and arenas. The customers want tickets for concerts, plays, and sports events. The exercise guides students through the loading of the ticket office software. Ask students to demonstrate loading the software, point out the specific keys mentioned in question 2, and answer questions about the information read.

Practicing Computer Skills 1-2: Using the Ticket Office Simulation
The first customer would like four tickets to the September 15 matinee showing of the play *Annie*. The exercise lets students choose seats and print out the tickets. A printer should be available for this exercise. Ask students to describe or demonstrate selecting seats and printing tickets. Check that the correct tickets have been printed.

Practicing Computer Skills 1-3: Doing More Ticket Office Work
For this exercise, the student must use the simulation to perform prescribed tasks and answer questions regarding the steps taken and the results obtained.
Answers:
A.   1. Choose Sporting Events; choose Philadelphia Minuteman Hockey.
    2. This message appears: Tickets are not available for this event. Tickets will be available on October 1.
    3. Houston Barons
    4. Boston Tories
    5. Sept. 19, 20, 21, and 22, all at 7:15 p.m.
    6. This message appears: Sorry, those seats not available.
    7. Click on the Quit box, then on Return to preceeding menu, then on Return to TICKET MENU
B.   1. ten
    2. four
    3. Sept. 18, 21, 22, and 23
    4. six

TEACHING RESOURCES —————
(continued)

C.   1. Mary Goldstein
        2. Arthur Nichols
        3. Sept. 22 at 7 p.m. and Sept. 26 and 28
             at 8 p.m.
        4. This message appears: Tickets are not
available for this event. Tickets will be
available on October 1.
D.   1. Return to TICKET MENU, then Return to
MAIN MENU

LEARNING CHECK 1-3 ANSWERS —————

1. b
2. Click on the box next to the option.
3. Click on the box next to the option to return to the previous menu.
4. Please ready the printer, then click below to print.
5. Pull down the File menu and select Eject.
6. A medical student could practice diagnosing diseases or doing surgery.

PRACTICING COMPUTER SKILLS —————

1-1: Loading the WestSoft Software

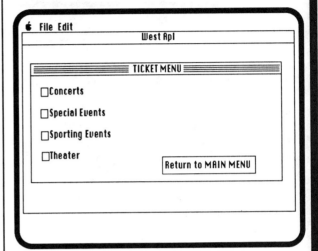

The TICKET MENU from the WestSoft program.

1-2: Using the Ticket Office Simulation

```
Annie
Sept 15  2:00pm  Matinee
Section 45  Row 26 Seat 12
```

A ticket printed using the Ticket Office simulation.

SKILLS TEST 1 ANSWERS —————

  1. Click on the box next to Ticket Office Manager
  2. 5
  3. Tickets are not available for this event. Tickets will be available on October 1.
  4. Mary Goldstein
  5. September 24 at 8:00 pm
  6. Houston Barons
  7. 7:15 pm
  8. This message appears: Sorry, those seats not available
  9. choose Return to MAIN MENU
10. choose Quit

● Chapter 1 Summary

SUMMARY POINTS

● Computers process data electronically and follow a basic flow: input, processing, and output.
● Computers cannot act like people, but can calculate, make comparisons, store data and return it to you more quickly than humans.
● The physical parts of a computer system are called hardware and include the computer itself and peripheral devices such as monitors, keyboards, disk drives, and printers.
● Software is the program or set of programs that make the computer do its work.
● Treat equipment and disks carefully to avoid damaging parts or losing data.
● A program that imitates an event that happens in real life is called a simulation. The WestSoft program lets you try some simulations.

DISCUSSION QUESTIONS

1. A calculator gets input when its keys are pressed, and does a variety of calculating jobs, commonly adding, subtracting, multiplying, and dividing. It produces output on a small flat screen display or on paper tape. A VCR receives input from a tape or when it is programmed to receive signals directly from a television. Processing involves reading the tape (retrieval) or storing the signal (storage). Output occurs when what is on the tape is shown on the TV screen.
A computer is different from a calculator in that it can do many jobs depending on the software, while a calculator is programmed internally to do only specific jobs. A computer is different from a VCR in that it does more than just play back what is input, it allows the user to interact with it.
2. A programmer has listed various responses that the computer can output, based on the kinds of input a user enters.
3. A computer cannot detect body language, or believe in a hero. It can offer a decision based on facts already input, but cannot detect a new factor.

4. Students may say they expect to learn word processing for writing reports in high school and college. They may want to use computers for communications, shopping, banking, and so on.
5. Proper care maintains the integrity of data and reduces repair and maintenance costs. It also reduces malfunctions and helps keep from losing all of the work done.
6. You must know how much internal memory is required, what equipment is needed--such as a joystick or mouse--and whether the software can be used on your system (for example, if you will be storing it on a hard disk drive). This information should be on the outside of the software package.
7. See Transparency Master 1C, Computer Room Guidelines, for suggestions.

ACTIVITIES

1. Accept valid responses, such as compiling sports statistics, making up address lists for Christmas cards or party invitations, putting membership cards in order, and so on. Students should also describe the input, processing, and output elements of each example.
2. Look for responses appropriate to the type of equipment the school has, the age and experience of the students, and the orientation-- toward business or hobbyists, for example.
3. For students, a computer could calculate grades, classify according to grade level or school activities, sort according to alphabet or residence, summarize attendance or enrollment statistics, and store in internal memory before outputting to disk or printer. For grocery stores, a computer could calculate total costs for customers; classify according to type or product--dairy, produce, or deli, for example, sort according to price, summarize daily sales, and store data temporarily in internal memory before using it for further processing or output. There may be questions about the difference between classify and sort. Generally, in computer use, to classify means to put into categories, and to sort means to put in some order such as alphabetical.
4. The posters should include specific information for your type of hardware and software disks.

ACTIVITIES ————————————
(continued)

Enrichment Activities.

1. An open system allows for the addition of accessories into the computer. A closed system does not have to allow for other accessories, so it can be more compact and faster.

2. The following are sample answers:
    a. Good job, Ben, yes, 9 x 8 = 72.
    b. No, try again or No, 9 x 9 = 81
    c. Have the computer flash the 68 and say "Try this again."

3. 1 Meg stands for one Megabyte of memory. A computer with one Meg has one million bytes of memory. This is the amount of storage available for programs and data. A program that requires one Meg of memory would need a computer with at least that much memory to run.

CHAPTER REVIEW ————————————

Vocabulary

1. c	5. g
2. e	6. b
3. a	7. h
4. f	8. d

Questions

1. store and retrieve data

2. Click on a box to choose a menu option such as THEATER. Type a row number.

3. Software and hardware must work together to be compatible.

4. a

5. The computer is set on a sturdy table away from cold, heat, and direct sunlight. The room temperature is moderate and the air is not so dry that static is a problem.

6. Avoid folding or bending disks. Keep fingers off exposed parts of the actual disk. Keep disks away from heat.

7. Put the disk into the disk drive carefully and close the drive door, if necessary. Turn on the equipment and wait for the computer to signal that it is ready for you to do something.

8. cannot

Chapter 2

 INTRODUCTION TO WORD PROCESSING

DESCRIPTION: Length 2:48. Heidi and Elliot, two eighth grade students, are introduced to word processing. Doing a report for Coach Johnson is more than they can handle with typewriter and white-out. Ms. McKinzie, the computer teacher, shows them how word processing can make their job easier. The Microsoft Works program is used.

Search to Chapter 2........Play

[barcode]

Suggested Additional Resources

- <u>Understanding Computers</u>, Third Edition, by Grace Murray Hopper and Steven L. Mandell, West Publishing Co.
- <u>Computer Skills Resource Guide: Microsoft Works for the Macintosh</u>, by Basil Melnyk, West Publishing Co.
- Computer magazines
- Microsoft Works manuals and documentation, Microsoft Corporation

PROJECTED LEARNING OUTCOMES

After studying the concepts and practicing the skills in this chapter, students should be able to:

- Explain the purpose of a word processor and name at least one job for which students would use a word processor.
- Understand files, the Desktop, and prompts.
- Use a menu.
- List two or three advantages of using a word processor rather than a pen or typewriter.
- Move freely through the Microsoft Works menus.
- Move the cursor by several methods throughout a document.
- Delete and insert text in a document.
- Start a new word processor document .

VOCABULARY TERMS

Word processor program	Filename
Database manager program	Prompt
	Dialog box
Electronic spreadsheet program	Document
	Scroll
Program disk	Delete
Write-protected	Insert
Data disk	Save
File	Format
Backup Copy	Word wrap

Getting Started With Microsoft Works and the Word Processor

CHAPTER OVERVIEW

● The Microsoft Works program has four parts: a word processor, a database manager, an electronic spreadsheet, and a telecommunications program.

● With the word processor, students can write, edit, store, and get text such as letters, reports, newsletters, tests, and other documents.

● A big advantage of using a word processor is that a document can be revised and mistakes can be corrected electronically rather than manually, as is necessary when handwriting a document or using a typewriter. A feature called word wrap lets students keep typing without worrying about the right margin. At the right margin, the cursor jumps down to the next line automatically and moves the word it was typing down to that line.

● In Microsoft Works, use the keys on the keyboard much like the keys on a typewriter. To choose a command, hold down the first key—for example, the [Command] key—and press the second key—for example, the [S] key for Save. Release both keys immediately.

● Students can do many jobs in Microsoft Works by choosing items from menus.

● Students can use the menu to start a new word processing document. After typing it in, save it using a filename that is a reminder of what is in the file.

TEACHING RESOURCES

Practicing Computer Skills 2-1: Getting Ready to Use Microsoft Works
Following detailed instructions, the student will load Microsoft Works and open an existing file.
Practicing Computer Skills 2-2: Moving the Cursor
Students gain experience in using the arrow keys and the mouse with the scroll bars to move the cursor in a word processed document.

TEACHING RESOURCES
(continued)

Practicing Computer Skills 2-3: Erasing Mistakes
Two methods for deleting text, using the [Delete] key and the Cut routine in the Edit menu are used to edit a document.
Practicing Computer Skills 2-4: Deleting More Mistakes
Additional practice in deleting text is provided.
Practicing Computer Skills 2-5: Inserting Some Text
Students practice adding text to a document.
Practicing Computer Skills 2-6: Inserting More Text
Additional practice in inserting text is provided.
Practicing Computer Skills 2-7: Saving the Spelling File on the West Disk
Students learn about saving a file and renaming a file to save a program with a different filename.
Practicing Computer Skills 2-8: Saving the Spelling File on a Formatted Blank Disk
Students learn about saving a file on a formatted blank disk that is provided by the teacher.
Practicing Computer Skills 2-9: Quitting the Session
This is the culminating activity for this set of computer skills activities.
Practicing Computer Skills 2-10: Creating a New Word Processor File
This exercise starts from the Open File screen and instructs students on how to begin a new document in the word processor.
Practicing Computer Skills 2-11: Typing Words in a Word Processor File
Students are given step-by-step instructions for typing a brief note about a club meeting.

Worksheet 2-1 COMPUTER. Using the Cars File: Students follow directions to practice inserting and deleting text in the Cars document.
Worksheet 2-2 ACTIVITY. Keys and Jobs in Microsoft Works: Students match the key or keys on the computer keyboard to the job they do.

TEACHING RESOURCES
(continued)

Worksheet 2-3 RETEACHING. A Word Processor Screen: A blank computer screen is shown and students are directed to indicate where certain messages appear on the screen.

Worksheet 2-4 RETEACHING. Typing the Home History File: Students are given step-by-step instructions for typing an assignment notebook page.

Worksheet 2-5 ENRICHMENT. Checking Spelling: The Microsoft Works spelling checker is introduced.

Transparency Master 2A. Word Processor Screen: Shows a blank word processor screen with the six parts numbered.

Assessment:

HyperCard Stack. Intro to the Mac: Introduces the Macintish to students in these areas: icons, menus, and the finder.

HyperCard Stack. About Windows: Introduces the concept of a Macintosh window, its parts, and the function of those parts.

HyperCard Worksheet. MACINTOSH: An Introduction: Students will explain the desktop and the use of the mouse, icons, and menus.

HyperCard Worksheet. Macintosh Windows: Students will describe the different parts of the window.

Test 2-A

Test 2-B

Portfolio 2. Getting Started with Microsoft Works/ Word Processor: This portfolio asks students to create a concept map about word processing, do an on-line word processing activity, and write responses to questions on word processing.

Skills Test 2. Students load the Palmtop file and follow directions on the Skills Test 2 sheet to make simple editing changes in the document. The document must be checked on the screen unless students have been taught to save or print the document.

TEACHING STRATEGIES

Opening. Students are often frustrated when they make mistakes while writing essays or reports. Talk about the kinds of things that discourage the beginning writer. Red marks, arrows, a letter grade, the word "Rewrite," and the words, "Recopy please" can trigger students to think "Don't take chances" and "I'm no writer." How many students crumple up several sheets of paper after writing a sentence or two, or even less? What is it about a clean sheet of paper that puts beginning writers on edge? How could the work be made easier for students? What items are on the "wish list" for a computer program that helps students write better?

Teaching Tips. Many jobs in Microsoft Works are done through menus. Discuss other menus. For example, restaurant menus help people choose what they would like without having to remember a long list of choices recited by a waiter. Other menus may be found at an auto repair shop where the services and their costs are displayed, at a theater where current films are posted, and at exits directing traffic in two or three different directions on an expressway. Some students may want to make their own menus, such as assignments for grades (so much work equals an A, so much equals a B, and so on), in choosing a favorite song out of the top ten, and in reading a book out of ten recommended books. Similarly, for beginners, the Microsoft Works menus are easier to use than remembering lots of key combinations.

Talk about the following keys: [Delete], [Return], [Command], and the arrow keys. Talk about the meaning of file and filename, Desktop, prompt, and menu. Students should remember that although the Desktop can hold up to 8 files, you can only view one at a time. Talk about using the arrow keys as well as the mouse and scroll bars to move through the file.

When & How.
1. Use the videodisc clip to introduce word processing and lead a discussion with ideas from the Opening strategy.
2. Discuss the Save routine for your particular computer set-up. For example, will students merely save the file to their data disk, or does the file need to be renamed first?
3. Many Practicing Computer Skills exercises are built on a previous session's work. Therefore, students should save their work each time they work at the computer so the file being used will be up-to-date for a later Practicing Computer Skills exercise.
4. Use the HyperCard Stacks "Intro to the Mac:" and "About Windows:," and their worksheets for assessment, review, or to introduce terms and ideas.

Computer Demonstration. Let students watch you perform the procedures discussed before they begin to work on their own, not necessarily with the same examples used in the Practicing Computer Skills exercises.

Classroom Management. Review your classroom methods (network, multiple loading, program disks for each computer, and so on) for handling files and accessing the Microsoft Works program. The instructions for the Practicing Computer Skills exercises assume the student is using a single disk drive. Otherwise, be sure students understand how and where your classroom procedure differs from the textbook directions. Discuss whether students will have to switch disks during loading. (Loading directions in later chapters are open-ended, telling students to access Microsoft Works and the file being used.)

Cooperative Learning. Students working in teams of two could help each other follow the exercises exactly without assuming a certain step comes next. One student would type and the other watch for typing errors or problems. Then the students would change roles. If steps are not followed exactly, students may get lost or do something that changes the column and line numbers used to help them find text.

Writing Activity. Request students to create a "wish list" for a computer program that would help them write better.

Trouble shooting. Remind students to press lightly or tap the keys. Holding keys down makes them repeat. Students should also spend time learning to become proficient at using the mouse.

Reteaching. Students should be given ample opportunity to slowly grow accustomed to working on a computer keyboard and with a mouse, particularly if they have never had keyboarding. Even repeating the same exercises may be beneficial.

Interdisciplinary Learning. Talk with teachers in other subject areas so that students can word process reports, notes, essays, or stories to be handed in.

Closing. Students can demonstrate an understanding of the chapter by producing a word processed document which describes what has been learned, lists the strengths of word processing, or details some of the characteristics of Microsoft Works.

 **Lesson 2 - 1**

p.26 - p.30

 PROJECTED LEARNING OUTCOMES

After studying the concepts and practicing the skills in this lesson, students should be able to:

● Explain the purpose of a word processor and name at least one job for which you would use a word processor.
● Understand files, the Desktop, and prompts.
● Use a menu.

 VOCABULARY TERMS

Word processor program	Data disk
Database manager program	File
	Backup copy
Electronic spreadsheet program	Filename
	Prompt
Program disk	Dialog box
Write-protected	

 **LESSON OVERVIEW**

● The Microsoft Works program has four parts: a word processor, a database manager, an electronic spreadsheet, and a telecommunications program.
● With the word processor, students can write, edit, store, and get text such as letters, reports, newsletters, tests, and other documents.

 **TEACHING RESOURCES**

Practicing Computer Skills 2-1: Getting Ready to Use Microsoft Works
Following detailed instructions, students will load Microsoft Works and open an existing file. Students may need additional help to recall proper procedures for handling diskettes, turning the computer system on and off, and using the keyboard. Students could demonstrate or describe how to begin using the Microsoft Works word processor for an existing document.

Transparency Master 2A. Word Processor Screen: Shows a blank word processor screen with the six parts numbered. Discuss the six areas of an Microsoft Works word processing screen. Across the top: 1 = menu names ; next line, center: 2 = current file; next line: 3 = ruler; at the right side: 4 = page number. Discuss with the students why each of the pieces of information is valuable.

Worksheet 2-3 RETEACHING. A Word Processor Screen: A blank computer screen is shown and students are directed to indicate where certain messages appear on the screen.
Answers:
<u>Number on screen</u>
3
2
4
1

A Word Processor Screen - part b

<u>Meaning</u>
ruler
current file
page number
menu names

LEARNING CHECK 2-1 ANSWERS

1. The original Microsoft Works disks are write-protected and should not not be used so the original program is not damaged or changed.
2. Two drives are recommended so there will be less disk switching.
3. hard drive
4. filename
5. d
6. A prompt is a message on the screen that tells you what to do next.
7. Reading Help information on a screen is easier and faster than looking it up in a book.

 ## PRACTICING COMPUTER SKILLS

2-1: Getting Ready to Use Microsoft Works

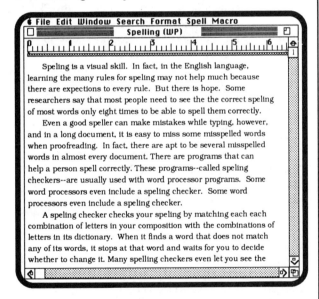

This is what the Spelling file looks like on the screen at the end of this exercise. Practicing Computer Skills exercises later in the chapter edit the document.

Lesson 2 - 2

p.31 - p.36

 ## PROJECTED LEARNING OUTCOMES

After studying the concepts and practicing the skills in this lesson, students should be able to:

● List two or three advantages of using a word processor rather than a pen or typewriter.
● Move freely through the Microsoft Works menus.
● Move the cursor by several methods throughout a document.
● Delete and insert text in a document.

 ## VOCABULARY TERMS

Document
Scroll
Delete
Insert
Save
Format

 ## LESSON OVERVIEW

● A big advantage of using a word processor is that a document can be revised and mistakes can be corrected electronically rather than manually, as is necessary when handwriting a document or using a typewriter. A feature called word wrap lets students keep typing without worrying about the right margin. At the right margin, the cursor jumps down to the next line automatically and moves the word it was typing down to that line.
● In Microsoft Works, use the keys on the keyboard much like the keys on a typewriter. To choose a command, hold down the first key—for example, the [Command] key—and press the second key—for example, the [S] key for Save. Release both keys immediately.
● Students can do many jobs in Microsoft Works by choosing items from menus.

 ## TEACHING RESOURCES

Practicing Computer Skills 2-2: Moving the Cursor
Students gain experience in using the arrow keys and the mouse with the scroll bars to move the cursor in a word processed document. Students may need review on loading Microsoft Works and the Spelling file if they did not do Practicing Computer Skills 2-1 immediately prior to this one. They must be reminded to follow the directions exactly so that the cursor will be placed on the exact characters mentioned in the worksheet. Sufficient time should be given to practice using the mouse until they are familiar with it.

Practicing Computer Skills 2-3: Erasing Mistakes
Two methods for deleting text, using the [Delete] key and the Cut routine in the Edit menu, are used to edit a document. If this worksheet does not immediately follow Practicing Computer Skills 2-2, students may need help loading Microsoft Works and the Spelling file. Students must be reminded to follow the directions exactly so that the cursor will be placed on the exact characters mentioned in the worksheet. The lesson ends by indicating to the student to leave the screen as it is; ie, the changed document is not saved. If time is a problem, use Practicing Computer Skills 2-8 to show students how to save a file and 2-9 to show them how to Quit Microsoft Works.

Practicing Computer Skills 2-4: Deleting More Mistakes
Additional practice in deleting text is provided. Students may need help loading Microsoft Works and the Spelling file (or Spelling.C1 if they have already saved it). They must be reminded to follow the directions exactly so that the cursor will placed on the exact characters mentioned in the worksheet. The lesson ends by indicating to the student to leave the screen as it is; ie, the changed document is not saved. If time is a problem, use Practicing Computer Skills 2-8 to show students how to save a file and 2-9 to show them how to Quit Microsoft Works.

Practicing Computer Skills 2-5: Inserting Some Text
Students practice adding text to a document. Students may need help loading Microsoft Works and the Spelling file (or Spelling.C1 if they have already saved it).

TEACHING RESOURCES
(continued)

They must be reminded to follow the directions exactly so that the cursor will be placed on the exact characters mentioned in the worksheet. The lesson ends by indicating to the student to leave the screen as it is; ie, the changed document is not saved. If time is a problem, use Practicing Computer Skills 2-8 to show students how to save a file and 2-9 to show them how to Quit Microsoft Works.

Practicing Computer Skills 2-6: Inserting More Text
Additional practice in inserting text is provided. Students may need help loading Microsoft Works and the Spelling file (or Spelling.C1 if they have already saved it). They must be reminded to follow the directions exactly so that the cursor will be placed on the exact characters mentioned in the worksheet. The lesson ends by indicating to the student to leave the screen as it is; ie, the changed document is not saved. If time is a problem, use either Practicing Computer Skills 2-7 or 2-8 to show students how to save a file and 2-9 to show them how to Quit Microsoft Works.

Practicing Computer Skills 2-7: Saving the Spelling File on the West Disk
Students learn about saving a file and renaming a file to save a program with a different filename.

Practicing Computer Skills 2-8: Saving the Spelling File on a Formatted Blank Disk
Students learn about saving a file on a formatted blank disk that is provided by the teacher. Depending on the age of the students and the classroom situation, you may want to have them format their own diskette rather than doing it for them.

Practicing Computer Skills 2-9: Quitting the Session
This is the culminating activity for this set of computer skills activities.

Worksheet 2-1 COMPUTER. Using the Cars File: Students follow directions to practice inserting and deleting text in the Cars document. Can be used to review at the end of the chapter or after Practicing Computer Skills 2-6 or 2-9.

Worksheet 2-2 ACTIVITY. Keys and Jobs in Microsoft Works: Students match the key or keys on the computer keyboard to the job they do. Can be used for a chapter review or as desk work while other students are using the computer.

TEACHING RESOURCES
(continued)

Answers:
1. f	6. d
2. a	7. c
3. i	8. b
4. h	9. g
5. e	

 LEARNING CHECK 2-2 ANSWERS

1. d
2. press [Delete]
3. c
4. in the exact location where you want the characters to be inserted
5. Press [Down Arrow] or use the mouse and the scroll bars.
6. File
7. Close, Quit
8. Answers will vary, but should include ease of editing, deleting, and inserting text.

 PRACTICING COMPUTER SKILLS

2-6: Inserting More Text

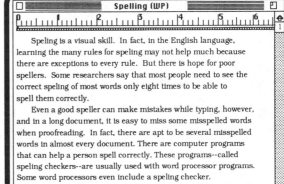

The Spelling file just before students save it to the disk in Practicing Computer Skills 2-7 and 2-8.

Lesson 2 - 3

p.36 - p.37

 ## PROJECTED LEARNING OUTCOMES

After studying the concepts and practicing the skills in this lesson, students should be able to:

● Start a new word processor document.

 ## VOCABULARY TERMS

Word wrap

 ## LESSON OVERVIEW

● Students can use the menu to start a new word processing document. After typing it in, save it using a filename that is a reminder of what is in the file.

 ## TEACHING RESOURCES

Practicing Computer Skills 2-10: Creating a New Word Processor File
This exercise starts from the Opening screen and instructs students on how to begin a new document in the word processor. Discuss naming files by using some systematic process or by some descriptive method so that they can be easily located in the future.

Practicing Computer Skills 2-11: Typing Words in a Word Processor File
Students are given step-by-step instructions for typing a brief note about a club meeting.

Worksheet 2-4 RETEACHING. Typing the Home History File: Students are given step-by-step instructions for typing an assignment notebook page. Use this as additional practice for entering a new file.

Worksheet 2-5 ENRICHMENT. Checking Spelling: The Microsoft Works spelling checker is introduced. Discuss the benefits and possible problems associated with using a spell checker. Explain what happens when homonyms are inadvertently used such as "their" and "there" or "two," "too," and "to." Have students give other examples.

LEARNING CHECK 2-3 ANSWERS

1. Letter.Vac; Letter.Phily; Letter.Philadelphia; and so on. The filename Letter would not be specific enough.
2. word wrap
3. Press [Return]
4. Using the mouse, pull down the menu, drag the pointer over the item and then release the mouse button. You could also use the [Command] key and the code letter, such as C for Copy.
5. Hold down [Command], press the other key, and release both keys immediately.
6. Press [Return]

PRACTICING COMPUTER SKILLS

2-11: Typing Words in a Word Processor File

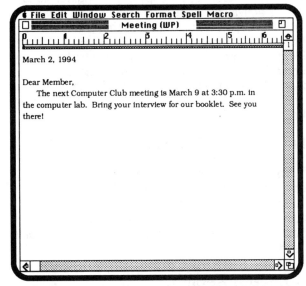

The Meeting file when the students are finished.

SKILLS TEST 2 ANSWERS

This is the Palmtop file with all of the changes made:

Student's Name

Big Things Expected Of Small Palmtop PCs

The first personal computers were clunky boxes dubbed desktops. Next came compact versions called laptops. Now there's a new technological wave - call them palmtops.
Companies are selling personal computers so small and light they can be held in the palm of your hand. They weigh 1 pound and do almost as much as a desktop computer. But don't expect tiny prices. These PCs will cost almost as much as their big siblings --$400 to $2500.

Experts say advances in computer screen technology and smaller, cheaper computer chips are paving the way for PCs that will fit in a coat pocket, purse or briefcase.

All agree that the miniatures won't replace desktops, since their size still means less power and memory. But they could be ideal as a supplement for the executive on the go, the field salesperson or the student dashing to class.

Kathy Rebello, <u>Understanding Computers</u>, West Publishing, page 90

● Chapter 2 Summary

SUMMARY POINTS

● The Microsoft Works program has four parts: a word processor, a database manager, an electronic spreadsheet, and a telecommunications program.
● With the word processor, students can write, edit, store, and get text such as letters, reports, newsletters, tests, and other documents.
● A big advantage of using a word processor is that a document can be revised and mistakes can be corrected electronically rather than manually. Word wrap lets students keep typing without worrying about the right margin.
● To enter a command, hold down the first key—for example, the [Command] key—and press the second key—for example, the [S] key for Save. Release both keys immediately.
● Students can do many jobs in Microsoft Works by choosing items from menus.
● Use the menu to start a new word processing document. After typing it in, save it using a filename that is a reminder of what is in the file.

DISCUSSION QUESTIONS

1. Menus are things that people already know about. People choose from restaurant menus, cost lists in car garages and beauty salons, television schedules, airline schedules, and even multiple-choice questions. So menus in a computer program let people see the choices, pick an item, and even return to a previous menu. This is unlike the effort required to memorize many key combinations.
2. Features may include menus; dialog boxes that show prompts that guide every step, filenames, procedures, and so on; and safety devices. For example, you cannot quit if some files are not saved. You cannot quit accidentally because there are two quit steps. There are also two methods of picking items from menus, so you can use the one you like better.

DISCUSSION QUESTIONS
(continued)

3. The documentation for a software program tells the user how many legal copies can be made. The copy function makes it easy. Unfortunately, it also makes it easy for people to take unfair advantage of the company and make illegal copies.
4. "Screen" means a display that lets you do a specific job. Some Microsoft Works screens are the Opening screen and the Word Processor screen.
5. Pressing the [Delete] key will let you go back to where you were.
6. The mouse allows you to select any option in the dialog box. The [Return] key lets you choose the double outlined button.

ACTIVITIES

1. Students need a new copy of the original file to do this activity because they should have saved their first copy with the changes they made in Practicing Computer Skills exercises. Help students identify the problem or problems they had originally and discuss how to overcome the difficulty.
2 and 3. Remind students that this is just a rough draft and they will be able to make other changes later.

Enrichment Activities.

1. To copy a file onto the same disk, choose the option Save As in the File menu. Then type a different name when prompted to do so.
2. Answers will vary depending on students' abilities and experiences and on the software being used.

CHAPTER REVIEW
Vocabulary

1. A menu is a list of choices shown on the screen from which the user picks a command or data to enter into the computer.
2. A filename is a name given to a file or document for storing on a disk and retrieving it later.
3. Delete means to erase or remove.
4. Save means to record on a disk or other storage medium.

CHAPTER REVIEW ————————————
(continued)

5. Scroll means that characters move off the screen to make room for new characters moving on to the screen while you are using a document that is longer than the screen can show at one time.
6. Word wrap is a feature in which the user can continue typing with no further activity even though the margin is reached because the cursor will automatically jump to the next line, taking with it any incomplete word.

Questions

1. The Desktop is an electronic version of the top of your desk or table on which you have laid out work to do. It may contain several items to work on, just as your table may contain several books for homework to do.
2. b
3. a
4. Word Processor
5. Save the file often. Make a backup copy on the same disk or another disk.
6. to have two copies of the same file on the same disk
7. [Return]
8. True

● Chapter 3

 DESKTOP PUBLISHING —————

DESCRIPTION: Length 2:18. Heidi and Elliot have developed a class newsletter with the word processor. Ms. McKinzie shows them how they can make their report more like a real newspaper by using a desktop publishing system. Page-Maker software, a scanner, and a laser printer are demonstrated.

Search to Chapter 3........Play

Suggested Additional Resources

● <u>Understanding Computers</u>, Third Edition, by Grace Murray Hopper and Steven L. Mandell, West Publishing Co.
● <u>Computer Skills Resources Guide: Microsoft Works for the Macintosh</u>, By Basil Melnyk, West Publishing Co.
● Computer magazines
● Microsoft Works manuals and documentation, Microsoft Corporation

 PROJECTED LEARNING OUTCOMES —————

After studying the concepts and practicing the skills in this chapter, students should be able to:

● Find text in a word processor file.
● Replace text in a word processor file.
● Move text within a word processor file.
● Format a word processor document using the Print and Format menus.
● Become familiar with adding, copying and deleting files from the disk.
● Define desktop publishing and tell its purpose.
● Explain the difference between typeface, font, size and style.

 VOCABULARY TERMS —————

Format	Graphics
Default	Clip Art
Justify	Typeface
Buffer	Point Size
Text	

Learning More about Word Processing and Desktop Publishing

🔍 CHAPTER OVERVIEW

● The Find routine lets students find text in a document that is any set of characters or a set of characters with specific upper and lower case letters. The Replace routine does the same and also replaces the text with other characters that you enter.

● Before printing a document, students might want to format it. To format a document means to set rules for the appearance of the document. Students might want to set line spacing, margin appearance, typeface, underlining, and so on.

● In Microsoft Works, there are default settings for the formats. These settings are the values the program uses when the users do not choose any formats of their own.

● Microsoft Works lets students list the files that are on the disk, and open, close, save as, and save on the disk.

● Desktop publishing uses computers and software to produce professional-quality publications.

● Designing a publication with desktop publishing software involves decisions about typefaces, sizes and styles; page format and margins; and placement of graphics.

📁 TEACHING RESOURCES

Practicing Computer Skills 3-1: Finding Text
Students use the Find routine to locate text in their copy of the Spelling file. They count how many times the word "computer" is used.

Practicing Computer Skills 3-2: Replacing Text
In this exercise, students use the Replace routine to correct the word "speling."

Practicing Computer Skills 3-3: Replacing More Text
Students get more practice with the Replace routine.

TEACHING RESOURCES
(continued)

Practicing Computer Skills 3-4: Moving a Sentence
Students highlight a sentence and use the Cut and Paste routines to place it in a different location in the document.

Practicing Computer Skills 3-5: Moving Paragraphs
Students highlight a paragraph in the Learn document and use the Cut and Paste routines to place it in a different location.

Practicing Computer Skills 3-6: Looking at the Format Menu
This exercise begins a series of exercises using the Spelling document that explore the various commands available on the Format menu.

Practicing Computer Skills 3-7: Choosing from the Format Menu and the Page Setup & Margins Menu
The Format menu is used to select double spacing, and the Page Setup & Margins menu is used to change the top margin.

Practicing Computer Skills 3-8: Justifying the Text
The Format menu is used to show students how to center a title for the document.

Practicing Computer Skills 3-9: Changing the Appearance of the Text
Two other options—bold and underline— are used from the Format menu for the Spelling file.

Practicing Computer Skills 3-10: Creating a Cover Page
Students will use formatting and Draw options to create a title page for the Spelling file.

Practicing Computer Skills 3-11: Printing a Document
This exercise concludes this set by asking the student to print the altered Spelling file.

Practicing Computer Skills 3-12: Working with Files
Students are instructed to delete the file named Meeting, using the mouse and the trash can.

TEACHING RESOURCES
(continued)

Worksheet 3-1 COMPUTER. Working with the CARS File: Follow the instructions to edit the CARS file.

Worksheet 3-2 COMPUTER. Formatting the CARS File: Use the Format menu and the Page Setup menu to format the CARS File.

Worksheet 3-3 RETEACH. Vocabulary Review: Students write one or two examples for terms from Microsoft Works.

Worksheet 3-4 RETEACH. Formatting: Answers to questions about formatting can be found in the textbook. Some changes are made to the Home History file.

Worksheet 3-5 ENRICHMENT. More Printer Options: Students are asked to try eight printer options not used in previous exercises.

Transparency Master 3A. An Example of a Prompt: Shows the Save prompt with possible responses.

Assessment:
HyperCard Stack. Desktop Publishing: Introduces, defines, and demonstrates desktop publishing, and its many special terms.
HyperCard Worksheet. Desktop Publishing: Students explain some of the concepts of desktop publishing, and define many of the special terms used in desktop publishing.

Test 3-A

Test 3-B

Portfolio 3. Learning More About Word Processing and Desktop Publishing: Students are asked to create a table showing the uses of replacing, searching, and moving in word processing. There is also an on-line activity using the format routine, and a concept map to be drawn listing the overlap between word processing and desktop publishing.

Skills Test 3. Students load the MOVIES file and follow directions on the Skills Test 3 sheet to edit, format, and print the document.

TEACHING STRATEGIES

Opening. Talk with students about the frustrations of cutting and pasting and retyping imperfect pages for a final copy of a paper. Let students discuss if learning to use a word processor is more or less frustrating than typing or handwriting a paper. When beginning desktop publishing, show examples of pamphlets or flyers done on a computer. Discuss why or why not this may be simpler and less expensive for individuals than going to a professional printer. Discuss who might use desktop publishing.

Teaching Tips. Discuss the differences between finding and replacing in the version of Microsoft Works you are using. Warn students to be careful when highlighting text to be moved. The inclusion or exclusion of blank spaces and carriage returns before and/or after the text must be considered. If this is not done, the moved text may be against words without spaces between or the area where the text was removed will have too many blank spaces. Remind students to always look at the areas of the document being effected and check for missing or additional blank spaces.

When & How.
1. Use suggestions from the Opening strategy to begin the discussion of the word processing portion of the chapter.
2. The section, Some Stuff That's Nice to Know about Microsoft Works, may be used as needed or as part of the requirements for this chapter. It discusses opening several files at once from the disk, using a file from the desktop, copying and deleting files.
3. Depending on software availability, the desktop publishing material can be expanded to include more computer applications.
4. Use suggestions from the Opening strategies to introduce desktop publishing.
5. Use the HyperCard stack "Desktop Publishing," and its worksheet to expand students knowledge on this art.

Observation. The Practicing Computer Skills in this chapter use work that the students should have completed in Chapter 2. As you monitor students at the computer, be sure they are using up-to-date files.

TEACHING STRATEGIES ——————
(continued)

Computer Demonstration. Let students watch you perform the procedures discussed before they begin to work on their own, not necessarily with the same examples used in the Practicing Computer Skills exercises.
Invite a parent who uses word processing or desktop publishing at home or at work to demonstrate advanced features of the program.

Cooperative Learning. Have two or three students work together and use the word processor to make up an exercise that includes some word processing, some editing, and some file maneuvers. Let groups exchange exercises and do them.

Writing Activity. Using the word processor, have students list their favorite commands or operations and why they like them. Write a letter to Apple Computer explaining why they like using a computer, or write a letter to Microsoft explaining why they like Microsoft Works.
Ask students to list the jobs discussed in the last section of the chapter. After each job, students should state specific occasions when they would use the routine.

Trouble shooting. Remind students that they can use the Cancel options to stop routines that are not completed and to exit menus or screens that are not needed. Use Transparency Master 3A to talk about prompts again. Some prompts list choices within the prompt area. Students should know what to expect when these prompts appear.

Interdisciplinary Learning. Arrange a field trip to a newspaper or other business that uses word processors or desktop publishing to produce their product. Students should interview someone at the business and word process a report about the information gained.

Closing. Students can demonstrate an understanding of the chapter by producing a word processed document which describes what has been learned, lists the strengths of word processing, or details some of the characteristics of Microsoft Works learned in this chapter. Similar information could be included for desktop publishing.

NOTES ——————

 # Lesson 3 - 1

p.42 - p.47

 PROJECTED LEARNING OUTCOMES

After studying the concepts and practicing the skills in this lesson, students should be able to:

● Find text in a word processor file.
● Replace text in a word processor file.
● Move text within a word processor file.

LESSON OVERVIEW

● The Find routine lets students find text in a document that is any set of characters or a set of characters with specific upper and lower case letters. The Replace routine does the same and also replaces the text with other characters that you enter.

 **TEACHING RESOURCES**

Practicing Computer Skills 3-1: Finding Text
Students use the Find routine to locate text in their copy of the Spelling file. They count how many times the word "computer" is used (Answer: 3 times). Students may require some review to remember how to load the Spelling document from their data disk. The last step in the exercise tells the student to leave the document on the computer screen.

Practicing Computer Skills 3-2: Replacing Text
In this exercise, students use the Replace routine to correct the word "speling." The exercise begins with the assumption that the Spelling file is on the screen. The choice Check Upper/Lowercase is used from the Replace routine. The last step in the exercise tells the student to leave the document on the computer screen.

Practicing Computer Skills 3-3: Replacing More Text
Students get more practice with the Replace routine by correcting the word "Speling." (Notice the capital "S".) The exercise begins with the assumption that the Spelling file is on the screen. The last step in the exercise tells the student to save the document on the data disk.

Practicing Computer Skills 3-4: Moving a Sentence
Using the Learn document, students highlight a sentence and use the Cut and Paste routines to place it in a different location in the document. Remind students to carefully highlight text to be moved so that the appropriate blank spaces are included with the text. The last step in the exercise tells the student to leave the document on the computer screen.

Practicing Computer Skills 3-5: Moving Paragraphs
Students highlight a paragraph in the Learn document and use the Cut and paste routines to place it in a different location. Remind students to carefully highlight text to be moved so that the appropriate blank spaces and carriage return are included with the text. The last step in the exercise tells the student to leave the document on the computer screen.

Worksheet 3-1 COMPUTER. Working with the CARS File: Follow the instructions to edit the CARS file. Students use the Find routine to replace a misspelled word and the Cut and Paste routines to move two sentences and a paragraph.

TEACHING RESOURCES
(continued)

Transparency Master 3A. Some Examples of Prompts: Shows three prompts with possible responses. Discuss the choice of responses. Is one choice better or faster than another?

LEARNING CHECK 3-1 ANSWERS

1. b
2. Pull down the Search menu and select Find
3. to locate a particular word or phrase in a document
4. Pull down the Search menu and select Replace
5. Move the cursor to the new location for the text and Paste it there.
6. The combination mmm would not appear in any known words, but mm might.

PRACTICING COMPUTER SKILLS

3-4: Moving a Sentence

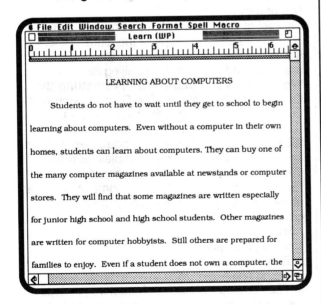

The screen after students have moved the sentence and are finished with the exercise.

PRACTICING COMPUTER SKILLS
(continued)

3-5: Moving Paragraphs

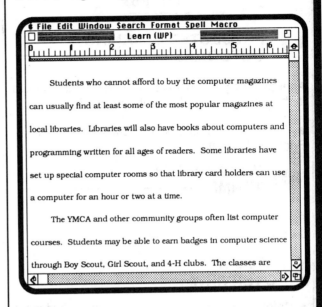

The screen after students have moved a paragraph correctly.

Lesson 3 - 2

p.47 - p.53

 ## PROJECTED LEARNING OUTCOMES

After studying the concepts and practicing the skills in this lesson, students should be able to:

● Format a word processor document using the Print and Format menus.

 ## VOCABULARY TERMS

Format	Default
Justify	Buffer

LESSON OVERVIEW

● Before printing a document, students might want to format it. To format a document means to set rules for the appearance of the document. Students might want to set line spacing, margin appearance, boldfacing, underlining, and so on.
● In Microsoft Works, there are default settings for the formats. These settings are the values the program uses when the users do not choose any formats of their own. Microsoft Works default settings are discussed in the text, p.48 - p.51.

 ## TEACHING RESOURCES

Practicing Computer Skills 3-6: Looking at the Format Menu
Students begin a series of exercises using the Spelling document that explore the various commands available on the Format menu. The file is left on the screen at the end.

Practicing Computer Skills 3-7: Choosing from the Format and the Print Menus
The Spelling document is on the screen. The student uses the Edit menu to Select All. The the Format menu is used to select double spacing. Then the Page Setup menu is used to change the top margin of the document. The last step in the exercise tells the student to leave the document on the computer screen.

TEACHING RESOURCES
(continued)

Practicing Computer Skills 3-8: Justifying the Text
This exercise assumes the Spelling document is on the screen when the student begins. It is used to show students how to center a title for the document, using the Format menu. The last step in the exercise tells the student to leave the document on the computer screen.

Practicing Computer Skills 3-9: Changing the Appearance of the Text
This exercise assumes the Spelling file is on the screen when the student begins. Two other printer options—bold and underline— are used from the Format menu for the Spelling file. Students should understand that the text must be highlighted first. The last step in the exercise tells the student to leave the document on the computer screen.

Practicing Computer Skills 3-10: Creating a Cover Page
This exercise assumes the Spelling file is on the screen when the student begins. Students will use formatting and Draw options to create a title page for the Spelling file. The exercise ends with the Spelling file being saved, but left on the screen.

Practicing Computer Skills 3-11: Printing a Document
This set of exercises concludes by instructing students to print one copy of the altered Spelling file. When the printer is finished, the students are instructed to close the Spelling file.

Worksheet 3-2 COMPUTER. Formatting the CARS File: Students use the Format menu and the Page Setup menu to format the Cars file. Several options are used and the file is printed.

Worksheet 3-3 RETEACH. Vocabulary Review: Students write one or two examples for terms from Microsoft Works. This can be used as a review lesson, desk work while some students are at the computers, or a reteach for a selected group of students.
Answers:
1. word processor
2. Desktop
3. typing text
4. The computer hunts for characters you type at the Find What prompt. The computer lines up text on the left and right margins when Justified is chosen.
5. Words appear on the screen.
6. Words appear on paper.

TEACHING RESOURCES

(continued)

7. [Command] and [S]
8. blinking bar
9. File, Format
10. Top margin-1 inch
11. Save document as:

Worksheet 3-4 RETEACH. Formatting: Answers to seven questions about formatting are found in the textbook. Some formatting changes are made to the Home History file which was begun in Chapter 2. This can be used as a review lesson, desk work while some students are at the computers, or a reteach for a selected group of students.
Answers:
1. Pull down the File menu
2. [Command] and [B]
3. Format
4. Highlight the text, then pull down the Format menu, select Spacing and choose Double
5. Page Setup
6. Highlight the text, then press [Command] and [B]
7. Highlight the text, then press [Command] and [U]

Worksheet 3-5 ENRICHMENT. More Printer Options: Students are asked to define eight printer options that are not used as often as others. They are also instructed to try each one in an existing file or a new file. The use of superscript and subscript is noted.
Answers:

1. Format/Style
2. Format/Style
3. Format/Font
4. Page Setup
5. Page Setup
6. Format/Size
7. Page Setup
8. Format/Style

LEARNING CHECK 3-2 ANSWERS

1. formatting
2. top , bottom, left, and right margins: 1 inch; single spaced; paper length: 11 inches; paper width: 8.5 inches (US Letter)
3. b
4. highlight
5. d
6. a justified margin has all characters aligned, a ragged margin does not
7. Answers will vary, however, they should include such items as a more professional document, and make it easier to read.

PRACTICING COMPUTER SKILLS

3-11: Printing a Document

Spelling Checkers: A Good Idea?

Spelling is a visual skill. In fact, in the English language, learning the many rules for spelling may not help much because there are exceptions to almost every rule. But there is hope for poor spellers. Some researchers say that most people need to see the correct spelling of most words only eight times to be able to spell them correctly.

Even a good speller can make mistakes when typing, however, and in a long document, it is easy to miss some misspelled words when proofreading. There are computer programs that can help a person spell correctly. These programs--called spelling checkers--are usually used with word processor programs. Some word processors even include a spelling checker.

A spelling checker checks your spelling by matching each combination of letters in your composition with the combinations of letters in its dictionary. When it finds a word that does not match any of its words, it stops at that word and waits for you to decide whether to change it. Many spelling checkers even let you see the correct spelling before you make your decision.

Now, some people say that spelling checkers will not help you to learn to spell. Instead, a spelling checker will make you into a lazy speller because you will depend on it too much. Spelling checkers do support individualized learning, however, because the computer picks out the words you tend to miss most often. Over time, you will mispell these words less and less often, because you receive visual reinforcement for the correct spelling. In other words, the more you see the correct spelling, the more likely you are to remember it!

One problem with spelling checkers is that they find only mispelled words, not words used incorrectly in context. For example, look at this sentence:

> Their willing to let they're students use
> spelling checkers, two.

Did you see the spelling mistakes? Many spelling checkers would not catch them because the three words used incorrectly here are in fact spelled correctly. It is up to you to see that the words "Their," "they're," and "two" are used incorrectly in context.

As you see, a spelling checker may not catch all of your mistakes, but they can help you with the words you mispell most often. Would a spelling checker help you? What do you think? What does your teacher think?

Main source: Garvey, Ian. Spelling checkers: can they actually teach spelling? Classroom Computer Learning. November/December 1984, pp. 62-65.

The completed Spelling file

 # Lesson 3 - 3, 4

p.54 - p.60

 ## PROJECTED LEARNING OUTCOMES

After studying the concepts and practicing the skills in these lessons, students should be able to:

● Become familiar with adding, copying and deleting files from the disk.
● Define desktop publishing and tell its purpose.
● Explain the difference between typeface , font, size and style.

 ## VOCABULARY TERMS

Text
Graphics
Clip Art
Typeface
Point Size

 ## LESSON OVERVIEW

● Microsoft Works lets students list the files that are on the disk, and open, close, save as, and save on the disk.
● Desktop publishing uses computers and software to produce professional-quality publications.
● Designing a publication with desktop publishing software involves decisions about typefaces, sizes and styles; page format and margins; and place-ment of graphics.

 ## TEACHING RESOURCES

Practicing Computer Skills 3- 11: Working with Files
The exercise begins at the system screen. Students are instructed to delete the file named Meeting, using the mouse and the trash can.

 ## LEARNING CHECK 3-3 ANSWERS

1. Use the Window menu and select the one you want.
2. If anything happens to damage or erase the file while editing, the original file still exits.
3. b
4. Closing a file on the Desktop removes it from the computer's memory, but not from the disk. Deleting a file from the disk removes the file completely.
5. Close All
6. to be able to get information from several documents

 ## LEARNING CHECK 3-4 ANSWERS

1. Desktop publishing is the process of creating a publication using a computer.
2. c
3. text and graphics
4. What-You-See-Is-What-You-Get
5. word processor software, graphics software (or clip art), page layout software, computer, and printer
6. d
7. The greater the point size, the easier the typeface should be to read because it will be printed larger.

SKILLS TEST 3 ANSWERS

The Movies file after changes have been made:

Student's Name

<u>Computers Take the Lead in Hollywood</u>

Two small World War II planes streak across the screen, diving and ascending, barely missing a collision. The heroic and handsome archaeologist Indiana Jones, is once again tracking down the bad guys in the movie "Indiana Jones and the Last Crusade"--only in this film sequence of an electrifying plane chase, it is not the actor Harrison Ford piloting the airplane, but a computer.

Many of the dangerous scenes from "The Last Crusade" were shot using computer-controlled models and animation. Industrial Light and Magic, the company that created the special effects, created detailed airplane models and clay models of Harrison Ford and other actors in the movie. The heads and upper bodies of the clay actors could be moved so that they looked like they were swaying with the motion of the planes.

Not only are computers used to help film exciting movie sequences, they are used to write them as well. Hollywood screenwriters use word processors to help them write and revise their work faster.

Computers are used to manage the business end of Hollywood as well. Software has been developed to meet the specific needs of movie-making, taking into consideration the jargon used in the movie industry. The assistant director for the movie "Karate Kid III" used a computer to set up a crew of eighty-five people.

Editors, set designers, and actors all use computers as well. There is no doubt that computers are here to stay in the movie industry.

● Chapter 3 Summary

SUMMARY POINTS

● The Find routine lets students find text in a document that is any set of characters or a set of characters with specific upper and lower case letters. The Replace routine does the same and also replaces the text with other characters that you enter.

● Before printing a document, students might want to format it. To format a document means to set rules for the appearance of the document. Students might want to set line spacing, margin appearance, boldfacing, underlining, and so on.

● In Microsoft Works, there are default settings for the formats. These settings are the values the program uses when the users do not choose any formats of their own.

● Microsoft Works lets students list the files that are on the disk.

● Desktop publishing uses computers and software to produce professional-quality publications.

● Designing a publication with desktop publishing software involves decisions about typefaces, sizes and styles; page format and margins; and placement of graphics.

DISCUSSION QUESTIONS

1. The advantages of using a word processor include the following: mistakes can be corrected electronically; large blocks of text can be moved easily; the Replace routine can help with correcting spelling or changing incorrect word usage; and a document can be custom format-ted and printed without the frustration of trying to type a perfect paper. Paper copies are handy during the revision process or when several people are going to be reading the text.

2. Students might suggest a copy function or an undo feature that returns work to the previous state after a routine has been completed by mistake.

DISCUSSION QUESTIONS
(continued)

3. On one hand, word processing skills can help the development of writing skills by making it less frustrating to produce a good final copy and by making revisions easy to do mechanically. Students may be willing to make major revisions when they know they will not have to rewrite the whole paper by hand. On the other hand, the ease of making corrections with a word processor may only encourage superficial, easy-to-do revisions.

4. Most students will probably think a spelling checker is wonderful. Some may say that with a spelling checker, they will never have to learn to spell. If the students use a spelling checker, however, they may find out that it takes more time to complete the checking process than they counted on, especially if their spelling is atrocious. Students may say spelling checkers should be used only after students acquire a basic profi-ciency in spelling. Then the spelling checker can help them learn to spell the word they still cannot spell correctly, because students will see the correct spelling on the screen.

5. Choosing Replace All tells the program to go ahead and change all occurrences of a set of letters even in cases where a whole word could be changed drastically. For example, if you changed the word "he" to "she," you would also change the word "rather to "ratsher."

6. You could name the disks for the types of files on them, or keep a paper list of the files on each disk. In the case of a large number of disks, you could use the Microsoft Works database module to keep a record of the files.

7. Advantages include less expense than using a graphics artist, more control over the appearance of the final document, quicker to produce in a short time frame, more interesting flyers or memos than previously, easy combination of text and graphics, etc.

8. Use the Highlight "Hints for Creating an Attrac-tive Publication" to critique the publications.

ACTIVITIES

The activities are self-explanatory. Posters may be substituted for the cards in Activity 5, if students want some Help instructions on the walls of the computer room.

ACTIVITIES

(continued)

Enrichment Activities.

1. Students may wish to use Worksheet 3-5 before doing the activity. They can try wide margins, different fonts if available, and so on, depending on the capabilities of the printer.
2. Students may want to make a backup copy of the Spelling file before doing this exercise.
3. Copy puts a copy of the text into the clipboard, which can later be pasted elsewhere. An item copied to the clipboard stays in the clipboard until another item is put into it or until the computer is turned off. (The clipboard is a special place in memory reserved for holding data temporarily. It can hold only one set of characters at a time.)
4. Students should word process information gained from the interview. Oral reports might be interesting, too.
5. crop - to trim or remove part of a graphic
   kerning - the space between individual letters
   landscape page layout - printing text lengthwise on paper (11" x 8.5")
   leading - vertical spacing between lines of text
   masthead - the area on the top of the first page of a newspaper that displays the name of the newspaper
   monospaced typeface - a typeface in which each character takes the same amount of space
   orphans - one or more initial lines (usually no more than 3) of a paragraph falling at the bottom of a column or page and separated from the rest of the paragraph
   portrait page layout - printing text in normal position on paper (8.5" x 11")
   proportionally spaced typeface - a typeface in which the characters are of varying sizes
   style sheet - a set of formatting information for a document
   widows - one or more ending lines (usually no more than 3) of a paragraph at the beginning of a column or page and separated from the rest of the paragraph

CHAPTER REVIEW

Vocabulary

1. format
2. margin
3. default
4. right justified
5. scrolling
6. desktop publishing
7. typeface

Questions

1. to delete text, or to remove it from one location and paste it in another
2. true
3. The Page Setup menu includes these defaults: margins are 1 inche, right margin is 1.2, unjustified, paper length is 11 inches, paper width is 8.5 inches. The Format menu includes single-spacing and left justified.
4. a
5. Type a code such as MMM every time the words "Mississippi River" are used. Use the Replace routine to replace the code with the words. (Using a space before and after the code and the replacement words can help isolate the code in case an unwise choice of codes is made.)
6. true
7. c
8. If anything happens to damage or erase the file while editing, the original file still exists.
9. A subscript is a smaller character that is lower on the line than the normal text. A superscript is a smaller character that is higher on the line than the normal text.
10. c

●Chapter 4

 DATABASE MANAGEMENT

DESCRIPTION: Length 4:50. Ms. McKinzie explains database programs to Heidi and Elliot and shows them how database programs can be used to access various kinds of information. Heidi and Elliot use the Microsoft Works program to set up their own database about students in their class.

Search to Chapter 4........Play

Suggested Additional ReSources

● <u>Understanding Computers</u>, Third Edition, by Grace Murray Hopper and Steven L. Mandell, West Publishing Co.
● <u>Computer Skills Resources Guide: Microsoft Works for the Macintosh</u>, By Basil Melnyk, West Publishing Co.
● Computer magazines
● Microsoft Works manuals and documentation, Microsoft Corporation

 PROJECTED LEARNING OUTCOMES

After studying the concepts and practicing the skills in this chapter, students should be able to:

● Name the purpose and parts of a database.
● Move the cursor freely in both the Form Window and the List Window.
● Change database entries.
● Insert and delete records.
● Sort records.
● Use the Match Records routine in a database.
● Enter fields and data in a new file.

 VOCABULARY TERMS

Database manager program	Entry
Database	Form Window
Retrieve	List Window
File	Open
Record	Update
Field	Comparison information

Using the Database Program

CHAPTER OVERVIEW

● A database is a collection of related facts. A database manager program helps with organizing and accessing the facts.
● Large units of data in a database are called files. The files are divided into units called records. A record has smaller units called fields. Each piece of data in a field is called an entry.
● Most database manager programs let the user do these jobs: a) add or delete data; b) search for data; c) change data; d) sort data into some order; and e) print a report.
● Students will be shown how to create their own new database.

TEACHING RESOURCES

Practicing Computer Skills 4-1: Opening the Volunteers File
In this exercise, students will use the Volunteers file, view the file, and move the cursor.
Practicing Computer Skills 4-2: Looking at List Window
Students will move the cursor around in a file that is shown in List Window.
Practicing Computer Skills 4-3: Looking at Form Window
Students will move the cursor around in a file that is shown in Form Window.
Practicing Computer Skills 4-4: Changing Entries
Students will practice changing some entries in the Volunteers file.
Practicing Computer Skills 4-5: Inserting a Record
Insert a record for Matt Redding. The Volunteers file should be on the screen in Form Window.
Practicing Computer Skills 4-6: Inserting Another Record
Add a record before Brice James to the Volunteers file.

TEACHING RESOURCES
(continued)

Practicing Computer Skills 4-7: Deleting Records
Delete a record in List Window.
Practicing Computer Skills 4-8: Deleting Another Record
Students delete another record in this exercise.
Practicing Computer Skills 4-9: Adding a Record at the End of a File
Add a record for Mike James to the Volunteers file.
Practicing Computer Skills 4-10: Adding Records at the End of a File
Add more records at the end of the Volunteers file.
Practicing Computer Skills 4-11: Sorting Records
Sort the Volunteers file alphabetically by last name.
Practicing Computer Skills 4-12: Finding Data
Use the Match Records routine in a database.
Practicing Computer Skills 4-13: Finding a Record and Deleting It
This exercise shows how to use the Match Records routine for practical purposes. The screen should show the Volunteers file.
Practicing Computer Skills 4-14: Finding Records and Changing Data
Find all of the records that have the entry, Monitor for lab, and make the entry shorter.
Practicing Computer Skills 4-15: Creating a New Database File
Students will create a new database file named Address from the Opening screen.
Practicing Computer Skills 4-16: Saving the Fields in the Address File
Save the fields for the Address file.
Practicing Computer Skills 4-17: Entering Data in a New File
Enter data in the Address file.

Worksheet 4-1 ACTIVITY. Cursor Moves:
Students write the job that each keystroke or key combination does in List Window. Then they do the same task for Form Window.

TEACHING RESOURCES
(continued)

Worksheet 4-2 COMPUTER. Starting the Sitter File: Students create a new database file with three records.

Worksheet 4-3 RETEACH. Data File Structure: Students are given several items to fit into a database in the appropriate place: file, field, or entry.

Worksheet 4-4 RETEACH. Database Commands: Reviews certain keystrokes for use in a database.

Worksheet 4-5 ENRICHMENT. Setting Values Formats: Students are shown how to change the way dates and times appear in the Address file.

Assessment:

HyperCard Stack. Database Intro: Types of databases, their parts, and their advantages are the focus of this stack.

HyperCard Worksheet. Database Introduction: Students will define database terms and list advantages of databases.

Test 4-A

Test 4-B

Portfolio 4. Using The Microsoft Works Database Program: Students will determine names for database files and fields, and draw a concept map to explain what a database is.

Skills Test 4. Students load the Colonies database and use the Skills Test 4 sheet to answer questions and make changes in it.

TEACHING STRATEGIES

Opening. Databases seem to be at the core of many controversies about computer use—information being used illegally, corrections being hard to make, too much information being collected. Yet many people reap the benefits of the databases used by pharmacists, physicians, and other professionals and the large commercial databases that they can connect to by telephone. Students might speculate about the databases that their names appear in—school, physicians, Social Security, and so on. Talk about the advantages of using databases. Show how to get information from the Volunteers file.

Teaching Tips. Students should be thinking about what hobbies or collections they have that could be recorded in a database file. The class may begin planning a database for another course, computer laboratory equipment, or some type of survey. Access to electronic databases through telecommunications is discussed in Chapter 5.
Ask students to talk to their parents and see if they use or maintain a database. Report findings to the class. Invite a parent to speak to the class.

When & How.
1. Use the videodisc clip to introduce the idea of a database. Students may have no knowledge base to work from on electronic databases.
2. Use analogies such as a phone book or a recipe book to explain parts of a database.
3. Discuss the file structure and the jobs that can be done in a database. Then have students learn to move the cursor through the Volunteers file.
4. Use the HyperCard stack "Database Intro," and its worksheet for assessment, review, or to introduce terms and ideas.

Computer Demonstration. Let students watch you perform the procedures discussed before they begin to work on their own, not necessarily with the same examples used in the Practicing Computer Skills exercises.

TEACHING STRATEGIES —————
(continued)

Cooperative Learning. Assign groups of students to find out how many school offices maintain files about them. Do the files hold the same data? Is any data incorrect? Who has access to the files: faculty members, students or parents? Check the principal's office, counselor's office, library, central administration office, etc.

Writing Activity. Ask students to describe completely one database that their name appears in. What is the filename? Where is the file located? What are some of the fields? How often is the file updated? etc.

Trouble shooting. Remind students that they can edit database entries much as they do text in word processors. The [Delete] key and the Cut command in the Edit menu are handy for deleting characters and database entries.
Students must be reminded to type characters exactly when using the Match Records routine.

Interdisciplinary Learning. Invite someone to speak about using a database program for recording family trees, recording research for a book, or keeping track of hobbies such as birdwatching or collecting stamps.
Discuss how people in professions such as construction, law enforcement, teaching, or environmental studies might benefit from accessing databases. A person in one of these professions might speak to the class about using a database.

Closing. Students can demonstrate an understanding of the chapter by creating a database on some topic of interest such as hobbies or collections they have. Other curriculum teachers in Social Studies or Science may develop projects that could be done with a database.

NOTES —————

# ● Lesson 4 - 1

p.66 - p.70

➡ PROJECTED LEARNING OUTCOMES

After studying the concepts and practicing the skills in this lesson, students should be able to:

● Name the purpose and parts of a database.
● Move the cursor freely in both Form Window and List Window.

📖 VOCABULARY TERMS

Database manager program	Field
	Entry
Database	Form Window
Retrieve	List Window
File	Open
Record	

🔍 LESSON OVERVIEW

● A database is a collection of related facts. A database manager program helps with organizing and accessing the facts.
● Large units of data in a database are called files. The files are divided into units called records. A record has smaller units called fields. Each piece of data in a field is called an entry.

# 📚 TEACHING RESOURCES

Practicing Computer Skills 4-1: Opening the Volunteers File
In this exercise, students will open the Volunteers file and view the file. The Volunteers file is left on the screen.

Practicing Computer Skills 4-2: Looking at List Window
Students will move the cursor around in a file that is shown in List Window. The exercise begins and ends with the Volunteers file on the screen.

Practicing Computer Skills 4-3: Looking at Form Window
Students will move the cursor around in a file that is shown in Form Window. The exercise begins and ends with the Volunteers file on the screen.

Worksheet 4-1 ACTIVITY. Cursor Moves:
Students write the job that each keystroke or key combination does in List Window. Then they do the same task for Form Window. Students could record these cursor moves for future reference. Students may work at the computer to try each keystroke or key combination.
Answers:
  1. down the entries in a field
  2. up the entries in a field
  3. right one field at a time
  4. left one field at a time
  5. right one field at a time
  6. down the entries in a field
  7. left one field at a time
  8. up the entries in a field
  9. down to the next field
10. up to the next field
11. down to the next field
12. up to the next field
13. down to the next field
14. up to the next field
15. down to the next field
16. up to the next field

TEACHING RESOURCES
(continued)

Worksheet 4-3 RETEACH. Data File Structure:
Students are given several items to fit into a database in the appropriate place: file, field, or entry. Can be used as reteach or as review at the end of the chapter.
Answers:

File:	Early Explorers
Fields:	Discovery
	Nationality
	Year
	Explorer
	Employer
Entries:	Juan Ponce de Leon
	Spanish
	Christopher Columbus
	Spain
	1498
	Spain
	Italian
	1513
	Florida
	Trinidad

1. The individual records in this particular file would be identified by each explorer's name.
2. In some database files, each record is assigned a number.
3. This file could be sorted by employer or by year.
4. You might find how many times the explorer Christopher Columbus is found or the number of times Spain sponsored a trip.

 LEARNING CHECK 4-1 ANSWERS

1. records
2. entries
3. Using the mouse, pull down the menu, move the cursor to the command and release the mouse button. You can also press the [Command] key with the code key for that command, such as [S] for Save.
4. pulling down the Format menu and selecting Show List.
5. down to the entry in the next field; down to the next entry in the same field
6. d
7. Answers will vary. However, security of private information about individual students should be mentioned.

PRACTICING COMPUTER SKILLS

4-1: Opening the Volunteers File

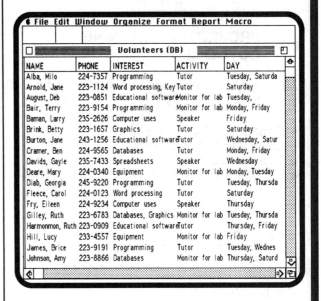

NAME	PHONE	INTEREST	ACTIVITY	DAY
Alba, Milo	224-7357	Programming	Tutor	Tuesday, Saturda
Arnold, Jane	223-1124	Word processing, Key	Tutor	Saturday
August, Deb	223-0851	Educational software	Monitor for lab	Tuesday,
Bair, Terry	223-9154	Programming	Monitor for lab	Monday, Friday
Baman, Larry	235-2626	Computer uses	Speaker	Friday
Brink, Betty	223-1657	Graphics	Tutor	Saturday
Burton, Jane	243-1256	Educational software	Tutor	Wednesday, Satur
Cramer, Ben	224-9565	Databases	Tutor	Monday, Friday
Davids, Gayle	235-7433	Spreadsheets	Speaker	Wednesday
Deare, Mary	224-0340	Equipment	Monitor for lab	Monday, Tuesday
Diab, Georgia	245-9220	Programming	Tutor	Tuesday, Thursda
Fleece, Carol	224-0123	Word processing	Tutor	Saturday
Fry, Eileen	224-9234	Computer uses	Speaker	Thursday
Gilley, Ruth	223-6783	Databases, Graphics	Monitor for lab	Tuesday, Thursda
Harmonmon, Ruth	223-0909	Educational software	Tutor	Thursday, Friday
Hill, Lucy	233-4557	Equipment	Monitor for lab	Friday
James, Brice	223-9191	Programming	Tutor	Tuesday, Wednes
Johnson, Amy	223-8866	Databases	Monitor for lab	Thursday, Saturd

The Volunteers file when students open it.

 # Lesson 4 - 2

p.70 - p.75

 ## PROJECTED LEARNING OUTCOMES

After studying the concepts and practicing the skills in this lesson, students should be able to:

- Change database entries.
- Insert and delete records.
- Sort records.
- Use the Match Records routine in a database.

 ## VOCABULARY TERMS

Update
Comparison information

 ## LESSON OVERVIEW

- Most database manager programs let the user do these jobs: a) add or delete data; b) search for data; c) change data; d) sort data into some order; and e) print a report.

 ## TEACHING RESOURCES

Practicing Computer Skills 4-4: Changing Entries
Students will practice changing some entries in the Volunteers file. This exercise begins and ends with the Volunteers file on the screen.

Practicing Computer Skills 4-5: Inserting a Record
Insert a record for Matt Rodding. The Volunteers file should be on the screen in Form Window. This exercise begins and ends with the Volunteers file on the screen.

Practicing Computer Skills 4-6: Inserting Another Record
Add a record before Brice James in the Volunteers file. This exercise begins and ends with the Volunteers file on the screen.

Practicing Computer Skills 4-7: Deleting Records
Delete a record in List Window. This exercise begins and ends with the Volunteers file on the screen.

Practicing Computer Skills 4-8: Deleting Another Record
Students will delete another record in this exercise. This exercise begins and ends with the Volunteers file on the screen.

Practicing Computer Skills 4-9: Adding a Record at the End of a File
Add a record for Mike James in the Volunteers file. This exercise begins and ends with the Volunteers file on the screen.

Practicing Computer Skills 4-10: Adding Records at the End of a File
Add more records at the end of the Volunteers file. This exercise begins and ends with the Volunteers file on the screen.

Practicing Computer Skills 4-11: Sorting Records
Sort the Volunteers file alphabetically by last name. This exercise begins and ends with the Volunteers file on the screen.

Practicing Computer Skills 4-12: Finding Data
Use the Match Records routine in a database. The exercise begins with the Volunteers file on the screen. At the end of the exercise, students are directed to leave the file on the screen.

TEACHING RESOURCES ───────
(continued)

Practicing Computer Skills 4-13: Finding a Record and Deleting It
This exercise shows how to use the Match Records routine for practical purposes. The screen should show the Volunteers file. At the end of the exercise, students are instructed to save the file and to leave the file on the screen.

Practicing Computer Skills 4-14: Finding Records and Changing Data
Find all of the records that have the entry, Monitor for lab, and make the entry shorter. At the end of the exercise, students save the file.

LEARNING CHECK 4-2 ANSWERS ───────

1. Click the mouse button once
2. They move move you out of the entry
3. Pull down the Edit menu, then select Insert Record
4. Highlight the entire record by clicking on the box at the left side of the record. Pull down the Edit menu, then select Cut.
5. Match Records
6. Pull down the Organize menu, then select Show All Records.
7. Answers will vary, however they should include items like to Match Records for persons who live in a particular neighborhood, or to set up a delivery route.

PRACTICING COMPUTER SKILLS ───────

4-12: Finding Data

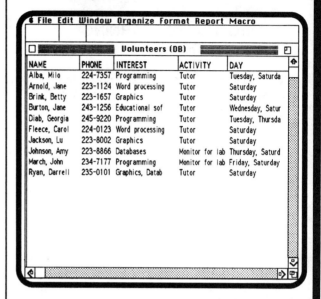

All records shown on the screen contain Saturday. On Georgia Diab's record, Saturday does not appear on the screen because there is not enough room to see it.

Lesson 4 - 3

p.75 - p.78

PROJECTED LEARNING OUTCOMES

After studying the concepts and practicing the skills in this lesson, students should be able to:

● Enter fields and data in a new database file.

LESSON OVERVIEW

● Students will be shown how to create their own new database.

 ### TEACHING RESOURCES

Practicing Computer Skills 4-15: Creating a New Database File
Students will create a database file named Address from the Opening screen, and type some fields . At the end of the exercise, students are directed to leave the screen as it is.

Practicing Computer Skills 4-16: Saving the Fields in the Address File
Students finish adding fields and save them for the Address file. At the end of the exercise, students are directed to leave the screen as it is.

Practicing Computer Skills 4-17: Entering Data in a New File
Students enter data in the Address file. At the end of the exercise, students are directed to save the file and Quit Microsoft Works.

Worksheet 4-2 COMPUTER. Starting the Sitter File: Students create a new database file with three records. This provides additional practice in entering fields and data.
Answers:
Parents might ask who can babysit on Fridays and charges $2.00 or less. Other fields could include more specific times (such as mornings, afternoons, and evenings), references, or interests.

Worksheet 4-4 RETEACH. Database Commands: Reviews certain keystrokes for use in a database. Use to reinforce, reteach, or review at the end of the chapter.
Answers:
Top
1. Move the cursor ahead to the next entry.
2. Change layouts
3. Cut a record or an entry
4. Start the Match Records routine
Bottom
1. Press the [Left Arrow] key to go back to the previous entry in the same record. Press [Up Arrow] to go back to the previous entry in just one field.
2. Move the page box in the scroll bar all the way down
3. Pull down the Edit menu, then select Insert Record
4. Pull down the Organize menu, then select Sort
5. Press an arrow or the [return] key

TEACHING RESOURCES
(continued)

Worksheet 4-5 ENRICHMENT. Setting Values Formats: Students are shown how to change the way dates and times appear in the Address file.

LEARNING CHECK 4-3 ANSWERS

1. Select the type of file, such as New Word Processor, New Database, etc..
2. Add Field
3. It tells the computer that you are finished typing one field name and are ready to move on to the next one.
4. You can insert a field name that you left out, or you can insert a record that you omitted while typing entries.
5. Press [Return] to leave the entry blank.
6. Answers will vary, however some reference to simplifying the layout and including all necessary data should be made.

PRACTICING COMPUTER SKILLS

4-17: Entering Data in a New File

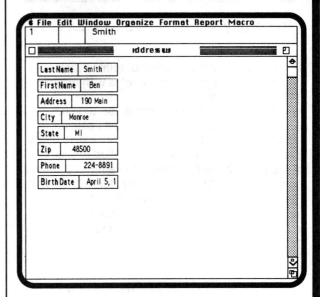

Ben Smith's record is shown in Form Window at the end of the exercise.

SKILLS TEST 4 ANSWERS

2. 12
3. 10
6. Sweden
7. Virginia
8. Virginia
9. Virginia, Maryland, Carolinas, Georgia

● Chapter 4 Summary

SUMMARY POINTS

● A database is a collection of related facts. A database manager program helps with organizing and accessing the facts.
● Large units of data in a database are called files. The files are divided into units called records. A record has smaller units called fields. Each piece of data in a field is called an entry.
● Most database manager programs let the user do these jobs: a) add or delete data; b) Match Records for data; c) change data; d) sort data into some order; and e) print a report.
● Students will be shown how to create their own new database.

DISCUSSION QUESTIONS

1. A database could hold information and show relationships between locations, flora, fauna, and environmental conditions. It could force students to organize and classify information. Users can ask for different types and combinations of information. A filename might be Vertebrate. Fields might include species; Latin names; characteristics; environmental needs; locations; remaining numbers; danger to species; and so on.
2. A database is no longer useful when the information is out-of-date, inaccurate, or incomplete. Updating the file improves it. Updating involves erasing errors and old data and writing in new data. Perhaps entire records may be deleted.
3. Redundancy is having too much of the same data in too many fields held by just one organization. With a single complete database, many people and departments in an organization can access the same database rather than having the same data in many files. Data in a single database is apt to be more accurate than similar data held in many database files.

DISCUSSION QUESTIONS
(continued)

4. The database screen is like the word processor screen in that it tells the file, the job, the prompt, and the menu names. It also tells the record number, and shows the prompts and dialog boxes as needed.

ACTIVITIES

1. Students may begin discussing similarities between the key commands in the word processor and the database modules.
2. Answers will vary, but can be about hobbies, important family records, possessions, or collections.
3. The student doing the exercises will probably catch errors.

Enrichment Activities

These activities are self-explanatory.

CHAPTER REVIEW

Vocabulary

1. A database is a collection of facts that are stored in a well-organized way.
2. A database manager program is software that lets you record, organize, and store information in a file.
3. A record is all of the information in a file about one person, animal, thing, or event.
4. A field is the part of a record that stored one characteristic of the person, thing, or event that the record is about.
5. An entry is the data put into one field of one record.

Questions

1. A file is a collection of related data such as Customer Billing. A record—the information about one of the entities in the file—could be the credit record of one customer. A field could be the customer's current balance; the field tells about just one aspect of each record.
2. List Window

CHAPTER REVIEW ─────────────
(continued)

3. Remove a record by highlighting the entire record and then select Cut from the Edit menu. Remove an entry by pressing [Delete].
4. Click on the entry to select it, then highlight the error with the mouse and cursor and type in the correct information.
5. the topic sports or the author Collier
6. Arrow keys
7. [X] Cut; [C] Copy; [S] Save
8. make the record current

NOTES ─────────────

● Chapter 5

TELECOMMUNICATIONS ⎯⎯

DESCRIPTION: Length 3:20. In this program, the hardware and terminology of data communications is introduced. A local bulletin board and the Prodigy Information Service are demonstrated.

Search to Chapter 5........Play

Suggested Additional Resources

● <u>Understanding Computers</u>, Third Edition, by Grace Murray Hopper and Steven L. Mandell, West Publishing Co.
● <u>Computer Skills Resources Guide: Microsoft Works for the Macintosh</u>, by Basil Melnyk, West Publishing Co.
● Computer magazines
● Microsoft Works manuals and documentation, Microsoft Corporation
● Telecommunications networks and bulletin boards - CREN, TENET, DIALOG, PRODIGY, or a local bulletin board for your city/state.

PROJECTED LEARNING OUTCOMES ⎯⎯⎯

After studying the concepts and practicing the skills in this chapter, students should be able to:

● Select records that fit one, two, or three rules for comparison in a database file.
● Create, format, and print a table report.
● List some ways to use database manager software.
● Describe telecommunications, including equipment and uses.
● Describe E-mail, electronic bulletin boards, and information services.

VOCABULARY TERMS ⎯⎯⎯

Comparison criteria	Start Bit
Format	Stop bits
Telecommunications	Data bits
Communication channel	Noise
	Parity
Modem	Odd parity
Digital signals	Even parity
Analog signals	Electronic bulletin board
Protocol	E-mail
Baud rate	Commercial database
BPS	Information network
Packet	Password

Using Advanced Features of the Database and Telecommunications

CHAPTER OVERVIEW

● With a database manager program, students can find records that have two or three entries in common. For example, students can set up rules that find records that have specific characteristics in common. Using the connectors And and Or provide different combinations of characteristics to find common records.

● A database file can be the basis for a report. A report format, or plan, includes only the fields and records needed, in the order desired. Options for the appearance of the page can be picked, too. The report format can be saved so that it can be used again.

● Telecommunications means to talk at a distance. Telecommunications, using computers, involves two computers with modems, telecommunications software, and telephones.

● A telephone can only accept tones or analog signals. Computers can only accept digital signals. A modem converts these signals back and forth.

● Protocol includes how fast information is transmitted as a baud rate; how bits are to be framed into characters as packets that include start bits, data bits, and stop bits; and how errors are checked through parity.

● An electronic bulletin board is an information service which is commonly shared by people with special interests.

● Electronic Mail can be a cost effective way of rapidly exchanging information.

● On-line information services use a computer, a modem, and a telephone to connect for varying kinds of information - including electronic mail, databases with an assortment of titles, newspapers, magazines, business information, and encyclopedias.

● The cost of an on-line service varies according to the services offered and the amount of time spent "on-line."

 TEACHING RESOURCES

Practicing Computer Skills 5-1: Selecting Data That Fits Two Rules
In this exercise, students will find the names of volunteers who will help with programming on Fridays, using the Volunteers file.

Practicing Computer Skills 5-2: Selecting Data That Fits Three Rules
Students will find data that fits three rules in the Volunteers file.

Practicing Computer Skills 5-3: Beginning a Report
In this exercise, students will begin a report that lists volunteers who can tutor in programming. Use the Volunteers file.

Practicing Computer Skills 5-4: Arranging the Report
Change some column widths and hide one field.

Practicing Computer Skills 5-5: Finishing the Report Format
Move a field, delete another field, and change some column widths using the Report Window.

Practicing Computer Skills 5-6: Selecting the Records for Printing
Choose only the records that contain the words "tutor" and "programming" for a report.

Practicing Computer Skills 5-7: Writing a Report Title
Add a title to the report, using the Report Window.

Practicing Computer Skills 5-8: Using the Page Setup Menu
Get the report ready for printing.

Practicing Computer Skills 5-9: Setting More Printer Options
Set margins for a report using the Print menu.

Practicing Computer Skills 5-10: Viewing a Report
Students will now view the report on the screen.

Practicing Computer Skills 5-11: Using a Printer
Now print the report on paper.

TEACHING RESOURCES
(continued)

Practicing Computer Skills 5-12: Starting the WestSoft On-Line Simulation
The WestSoft Information Network Simulation shows how to use a service that stores information and lists items that can be ordered. A modem is not needed (this is a simulated on-line service).

Practicing Computer Skills 5-13: Using the Buyer's Service
Students will see what products can be ordered through the Buyer's Service this month.

Practicing Computer Skills 5-14: Finding Other Information
Use the information network to find the answers to questions. Students must make choices from the menus until they reach the information needed.

Worksheet 5-1 ACTIVITY. Comparison Options and Connectors: Students are instructed to write selection rules using ten different comparison options and connectors. A chart with information on lakes throughout the world is used.

Worksheet 5-2 ACTIVITY. Database Menus: Six menus and screens are listed and students are directed to name three jobs that can be done or started at each.

Worksheet 5-3 RETEACH. Selecting Records in the Sources File: Additional questions concerning selection criteria help students to understand the steps.

Worksheet 5-4 RETEACH. Commands for a Report: Students write the keys or commandss used to do or start jobs associated with designing a report format.

Worksheet 5-5 ENRICHMENT. Calculations: Students are given information step-by-step to create a database and perform calculations on certain fields.

Worksheet 5-6 ACTIVITY. Telecommunications: Students define twelve telecommunications terms.

Transparency Master 5A. Using a Connector: Shows the choices available to select fields containing "Friday".

TEACHING RESOURCES
(continued)

Assessment:
HyperCard Stack. Telecommunications: Defines telecommunications and what is needed for telecommunications to take place.
HyperCard Worksheet. Telecommunications: Students will define telecommunications, explain what a modem does, and describe e-mail and electronic bulletin boards.

Test 5-A

Test 5-B

Portfolio 5. Using Advanced Features of the Database and Telecommunications: Students will create a database, respond to questions about telecommunications, and draw a concept map about telecommunications.

Skills Test 5. Students use the Skills Test 5 sheet to create the CAPS database and answer questions about it.

 ## TEACHING STRATEGIES

Opening. Selecting records in a database is a feature that lets people find the best statistics and players for a football season, the albums or videos that sell the best in a music store, and parents who are willing to tutor in English after school on Mondays. This feature is a major advantage of using a computer versus a filing cabinet. It is also the feature that causes problems—for example, when governments crosscheck files of various agencies and mail order companies buy lists of prospective customers based on previous buying habits. Discuss the meanings of the criteria contains, equals, is greater than, is less than, and the connectors And, and Or. Solicit examples of connectors using albums, football scores, or grades.
Introduce telecommunications by discussing the connection between databases and commercial networks. For example, talk about travel agencies, airlines, and publications. Other business use of communication channels can be mentioned such as publications and telecommuting employees.

Teaching Tips. Emphasize the fact that learning to make a report may take some effort, but like the word processor, the program eliminates the frustration of trying to type a perfect paper. Any report format is saved with the file, so it can be used over and over. Examine the style of the report, and ask for similar examples that students may have seen, for example, charts, tables of statistics, and so on. Since some students may already be involved in electronic bulletin boards, they might be willing to report on their experiences.
Students should access a commercial database network or an electronic bulletin board, if either is available.

When & How.
1. Open the chapter with a discussion of why Record Selection is a valuable aspect of databases. Use examples from the Opening strategy. Reinforce open-ended questioning during discusion.
2. Record Selection and report creation are detailed procedures. Be sure to demonstrate each of these on the computer before students try them.
3. As students work on Record Selection and report formats, talk about how the information on the screen helps prepare the report.
4. Open lesson 5-3 on telecommunications with the videodisc clip to get students' attention. Involve students who may already be using a commercial or private electronic bulletin board system.
5. Use the HyperCard stack Telecommunications, to demonstrate the availability and capabilities of commercial information systems.

Computer Demonstration. Let students watch you perform the procedures discussed before they begin to work on their own, not necessarily with the same examples used in the Practicing Computer Skills exercises.
Use classroom computer equipment or invite a guest to demonstrate his or her telecommunications equipment.

Cooperative Learning. Ask teams of students to use one of the database files in this chapter and create a word processor document with questions to be answered by selecting records. Let teams exchange questions to check the correctness of the questions and to review the selection process.

Assign a commercial database network such as The Source, CompuServe, Prodigy, StarText, or Iris to a group of students to investigate and word process a report. What services are offered? What equipment is needed? How much does it cost to subscribe? What kinds of information can you access? Do the phone companies in your area charge extra fees if you use a modem?

Writing Activity. Students may write a persuasive letter to their principal to purchase the necessary equipment and phone line for telecommunications in the computer lab (or social studies room or science room or library, etc.). They should include the equipment needed and clearly justify the purchase.

Trouble shooting. The connectors And, and Or can sometimes confuse students. Use an existing database and determine which records are chosen when each connector is used. Explain how each of the connectors exclude or include certain selections. Combinations of connectors should only be attemped for more advanced students.

Interdisciplinary Learning. Have students plan and complete a database file for another class they are taking.
Assign some research on fiber optics. Search out advantages of fiber optics over regular telephone wires. Search out whether your area has installed fiber optic cables. Search out information about new chips based on fiber optics.

Closing. Students can demonstrate an understanding of the chapter by creating a report from a database that gives exact information requested by you (or another teacher).

Lesson 5 - 1

p.84 - p.87

PROJECTED LEARNING OUTCOMES

After studying the concepts and practicing the skills in this lesson, students should be able to:

● Select records that fit one, two, or three rules for comparison in a database file.

VOCABULARY TERMS

Comparison criteria

LESSON OVERVIEW

● With a database manager program, students can find records that have two or three entries in common. For example, students can set up rules that find records that have specific characteristics in common. Using connectors such as And, and Or provide different combinations of characteristics to find common records.

Practicing Computer Skills 5-1: Selecting Data That Fits Two Rules
Students begin by loading Microsoft Works and the Volunteers file. They will find the names of volunteers who will help with programming on Fridays, using the Volunteers file. Students are directed to show the teacher the set of names (see answer, page 55.) The file is left on the screen at the end of the exercise.

Practicing Computer Skills 5-2: Selecting Data That Fits Three Rules
Students will find data that fits three rules in the Volunteers file. This exercise assumes the file is already open. Students are directed to show the teacher the set of names (see answer, page 55.) It ends by directing the student to save the Volunteers file.

Worksheet 5-1 ACTIVITY. Comparison Options and Connectors: Students are instructed to write selection rules using ten different comparison options and connectors. A chart with information on lakes throughout the world is used. Reinforces Record Selection techniques.
Answers: Answers will vary, suggestions are listed below.

1. Length equals 350
2. Length is greater than 300
3. Depth is less than 500
4. Elevation is not equal 0 (zero)
5. Name contains Aral Sea
6. Continen: begins with A
7. Continent does not contain Asia"
8. Continent contains Africa and Area is greater than 20000
9. Continent: contains Africa Or contains Asia
10. Elev is greater than 200 And is less than 800

In an Address file, you hunt in the Birth Date field for blank places: select is blank. In an magazine subscriber file, you hunt for persons who own a motorcycle: select is not blank. In an Address file, you could drop all of the addresses whose zip codes do not begin with 456 for this particular mailing.

TEACHING RESOURCES ———————
(continued)

Worksheet 5-3 RETEACH. Selecting Records in the Sources File: Additional questions concerning selection criteria help students to understand the steps. Students may try these exercises with the computer.
Answers:
1.   Date; is greater than or equal to; Jan 1, 1989; And; Date; is less than or equal to; Dec 31, 1989
2.   Date; equals; 1988; And; Subject; contains; hardware
3.   a. Pull down the Organize menu, then select Record Selection
     b. choose the Subject field
     c. choose contains
     d. Type in Ethics and click on Select

Transparency Master 5A. Using a Connector: Shows the choices available to select fields containing "Friday". Use if more direction is needed while students are doing the Practicing Computer Skills exercise Selecting Data That Fits Two Rules.

 LEARNING CHECK 5-1 ANSWERS ———————

1. Many items that you are not interested in may contain the same characters that you are looking for elsewhere.
2. c
3. b
4. a
5. Answers will vary, but should contain items like:
     - to store information on experiments
     - to store data on weather observations
     - to search for animals in a particular species
6. The rules could exclude many pertinent records from being found.

 PRACTICING COMPUTER SKILLS ———————

5-1: Selecting Data That Fits Two Rules

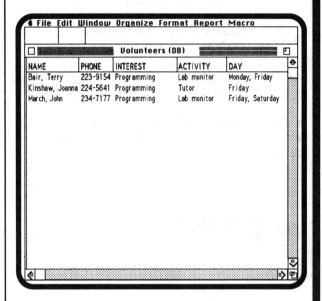

The three entries shown fit both rules.

5-2: Selecting Data That Fits Three Rules

Larry Bachman's entry is the only one that meets all of the selection rules.

Lesson 5 - 2

p.87 - p.94

 ## PROJECTED LEARNING OUTCOMES

After studying the concepts and practicing the skills in this lesson, students should be able to:

● Create, format, and print a table report.
● List some ways to use database manager software.

 ## VOCABULARY TERMS

Format

 ## LESSON OVERVIEW

● A database file can be the basis for a report. A report format, or plan, includes only the fields and records needed, in the order desired. Options for the appearance of the page can be picked, too. The report format can be saved so that it can be used again.

 ## TEACHING RESOURCES

Practicing Computer Skills 5-3: Beginning a Report
In this exercise, students will begin a report that lists volunteers who can tutor in programming. Use the Volunteers file. The exercise assumes the file is already open. At the end, students are directed to leave the file on the screen in Report Window.

Practicing Computer Skills 5-4: Arranging the Table
Starting in Report Window, students change some column widths and hide a field. The exercise ends in Report Window.

Practicing Computer Skills 5-5: Finishing the Report Format
Starting in Report Window, students move a field, change a column width and hide another field. The exercise ends in Report Window.

Practicing Computer Skills 5-6: Selecting the Records for Printing
Starting in Report Window, students use the Record Selection routine to choose only the records that contain the words "Tutor" and "Programming." The exercise ends in Report Window.

Practicing Computer Skills 5-7: Writing a Report Title
Starting in Report Window, students add a title to the report. The exercise ends in Report Window.

Practicing Computer Skills 5-8: Using the Page Setup Menu
Starting in Report Window, students get the report ready for printing. The exercise ends in Report Window.

Practicing Computer Skills 5-9: Setting More Printer Options
Starting in Report Window, students set margins. The exercise ends in Report Window.

Practicing Computer Skills 5-10: Viewing a Report
Starting in Report Window, students view the report on the screen. The exercise ends in Report Window.

Practicing Computer Skills 5-11: Using a Printer
The Volunteers file should be on the screen in Report Window. Now print the report on paper (see printout, page 57.) The exercise ends by directing students to Quit Microsoft Works.

TEACHING RESOURCES ——————
(continued)

Worksheet 5-2 ACTIVITY. Database Menus: Five menus and screens are listed. Students are directed to name three common jobs that can be done or started at each. In some cases, there are more than three correct answers. Sample answers:
1. Insert or Delete a field or record; change an entry
2. Get a report format; erase a format; print a report
3. Show Grid, change font, change type size
4. Change margins; change paper size; print headers
5. Choose to preview on the screen; choose which pages to print; choose to print on the printer

Worksheet 5-4 RETEACH. Commands for a Report: Students list keys or steps used for designing a report format. Use as review or reteach to remember what key combinations do.
Answers:
1. Select New Report from the Report menu
2. Move the field off the page
3. Move the dividing line to widen the column
4. Move the dividing line to shrink the column
5. Move it using the hand icon
6. Select Record Selection from the Organize menu
7. Select Page Setup from the File menu
8. Pull down the File menu
9. Type in 1 for Left margin
10. Select Print from the File menu
11. Click on OK

Worksheet 5-5 ENRICHMENT. Calculations: Students are given step-by-step information to create a database, perform calculations on certain fields, and print the report to the screen. You may want them to make a hardcopy.

LEARNING CHECK 5-2 ANSWERS ——————————

1. 8
2. a, b, and e
3. d
4. c
5. Place the cursor at the dividing line to the right of the field name. Then drag the line left.
6. Answers will vary, but should include items like:
   - to include the data in a letter
   - to use it in a form letter

PRACTICING COMPUTER SKILLS ——————————

5-11: Using a Printer

Volunteers Who Can Tutor in Programming

DAY	NAME	PHONE
Tuesday, Saturday	Alba, Milo	224-7357
Saturday	Arnold, Jane	223-1124
Tuesday, Thursday, Saturday	Diab, Georgia	245-9220
Tuesday, Wednesday	James, Brice	223-9191
Friday	Kinshaw, Joanna	224-5641
Monday	Redding, Matt	223-6767
Monday	Rose, Barbara	224-5423

Page – 1 – October 10, 1994

All of the records of volunteers who can tutor in programming are printed on a printer.

Lesson 5 - 3

p.94 - p.99

 ## PROJECTED LEARNING OUTCOMES

After studying the concepts and practicing the skills in this lesson, students should be able to:

● Describe telecommunications, including equipment and uses.

 ## VOCABULARY TERMS

Telecommunications	Packet
Communication channel	Start bit
Modem	Stop bits
Digital signals	Data bits
Analog signals	Noise
Protocol	Parity
Baud rate	Odd parity
BPS	Even parity

 ## LESSON OVERVIEW

● Telecommunications means to talk at a distance. Telecommunications, using computers, involves two computers with modems, telecommunications software, and telephones.
● A telephone can only accept tones or analog signals. Computers can only accept digital signals. A modem converts these signals back and forth.
● Protocol includes how fast information is transmitted as a baud rate; how bits are to be framed into characters as packets that include start bits, data bits, and stop bits; and how errors are checked through parity.

 ## TEACHING RESOURCES

Worksheet 5-6 VOCABULARY. Telecommunications: Students define twelve telecommunications terms. Use as an introductory or review activity depending on the knowledge base of the students.

Answers:
1. sending data to the host computer
2. putting data from the host computer on secondary storage
3. basic analog signal used to transmit data over telecommunications lines
4. means of sending data in a telecommunication network: contains start and stop information, origin and destination, and error check bits
5. transmission in which data is sent one character at a time
6. a bit that checks for errors in transmission
7. rules and procedures for sending data between two computers
8. rate at which data is sent
9. term that describes the rate at which data is sent
10. transmission in which data is sent in two directions at the same time
11. shared software offered at no charge except a modest sum or the price of the user's manual if the user likes the software
12. establishing and acknowledging connections between two computers

LEARNING CHECK 5-3
ANSWERS ——————————

1. computer, modem, telephone, telephone lines
2. helps one computer become part of another computer by "tricking" it into becoming an input/ output tool for the other computer; acts as a translator
3. allows computer to exchange information over a phone line
4. baud rate - number of bits being transmitted or received per second; packets - small chunks of data; parity - how bits in a packet add to check for errors
5. telephone line interference
6. method used to detect errors in data transmission
7. a person who translates from one language to another

Lesson 5 - 4

p.99 - p.102

 ## PROJECTED LEARNING OUTCOMES

After studying the concepts and practicing the skills in this lesson, students should be able to:

● Describe E-mail, electronic bulletin boards, and information services.

 ## VOCABULARY TERMS

Electronic bulletin board
E-mail
Commercial database
Information network
Password

 ## LESSON OVERVIEW

● An electronic bulletin board is an information service which is commonly shared by people with special interests.
● Electronic Mail can be a cost effective way of rapidly exchanging information.
● On-line information services use a computer, a modem, and a telephone to connect for varying kinds of information - including electronic mail, databases with an assortment of titles, newspapers, magazines, business information, and encyclopedias.
● The cost of an on-line service varies according to the services offered and the amount of time spent "on-line."

 ## TEACHING RESOURCES

Practicing Computer Skills 5-12: Starting the WestSoft On-Line Simulation
The WestSoft Information Network Simulation shows how to use a service that stores information and lists items that can be ordered. A modem is not needed (this is a simulated on-line service). Students are directed to the Network Menu and then the exercise ends.

Practicing Computer Skills 5-13: Using the Buyer's Service
Students will see what products can be ordered through the Buyer's Service this month. The exercise begins and ends at the Network Menu. Students may print a summary of the order if you choose. Orders will be different since students are allowed to select items for purchase from a list.

Practicing Computer Skills 5-14: Finding Other Information
Use the information network to find the answers to questions. Students must make choices from the menus until they reach the information needed.
Answers:
 1. 72/40 sunny
 2. 65/47 showers
 3. Babe Ruth, 15
 4. Roundball, Townball
 5. New York 30, Chicago 13; 35,059 fans
 6. Nancy Hogshead, Carrie Steinseifer
 7. Gorbachev; provides India with $1.2 billion in credit for major industrial projects and trade through 2001.
 8. a. Smoking is the leading single cause of death.
     b. Four out of five leading causes of death are related to cigarette smoking.
     c. About one in six deaths are related to smoking.

LEARNING CHECK 5-4 ANSWERS ─────────

1. try out different software programs; search information on a subject; exchange messages, etc.
2. electronic mail - personal or business messages that are sent electronically
3. offers news or information; provide movie reviews, sports news, weather information, etc.
4. used by on-line information services; if used, must be paid for
5. business people, individuals, etc.
6. membership fee, monthly fee, access fee, long-distance phone charge, etc.

 ## PRACTICING COMPUTER SKILLS ─────────

5-13: Using the Buyer's Service

```
-----------------------------------------
                   INVOICE

             WestSoft Buying Service

Sold to:
Sally Spectrum
401 Miramar
Las Cruces, NM 80018

-----------------------------------------
                      Sugg.
Inv       Brand/      Retail    Discount
*         Model       Price     Price

(1) 3011  Sony Walkman  $ 170    $ 102

-----------------------------------------

Charge to: Visa
Account No. 1234-123456-123

-----------------------------------------
```

This is a summary of a typical transaction. The summaries printed by students will show their names and the items that they ordered.

SKILLS TEST 5 ANSWERS ─────────

3a. 2   b. 3   c. 2
4. 1
5. 1
6a. 2   b. 1

● Chapter 5 Summary

SUMMARY POINTS

● A database manager program can find records that have two or three specific characteristics in common. Using connectors such as And, and Or provide different combinations of characteristics to find common records.

● A database report format, or plan, includes only the fields and records needed, in the order desired. Options for the appearance of the page can be picked, too.

● Telecommunications, using computers, involves two computers with modems, telecommunications software, and telephones.

● A telephone can only accept tones or analog signals. Computers can only accept digital signals. A modem converts these signals back and forth.

● Protocol includes how fast information is transmitted as a baud rate; how bits are to be framed into characters as packets that include start bits, data bits, and stop bits; and how errors are checked through parity.

● An electronic bulletin board is an information service which is commonly shared by people with special interests.

● Electronic Mail can be a cost effective way of rapidly exchanging information.

● On-line information services use a computer, a modem, and a telephone to connect for varying kinds of information - including electronic mail, databases with an assortment of titles, newspapers, magazines, business information, and encyclopedias.

DISCUSSION QUESTIONS

1. In a store, ask for a ruler and a notebook, a pencil or a pen, or a notebook that costs from $.75 through $2. Find a recipe that uses nuts and chocolate, a recipe that uses milk or buttermilk, a dessert recipe that has from 100 through 200 calories per serving. At the kennels, choose a dog that is small and white, a boxer or a Great Dane, or a female that weighs between 15 and 25 pounds.

DISCUSSION QUESTIONS
(continued)

2. Use the Match Records routine or the Record Selection routine. Use Match Records to locate one set of characters. Use Record Selection to locate data that meets more than one rule. The Record Selection routine can be used in preparing a report, too, so that the data found will be saved for later use.

3. That choice eliminates Volunteers whose list of days includes other days as well as Monday.

4. You may wish to create another report using some of the format of the first report.

5. There are many examples. Some are: to create a report of all honors students for the Honor Roll, to select athletes to be notified for scholarships, to print reports by teachers of classes, etc.

6. Most commercial information services are large, complex databases.

7. Students may answer this question on prior experience or on classroom work. Accept valid reasons for the selection.

8. A modem is needed to convert analog and digital signals to and from computers over telephone lines.

9. It checks for errors to assure the accuracy of the transmission. Information from a bank would contain many numbers and an incorrect transmission would cause many problems for customers.

10. Students may answer this question on prior experience or classwork. Accept valid reasons.

11. To obtain information without leaving your business or home, to communicate with people easily without "telephone tag," to quickly send information great distances, etc.

12. To obtain information not contained in your library, search out about new software packages, to get help on a project, etc. Science classes could communicate with SpaceLink, the free electronic bulletin board from NASA. Foreign Language students could send and receive messages in another language. English students could establish pen-pals and improve writing skills.

13. Students could interview parents who use telecomunications and report on benefits. A parent could talk to the class about benefits.

14. Similar recommendations as question #13.

15. Send notes to friends, search out homework assignments, contact a teacher for additional help, contact a professional for help on a difficult project, etc.

ACTIVITIES

1. Also see worksheet 5-1, Comparison Options and Connectors.
2. If students began notebooks, copies of the articles could be added, as well as a printout of the Sources file.
3. Students should write down the comparison options so they can study the differences between the two lists without using the computer.
4. After students are through using the Sources file for exercises, including those in later chapters, they can adapt the file to their own use or class-room use.
5. You may want students to produce a hardcopy of the report.
6. Information obtained will vary.
7. Ability to complete this exercise depends on availability of telecommunications.

Enrichment Activities.

1. Match the database programs to the student's abilities. Some programs are very different from Microsoft Works.
2. This exercise can mushroom into an unwieldy, large-scale project. Putting limits on the data is advisable.
3. Changes to input can make information that is used the most in a database visible on the screen as soon as the file is opened.
4. and 5. Ability to complete depends on availability of telecommunications.
6. Students can word process their findings or give oral reports.
7. Students can word process a summary of the article. Several students or the class could produce a booklet of telecommunications information.

CHAPTER REVIEW

Vocabulary

1. A format is a plan or design for a document.
2. A menu is a list of choices shown on the screen from which the user picks a command or data to enter into the computer..
3. A connector is a logic device that links comparisons for selection rules. The three connectors used in Microsoft Works are and, or, and not.
4. Telecommunications software is used so that one computer can communicate with another using a modem and phone lines.

CHAPTER REVIEW
(continued)

5. A modem is a device that allows a computer to exchange information over telephone lines.
6. Protocol is the set of rules that govern how signals are transmitted.
7. The ASCII character A with
even parity: 01000001
odd parity: 11000001
8. An electronic bulletin board is an information source and reference accessed electronically.
9. E-mail is electronic-mail; personal or business messages that are sent electronically.
10. An on-line information service is a commercial database or information network that can be accessed using a computer.

Questions

1. Use the connector And to link the comparison information "speak" and "computer uses."
2. Record Selection lets the user be much more specific about the information wanted.
3. to move a field to another location
4. List Window, Form Window, Report Window
5. Print the report on a printer, preview the report on the screen.
6. Purchase a modem and telecommunications software.
7. A modem translates a computer's digital signals into analog signals and then sends them over the phone line. The receiving modem does just the opposite.
8. Protocol is the set of rules that govern how signals are transmitted.
9. Baud rate is the speed at which information is sent/received. For successful transmission the two computers must operate at the same baud rate.
10. Lists telephone numbers of other boards, lists daily information or schedules, gives information on a particular subject, exchanges messages, etc.
11. Messages and information can be rapidly transmitted.
12. A password is used to get access to a network. It prevents someone else from using your subscription.
13. Anyone can use an electronic bulletin board who has the correct equipment, software, knowledge, and permission.

●Chapter 6

 ELECTRONIC SPREADSHEETS

DESCRIPTION: Length 2:28. Heidi and Elliot use the Microsoft Works spreadsheet to plan a school picnic for their class. The spreadsheet is used to keep track of food items needed for the picnic, calculate the number of each item needed, the costs, and the amount that each student must contribute to pay for the picnic.

Search to Chapter 6........Play

Suggested Additional Resources

● <u>Understanding Computers</u>, Third Edition, by Grace Murray Hopper and Steven L. Mandell, West Publishing Co.
● <u>Computer Skills Resources Guide: Microsoft Works for the Macintosh</u>, By Basil Melnyk, West Publishing Co.
● Computer magazines
● Microsoft Works manuals and documentation, Microsoft Corporation

→ PROJECTED LEARNING OUTCOMES

After studying the concepts and practicing the skills in this chapter, students should be able to:

● Recognize an electronic spreadsheet and list some of its uses.
● Enter labels, values, and formulas into an electronic spreadsheet.
● Format a spreadsheet so that it is easy to read.
● Explain how a spreadsheet can be used for forecasting.

 VOCABULARY TERMS

Electronic spreadsheet program	Value
	Entry
Cell	Formula
Coordinates	Function
Label	Forecast

Using the Spreadsheet Program

CHAPTER OVERVIEW

- Spreadsheet programs help solve math problems. They look like a table, with numbers and words arranged in rows and columns.
- Each entry in a spreadsheet goes into a cell. The first character that is typed into a cell tells the program whether a label or a value is being entered. A label tells about a part of the spreadsheet. A value can be a number or the result of a formula or a function. A formula is a math expression, and a function is a short-cut formula that is built into the program. Once all of the entries have been made, the program automatically refigures any changes.
- The spreadsheet can be formatted so that it is easier to understand. Labels can be left justified, right justified, or centered. Values can be given a fixed number of decimal points, shown as dollars or percentages, or shown with commas between thousands. Rows and columns can be added or deleted; columns can be made wider or narrower.
- A spreadsheet is ideal for preparing a forecast, that is, a plan that helps decide a course for the future. Students can try out various numbers to see what will happen to other numbers when the changes are made, and therefore predict how earnings or other numbers will be affected under certain circumstances.

TEACHING RESOURCES

Practicing Computer Skills 6-1: Opening a Spreadsheet File
Students will learn about the parts of a spreadsheet and how to move the cursor in a spreadsheet, using the Basketball file.

Practicing Computer Skills 6-2: Looking at a Spreadsheet File
Students will follow instructions and answer questions about the spreadsheet.

Practicing Computer Skills 6-3: Looking at Labels and Values
Students learn about labels and values and also enter some data into cells.

TEACHING RESOURCES
(continued)

Practicing Computer Skills 6-4: Starting a New Spreadsheet File
This exercise lets students start a Budget file.

Practicing Computer Skills 6-5: Entering Some Labels
This exercise lets students enter some labels.

Practicing Computer Skills 6-6: Entering Labels That Do Not Start with Letters
Students will enter labels starting with non-alpha characters.

Practicing Computer Skills 6-7: Entering Values
This exercise helps students enter values into the Budget file.

Practicing Computer Skills 6-8: Entering Formulas
This exercise helps students enter formulas into the Budget file.

Practicing Computer Skills 6-9: Entering Functions
Students will learn how to enter a function.

Practicing Computer Skills 6-10: Formatting Some Labels
Students try some formatting options for the labels on the spreadsheet.

Practicing Computer Skills 6-11: Formatting Some Values
Students try some formatting options for the values on the spreadsheet.

Practicing Computer Skills 6-12: Inserting Some Rows
Students add some blank rows to the spreadsheet.

Practicing Computer Skills 6-13: Adding a Decorative Line
Students will learn a trick to add a decorative line in one of the blank rows.

Practicing Computer Skills 6-14: Widening a Column
Students will widen a column to improve the appearance of the spreadsheet.

Practicing Computer Skills 6-15: Printing the Spreadsheet
Print the spreadsheet using a printer.

TEACHING RESOURCES
(continued)

Practicing Computer Skills 6-16: Forecasting with Cody's Spreadsheet
Students will change some of the values in the spreadsheet in order to forecast changes in this "what if" exercise.

Worksheet 6-1 VOCABULARY. Matching: Spreadsheet terminology is matched with brief definitions and characteristics.

Worksheet 6-2 ACTIVITY. Where Would You Use?: Eighteen jobs or items from Microsoft Works must be categorized as to which module it belongs to: word processor, database, or spreadsheet.

Worksheet 6-3 RETEACH. Spreadsheet Examples: An example of fifteen spreadsheet items must be given.

Worksheet 6-4 RETEACH. What Happens If?: Sixteen keystrokes are listed and students are instructed to tell what happens or what the program expects when those keys are pressed.

Worksheet 6-5 ENRICHMENT. Formatting: Students are instructed to create a spreadsheet file to investigate various formats for labels, values, and columns. Five functions are listed.

Transparency 6A Budget File without Formats: Shows a spreadsheet file that has not been formatted.

Assessment:
HyperCard Stack. Spreadsheet Intro: Covers general spreadsheet vocabulary and simple examples of how a spreadsheet is set up and used.

HyperCard Worksheet. Spreadsheet Introduction: Students will describe parts of a spreadsheet, list advantages, and sketch spreadsheet on a screen.

Test 6-A

Test 6-B

Portfolio 6. Using the Microsoft Works Spreadsheet Program: Students will create a concept map and answer questions about spreadsheets.

Skills Test 6. Students will create the Bowling spreadsheet, edit, format, and print it.

TEACHING STRATEGIES

Opening. Students will be confronted with a format that may be different from anything they have ever used. Show how a paper spreadsheet is used to keep track of numbers. Discuss cases when numbers will change during a year's time, such as the price of gasoline, the test scores needed to bring grades up to A's or B's, and so on. Discuss how a spreadsheet could help plan ahead.
Ask students to talk to their parents and see if they use or maintain a spreadsheet. Report findings to the class. Invite a parent to speak to the class.

Teaching Tips. Use relevant examples of spreadsheets with students rather than business ones which they may not have enough background to understand. Good examples can come from sports statistics or grade averages.

When & How.
1. Open the lesson with the videodisc clip to get students interested in spreadsheets. Continue with ideas from the Opening strategies.
2. Explain the cells, rows, and columns. Show labels and values. Then show the same parts in the Basketball file.
3. Erase all of the formulas and functions in the Basketball file. Have students try the Copy routine discussed in the Highlight about Copying Formulas to add formulas or functions to the file. Also, use the Copy routine to add two columns of six figures each, and then multiply each pair in each row.
4. Use Transparency Master 6A to introduce the section Changing the Looks of the Spreadsheet. Talk about how hard it is to read the spreadsheet when it looks so jumbled. Discuss what could be done to improve it.
5. Use the HyperCard stack "Spreadsheet Intro," and its worksheet for assessment, review, or to introduce terms and ideas.

Computer Demonstration. Let students watch you perform the procedures discussed before they begin to work on their own, not necessarily with the same examples used in the Practicing Computer Skills exercises.
Enter a short spreadsheet file. Allow students to format the cells. Ask students why they made their formatting choices.

Demonstrate the Find Cell and the Go To Cell routines in the Basketball file. Show how a set of characters or a particular cell can be found. Demonstrate how to select a cell and place the cursor in the active cell contents box to edit the contents of a cell without retyping the entire entry.

Cooperative Learning. In groups, allow students to figure out on paper (perhaps on a paper spreadsheet) what labels, values, formulas, and functions are needed for figuring grades for three students, Amy, Ben, and Carol. Use a small number of grades. Also, figure out how to write formulas for semester grades and the year's final grade.

Writing Activity. Have students interview someone who uses a spreadsheet and word process a report. What do they use it for? How often do they update it? How many columns and rows does it contain? What is the name of the software package? etc.

Trouble shooting. Before doing the Practicing Computer Skills exercises, discuss the arithmetic operators: +, -, *, /, and =. Then discuss the location of the keys that make the arithmetic operator symbols and also these: ", (, and).

Interdisciplinary Learning. Figure out how to use a spreadsheet to decide which department store or grocery store to shop. Rate five stores on their prices for five products that teenagers buy. The newspaper should be helpful to get prices, but trips to the stores would also work. The products must be the same brand at each store. For best results, check prices over a period of time.
To carry the activity further, weigh factors such as service, return policy, location, popularity, atmosphere, restrooms, and prices in order to rate on a scale of 1 to 10 which store is best. See how some groups come up with a different rating than others. Talk about how factors are weighed by opinion or need, for example. Do other types of rating, too. For example, rate three television shows for characters, plot, amount of violence, amount of sex, quality of music, appropriateness of music, and so on.

Closing. Students can demonstrate an understanding of the chapter by creating a spreadsheet using labels, values, formulas, and functions. A spreadsheet to calculate their grade over one reporting period would be useful.

Lesson 6 - 1

p.108 - p.112

 PROJECTED LEARNING OUTCOMES

After studying the concepts and practicing the skills in this lesson, students should be able to.

● Recognize an electronic spreadsheet and list some of its uses.

 VOCABULARY TERMS

Electronic spreadsheet program
Cell
Coordinates

 **LESSON OVERVIEW**

● Spreadsheet programs help solve math problems. They look like a table, with numbers and words arranged in rows and columns.

 **TEACHING RESOURCES**

Practicing Computer Skills 6-1: Opening a Spreadsheet File
Students will learn about the parts of a spreadsheet and how to move around in a spreadsheet, using the Basketball file. Students open the file and leave it on the screen.

Practicing Computer Skills 6-2: Looking at a Spreadsheet File
Students view the Basketball file and will follow instructions and answer questions about the spreadsheet. The file is left on the screen at the end of the exercise.
Answers:
1. top, center
2. Active cell indicator, entry bar
3. row 11
4. column D

Practicing Computer Skills 6-3: Looking at Labels and Values
Students learn about labels and values and also enter some data into cells. Students are directed to show the teacher the altered file (see answer, page 69). The exercise ends by quitting Works.
Answers:
4. Students should list any of the team names, the word Opponent, Hawks, etc.

 LEARNING CHECK 6-1 ANSWERS

1. When you change a value, any figures that are affected by the change are recalculated automatically.
2. b
3. Rows are labeled with numbers and columns are labeled with letters.
4. Enter or change data in it.
5. Press the [Delete] key to erase the mistake, then retype it. If you already pressed [Return], simply highlight the cell and place the cursor at the appropriate character in the active cell contents box, then correct the data.
6. Answers will vary; however some point about not losing all information about the business's inventory, sales, accounts, etc. should be noted.

PRACTICING COMPUTER SKILLS

6-1: Opening a Spreadsheet File

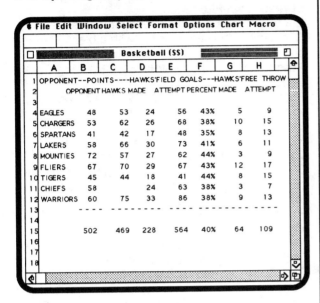

The Basketball file should be on the screen at the end of this exercise.

6-3: Looking at Labels and Values

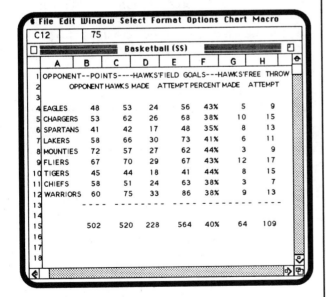

Students add an entry to the Basketball file.

Lesson 6 - 2

p.112 - p.116

 PROJECTED LEARNING OUTCOMES

After studying the concepts and practicing the skills in this lesson, students should be able to:

● Enter labels, values, and formulas into an electronic spreadsheet.

 VOCABULARY TERMS

Label
Value
Entry
Formula
Function

 **LESSON OVERVIEW**

● Each entry in a spreadsheet goes into a cell. The first character that is typed into a cell tells the program whether a label or a value is being entered. A label tells about a part of the spreadsheet. A value can be a number or the result of a formula or a function. A formula is a math expression, and a function is a short-cut formula that is built into the program. Once all of the entries have been made, the program automatically refigures any changes.

 TEACHING RESOURCES

Practicing Computer Skills 6-4: Starting a New Spreadsheet File
Starting at the Opening screen, students create a Budget file. The screen is left with a blank spreadsheet on it.

Practicing Computer Skills 6-5: Entering Some Labels
Starting with a blank spreadsheet, this exercise lets students enter some labels. The screen is left as is.

Practicing Computer Skills 6-6: Entering Labels That Do Not Start with Letters
Students will enter labels starting with non-alpha characters into the Budget file. The file is left on the screen.

Practicing Computer Skills 6-7: Entering Values
This exercise helps students enter values into the Budget file. The file is left on the screen.

Practicing Computer Skills 6-8: Entering Formulas
This exercise helps students enter formulas into the Budget file. Students are directed to show the teacher the file (see answer, page 71). The file is left on the screen.

Practicing Computer Skills 6-9: Entering Functions
In this exercise students will learn how to enter a function. The exercise ends by directing students to save the file and leave the screen as is. The file now looks like Transparency Master 6A.

 LEARNING CHECK 6-2 ANSWERS

1. arrow keys
2. Type " (quotation mark) using [Shift].
3. a
4. = (equals sign)
5. Use the mouse and click on the option.
6. Answers will vary; however the student might mention:

   - =COUNT - count the number of items in inventory listed in a column or row
   - =MAX - find the salesman with the largest commission
   - =MIN - find the salesman with the smallest commission

6-5: Entering Some Labels

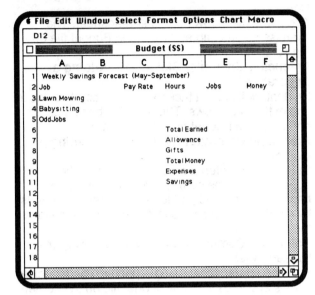

Labels have all been entered into the Budget file.

6-8: Entering Formulas

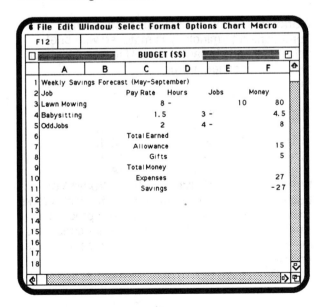

The labels, values and formulas have all been added to the Budget file.

6-9: Entering Functions

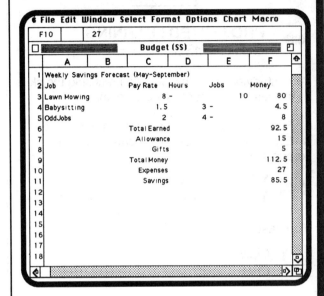

The Budget file with all of the labels, values, functions and formulas. If Cody can do the work shown above, he will save $85.50 each week.

Lesson 6 - 3

p.116 - p.121

 ## PROJECTED LEARNING OUTCOMES

After studying the concepts and practicing the skills in this lesson, students should be able to:

● Format a spreadsheet so that it is easy to read.
● Explain how a spreadsheet can be used for forecasting.

VOCABULARY TERMS

Forecast

 ## LESSON OVERVIEW

● The spreadsheet can be formatted so that it is easier to understand. Labels can be left justified, right justified, or centered. Values can be given a fixed number of decimal points, shown as dollars or percentages, or shown with commas between thousands. Rows and columns can be added or deleted; and columns can be made wider or narrower.
● A spreadsheet is ideal for preparing a forecast, that is, a plan that helps decide a course for the future. Students can try out various numbers to see what will happen to other numbers when the changes are made, and therefore predict how earnings or other numbers will be affected under certain circumstances.

 ## TEACHING RESOURCES

Practicing Computer Skills 6-10: Formatting Some Labels
Try some formatting options for the labels on the spreadsheet. The exercise begins and ends with the Budget file on the screen.

Practicing Computer Skills 6-11: Formatting Some Values
Try some formatting options for the values on the spreadsheet. The exercise begins and ends with the Budget file on the screen.

TEACHING RESOURCES
(continued)

Practicing Computer Skills 6-12: Inserting Some Rows
Add some blank rows to the spreadsheet. The exercise begins and ends with the Budget file on the screen.

Practicing Computer Skills 6-13: Adding a Decorative Line
Students will learn a trick to add a decorative line in one of the blank rows. The exercise begins and ends with the Budget file on the screen.

Practicing Computer Skills 6-14: Widening a Column
Students will widen a column to improve the appearance of the spreadsheet. The exercise begins with the Budget file on the screen and ends by directing the students to save the file and leave the screen as is.

Practicing Computer Skills 6-15: Printing the Spreadsheet
Print the spreadsheet using a printer. The exercise begins and ends with the Budget file on the screen.

Practicing Computer Skills 6-16: Forecasting with Cody's Spreadsheet
Students will change some of the values in the spreadsheet in order to forecast changes in this "what if" exercise. The students are directed to quit at the end of the exercise.

Worksheet 6-1 VOCABULARY. Matching:
Spreadsheet terminology is matched with brief definitions and characteristics. Use to reinforce or review spreadsheet terms.
Answers:

1. e	7. g	13. f
2. j, i	8. c	14. g
3. c	9. b	15. a
4. d	10. d	16. h
5. i	11. c	17. f
6. a	12. d	18. j

Worksheet 6-2 ACTIVITY. Where Would You Use?: Eighteen jobs or items from Microsoft Works must be categorized by module: word processor, database, or spreadsheet. This chapter concludes the study of major components of Microsoft Works.
Answers:

Word Processor: Match Whole Words Only
Replace routine
Superscript
Check Upper/Lowercase
Double space

Database: and, or
                             is less than or equal to
                             fields
                             Report Window
                             Record Selection
                             List Window
                             connector
Spreadsheet: =SUM
                             active cell
                             coordinates
                             functions
                             forecasting
                             true/false

Worksheet 6-3 RETEACH. Spreadsheet Examples: An example of fifteen spreadsheet items must be given. This can be used for reteach or review of the parts of a spreadsheet.
Answers on some questions may vary:

1. G12   9. A
2. Cost   10. 10
3. 35.65   11. 36
4. =C3+C4/2   12. Down Arrow
5. =SUM(D2:D20)   13. recalculation
6. Copy   14. D5 to E7
7. with dollar signs 15. Go To Cell
8. centered

Worksheet 6-4 RETEACH. What Happens If?:
Sixteen keystrokes are listed; students must tell what happens or what the program expects when those keys are pressed. Use as reteach or review of the jobs in the spreadsheet module.
Answers:
1. Highlighting moves to the last column in the file
2. The entry is accepted and the program calculates.
3. The program expects a label, no matter what character follows the quotation mark.
4. The program expects a value, no matter what character follows the equals sign.
5. The highlighting moves to the cell below
6. The highlighting moves to the last row that has an entry.
7. The highlighting moves to the last row
8. The program expects to delete a row or column
9. The program expects you to enter the coordinates of a cell to Go To.
10. The program expects comparison information for the Search routine
11. The program expects you to insert a row or column

12. The program expects you to type in the number of digits after the decimal point.
13. The program expects you to change the filename.
14. The program shows printer options.
15. The program quits whatever job you were doing.
16. The screen shows all the formulas or functions.
Worksheet 6-5 ENRICHMENT. Formatting:
Students are instructed to create a spreadsheet file to investigate various formats for labels, values and columns. Five functions are listed also. A printout will show what formatting the students have done.
Answers:
1. The label hugs the right side of the cell
2. The label hugs the left side of the cell
3. The label is centered
4. The number of decimal points remains the same for each number
5. The value has a dollar sign in front of it
6. The value has a comma between thousands and hundreds
7. The value has a percent sign after it
8. The column width changes
9. The column moves to another location
10. - 13. Should all show ranges within the parentheses.
14. Should show one value within the parentheses

Transparency 6A Budget File without Formats:
Shows a spreadsheet file that has not been formatted. Use as an introduction to the section Changing the Looks of the Spreadsheet. Talk about how hard it is to read the spreadsheet when it looks so jumbled. Discuss what could be done to improve it.

 LEARNING CHECK 6-3 ANSWERS ————

1. format
2. b, d
3. Move the highlighting to the point where you want to do the job.
4. a
5. The number is too large to fit in the cell
6. Answers will vary; however students will probably mention changing a final test grade to see how it will affect the final average.

Lesson 6 - 3

(Continued)

 ## PRACTICING COMPUTER SKILLS

6-10: Formatting Some Labels

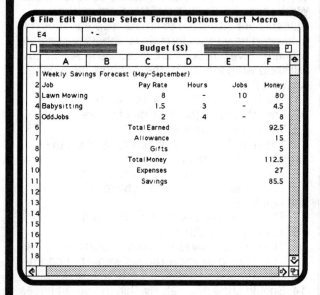

The labels are formatted to improve appearance.

6-11: Formatting Some Values

The values are formatted to improve appearance.

PRACTICING COMPUTER SKILLS
(continued)

6-12: Inserting Some Rows

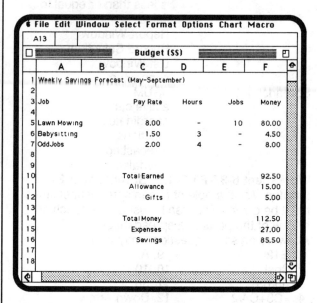

Blank rows have been added to separate the information in the spreadsheet and make it easier to read.

6-13: Adding a Decorative Line

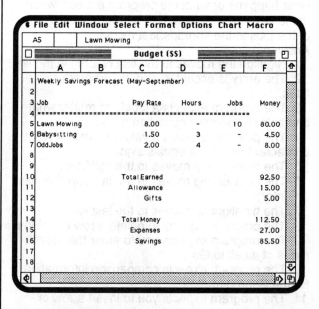

The decorative line separates the labels from the rest of the information.

PRACTICING COMPUTER SKILLS
(continued)

6-15: Printing the Spreadsheet

```
Weekly Savings Forecast (May-September)-

Job              Pay Rate Hours Jobs  Money
=============================================
Lawn Mowing        8.00     -    10    80.00
Babysitting        1.50     3    -      4.50
Odd Jobs           2.00     4    -      8.00


                      Total Earned     92.50
                      Allowance        15.00
                      Gifts             5.00

                      Total Money     112.50
                      Expenses         27.00
                      Savings          85.50
```

When printed to a printer, the final Budget spread-sheet looks like this.

6-16: Forecasting With Cody's Spreadsheet

Answer: No.
Students must change the values in the spread-sheet until the savings figure is at least $100. Each student's spreadsheet will reflect his/her own plan to achieve $100 savings.

SKILLS TEST 6 ANSWERS

The Bowling file will look like this when printed.

```
BIG LEAGUE BOWLING TEAM
         GAME 1  GAME 2  GAME 3  GAME 4  GAME 5   AVG
Tom        128     144     178     158     198   161.2
Kirk       109     145     123     133     100   122.0
Bev        210     178     166     189     150   178.6
Michele    121     100      98     144     140   114.6
Richie      97     101     150     158     135   128.2
```

● Chapter 6 Summary

SUMMARY POINTS

● Spreadsheet programs help solve math problems. They look like a table, with numbers and words arranged in rows and columns.
● Each entry in a spreadsheet goes into a cell. A label tells about a part of the spreadsheet. A value can be a number or the result of a formula or a function. A formula is a math expression, and a function is a short-cut formula that is built into the program. Once all of the entries have been made, the program automatically refigures any changes.
● A formatted spreadsheet is easier to understand. Labels can be left justified, right justified, or centered. Values can be given a fixed number of decimal points, shown as dollars or percentages, or shown with commas between thousands. Rows and columns can be added or deleted; columns can be made wider or narrower.
● A spreadsheet is ideal for preparing a forecast. Students can try out various numbers to see what will happen to other numbers when the changes are made, and therefore predict how earnings or other numbers will be affected under certain circumstances.

DISCUSSION QUESTIONS

1. Jobs include budgets, price comparisons, costs of buying and owning a car, costs of producing a school newspaper or yearbook, sports statistics for almost any sport, records on some types of physics experiments, checks for algebra or other math problems, and so on. Accept reasonable answers for planning ahead and making a job easier.
2. Press [Right Arrow]. Use the mouse and the scroll bar at the bottom of the screen. Use the Find Cell routine to find Rebounds. Use the Go To Cell routine to find a cell with coordinates off the screen.
3. Active cell is the highlighted cell that you can work in, that is, update or edit. Grid is a criss-cross of lines that make the cells. Worksheet is the actual file on the screen where you can make entries.

TEACHING RESOURCES
(continued)

4. When a formula contains references to many cells, using a function saves typing all of the cell references. You do not have to remember a real math formula, either, but can use the function and its format, which requires no math.
5. A school can use a spreadsheet to plan budgets by forecasting (or analyzing) costs and income for the following year. Officials can include projected money from taxes, federal programs, and grants, as well as allow for projected inflation and increases in wages and raw materials.

ACTIVITIES

1. This activity can follow Discussion Question 1. Students can plan their own spreadsheet project. Look at how students use labels, formulas, and functions, and see whether students included options for forecasting or analyzing data on the spreadsheet.
2. Some students may want to do this activity for use in classes other than math, such as physics.
3. Students should submit a very short word processed paper describing their observations.
4. Students may need considerable help, but some may be able to figure out what to do easily, based on their experiences with the other two Microsoft Works modules.

Enrichment Activities.

1. Students should submit a few examples on paper or on a word processor document.
2. Examples include the following:
=AVG(C5:C14) to average a column of ten test scores
=COUNT(A1:F16) to count cells in a block of the Budget file
=MAX(D2:D28) to find the highest score
=MIN(D2:D28) to find the lowest score
=SQRT(356) to find the square root of 356

CHAPTER REVIEW —————

Vocabulary

1. e
2. a
3. c
4. b
5. d

Questions

1. a
2. It automatically recalculates values as you make new entries or changes.
3. true
4. a, b
5. Type a quotation mark.
6. Start with an equals sign.
7. =SUM(B3:B7)
8. A spreadsheet can be used to find the expected interest on your savings account by the end of the year, based on rates and additional deposits. It can help decide what is necessary to save for a particular item such as a CD player or a weight machine.

● Chapter 7

 ## LOOKING BACK

DESCRIPTION: Length 4:24. This program provides an overview of the development of computers from the abacus through the CRAY supercomputer. Various computing devices including mechanical calculators, the ENIAC computer, second and third generation mainframe computers, and personal computers are shown.

Search to Chapter 7........Play

Suggested Additional Resources

● <u>Understanding Computers</u>, Third Edition, by Grace Murray Hopper and Steven L. Mandell, West Publishing Co.
● Computer magazines
● Blair, Marjorie. "Through the Looking Glass with Grace Hopper," Electronic Education, Vol 3, No. 4, Jan, 1984.
● Reid-Green, Keith. "The History of Census Tabulation," Scientific American, Feb, 1989.
● Cobblestone magazine, June, 1984, is devoted to computer history.

 ## PROJECTED LEARNING OUTCOMES

After studying the concepts and practicing the skills in this chapter, students should be able to:

● Describe how Pascal, von Leibniz, Jacquard, Babbage, and Hollerith contributed to the development of computers.
● Tell how the Mark I, ABC, ENIAC, and EDVAC led to the development of first-generation computers.
● List the chief characteristics of each of the four computer generations.
● Explain each important development in data processing in terms of specific needs for faster, more reliable methods.
● Access field names and edit them in an Microsoft Works database file.

 ## VOCABULARY TERMS

Calculator	Silicon
Punched cards	Real-time
Vacuum tube	Integrated circuit (IC)
Binary notation	Silicon chip
Electronic digital	Minicomputer
computer	Remote terminal
Stored-program	Large-scale integration
concept	(LSI)
Generation	Microprocessor
Language-translator	Personal computer
program	Very-large-scale integra-
Transistor	tion (VLSI)

Looking Back

CHAPTER OVERVIEW

● People have always looked for ways to handle data. Early devices used for counting and problem solving include the abacus, La Pascaline, and the Leibniz Calculator.

● The first "programmable" machine was a weaving loom, with punched cards to guide the loom. Hollerith also used punched cards in his Tabulating Machine that handled census data.

● Charles Babbage was called the Father of Computers because his plans for an Analytical Engine outlined ideas important in the design of computers. The first automatic calculator, the Mark I, used many of these ideas, but the first actual computers were the ABC and the ENIAC.

● Von Neumann outlined the stored-program concept, an idea for storing programs in computer memory rather than resetting switches and wires. The idea was used in the EDVAC.

● Electronic computers first used vacuum tubes for their circuits. These first-generation machines were huge, slow, and unreliable. The invention of transistors led to faster, smaller, second-generation computers. The use of silicon chips led to even faster and smaller third- and fourth-generation computers. Today's computers rely on large-scale integrated circuits and very-large-scale integrated circuits.

TEACHING RESOURCES

Practicing Computer Skills 7-1: Changing Field Names in the History Database File
Students will change some of the field names in the History database file.

Practicing Computer Skills 7-2: Adding Data to the History File
Students will fill in the blank spots in the History file.

TEACHING RESOURCES
(continued)

Worksheet 7-1 ACTIVITY. Chronology: Students must put three sets of events in chronological order.

Worksheet 7-2 ACTIVITY. Comparing Computer Generations: Students list the characteristics of each of the four generations of computing.

Worksheet 7-3 RETEACH. Summing Up: Students fill in the blanks with words or phrases that tell the history of computing.

Worksheet 7-4 RETEACH. Four Technologies: Students fill in the blanks with words or phrases and answer a question about trends in technology.

Worksheet 7-5 ENRICHMENT. Even More: Additional people and developments are included in this worksheet on computer history.

Transparency Master 7A . Chief Characteristic of Each Generation: Lists the four generations and an important characteristic of each.

Test 7-A

Test 7-B

Portfolio 7. Looking Back: Students will respond to questions about computer history, design their own computer, and create a concept map about the classification of computers.

Skills Test 7. Students use the History database and make changes to create a report.

TEACHING STRATEGIES

Opening. A demonstration with real machines can help students see how technology has advanced. If possible, bring to class an abacus, a crank-driven adding machine, a slide rule, an old manual typewriter, a hand-held electronic calculator, and other devices. Discuss the fact that each new development not only changed the speed with which jobs were done, but also changed the nature of the job itself. The problems workers had with La Pascaline and the Jacquard loom were harbingers of the problems labor has with robots and other automated machines today.

Teaching Tips. Discuss the length of time between the development of the abacus (about 500 B.C.) and the invention of paper (1000 A.D.). In early times, paper, writing, and knowledge were limited to a select few. Books were so valuable that they were carefully guarded in libraries. In 1458, Johann Gutenberg invented the printing press. The time difference between La Pascaline in 1642 and the ENIAC in 1943 is small compared to the time difference between the development of the abacus and La Pascaline. The time between the ENIAC and the Apple microcomputer in 1976 is even smaller. In less than 20 years, microcomputers have become more common in homes. As technology grew at a faster rate, more people had the benefits of learning and reading for themselves.
Show a vacuum tube, a transistor, and a computer chip. Perhaps someone in the community collects technology items.
Find some old encyclopedias and see what these volumes have to offer about computers. Also, ask students to ask grandparents and parents if they remember news articles about computers during the war years and in the late 1940s. Use *The Readers' Guide to Periodicals* for the late 1930s and early 1940s to find magazine articles about the machines.

When & How.
1. Open the lesson with the videodisc clip to get the students' attention.
2. Use ideas from the other Teaching Strategies for a variety of activities in this chapter. Studying history does not have to be boring.

TEACHING STRATEGIES
(continued)

3. Discuss the fact that part of Babbage's need was for accuracy, and he envisioned a machine that had the potential to eliminate human workers and their mistakes. Discuss the reasons why people and organizations were willing to invest in the development of computing machines.

Computer Demonstration. If you have access to a software program that does time lines such as Scholastic's *Point of View*, use it to show technology developments in the context of other social and governmental happenings.

Classroom Management. Incorporate as many activities as possible into this unit so that the history of technology will remain interesting. Allow students to continue to use the word processor to produce requested papers.

Cooperative Learning. Use teams of three or four students to create a computer history trivia game. Let the groups trade games and use as a review at the end of the chapter.

Writing Activity. Invite students to write "news articles" about the early inventions. They can use other sources and imagine interviews, too. If they have access to desktop publishing, allow them to publish their articles in a paper.
Students could imagine a character called "Father Time," who watches over the developments of Earth. As Father Time, students should write journals about the development of calculating devices. The journals can be serious or humorous. This activity can continue throughout the chapter. Treat the new computer developments as products and write advertisements for them. Use desktop publishing to produce a flyer selling the product.

Interdisciplinary Learning. Have students maintain a computer time line throughout this chapter. It could also include other relevant inventions. Students may insert important family events on the time line, too.

Closing. The Practicing Computer Skills exercises instruct students to use a database file about computer history. The finished database can be used to review for the chapter test and to answer relevant questions about computer history.

NOTES ————————————

NOTES ————————————

Lesson 7 - 1, 2

p.126 - p.134

 ## ➡ PROJECTED LEARNING OUTCOMES

After studying the concepts and practicing the skills in this lesson, students should be able to:

● Describe how Pascal, von Leibniz, Jacquard, Babbage, and Hollerith contributed to the development of computers.
● Tell how the Mark I, ABC, ENIAC, and EDVAC led to the development of first-generation computers.

📖 VOCABULARY TERMS

Calculator	Binary notation
Punched cards	Electronic digital computer
Vacuum tube	Stored-program concept

 ## 🔍 LESSON OVERVIEW

● People have always looked for ways to handle data. Early devices used for counting and problem solving include the abacus, La Pascaline, and the Leibniz Calculator.
● The first "programmable" machine was a weaving loom, with punched cards to guide the loom. Hollerith also used punched cards in his Tabulating Machine that handled census data.
● Charles Babbage was called the Father of Computers because his plans for an Analytical Engine outlined ideas important in the design of computers. The first automatic calculator, the Mark I, used many of these ideas, but the first actual computers were the ABC and the ENIAC.
● Von Neumann outlined the stored-program concept, an idea for storing programs in computer memory rather than resetting switches and wires. The idea was used in the EDVAC.

 ## 📁 TEACHING RESOURCES

Practicing Computer Skills 7-1: Changing Field Names in the History Database File
Students will change some of the field names in the History database file. Students begin by loading Microsoft Works and the History file. The exercise ends with the History file on the screen.

Practicing Computer Skills 7-2: Adding Data to the History File
Students will fill in the blank spots in the History file with information from the chapter. The exercise ends by directing students to quit Microsoft Works.

Worksheet 7-3 RETEACH. Summing Up:
Students fill in the blanks with words or phrases that tell the history of computing. This may help students who are having trouble remembering events. This activity could also be used by students as they read the material.
Answers:
La Pascaline
Babbage
figure taxes
more accurate math tables
punched
census
Mark I
ABC
vacuum tubes
general-purpose
von Neumann
stored-program

LEARNING CHECK 7-1 ANSWERS

1. add, subtract
2. add, subtract, multiply, divide, square roots
3. a loom
4. b
5. Augusta Ada Byron, Countess of Lovelace
6. Pascal, Ada
7. 1890
8. Answers will vary; however, students may respond that some people would react positively because the census would be counted faster; others may have responded negatively because their jobs were in jeopardy.

 ## LEARNING CHECK 7-2 ANSWERS

1. d
2. Howard Aiken
3. it used vacuum tubes, it was coded using binary notation
4. c
5. stored-program
6. Answers will vary; however students may reference the need for gunnery tables or weather analysis.

 ## PRACTICING COMPUTER SKILLS

7-1: Changing Field Names in the History Database File

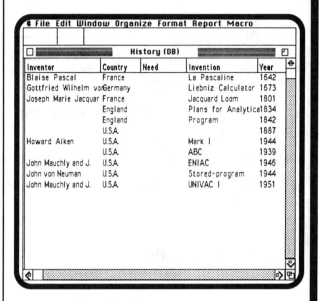

The History file appears like this after formatting changes have been made.

7-2: Adding Data to the History File

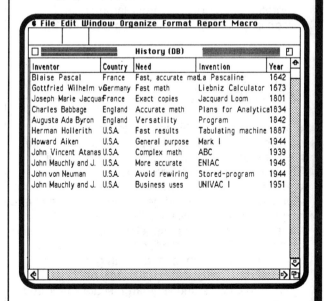

Students' additions to the History database should generally include this information.

 # Lesson 7 - 3

p.135 - p.141

 ## PROJECTED LEARNING OUTCOMES

After studying the concepts and practicing the skills in this lesson, students should be able to:

● List the chief characteristics of each of the four computer generations.
● Explain each important development in data processing in terms of specific needs for faster, more reliable methods.
● Access field names and edit them in an Microsoft Works database file.

 ## VOCABULARY TERMS

Generation
Language-translator program
Transistor
Silicon
Real-time
Integrated circuit (IC)
Silicon chip

Minicomputer
Remote terminal
Large-scale integration (LSI)
Microprocessor
Personal computer
Very-large-scale integration (VLSI)

 ## LESSON OVERVIEW

● Von Neumann outlined the stored-program concept, an idea for storing programs in computer memory rather than resetting switches and wires. The idea was used in the EDVAC.
● Electronic computers first used vacuum tubes for their circuits. These first-generation machines were huge, slow, and unreliable. The invention of transistors led to faster, smaller, second-generation computers. The use of silicon chips led to even faster and smaller third- and fourth-generation computers. Today's computers rely on large-scale integrated circuits and very-large-scale integrated circuits.

 ## TEACHING RESOURCES

Worksheet 7-1 ACTIVITY. Chronology: Students must put three sets of events in chronological order. This activity can be used as a review or as preparation for doing a computer time line.
Answers:
Group 1: 7, 10, 6, 3, 8, 2, 11, 1, 4, 12, 0, 9
Group 2: 6, 5, 1, 2, 3, 4, 8, 7
Group 3: 3, 4, 1, 2, 5, 6
Worksheet 7-2 ACTIVITY. Comparing Computer Generations: Students list the characteristics of each of the four generations of computers. This offers a good summary of computer developments in the last few decades.
Answers:
<u>First Generation</u>
used vacuum tubes
created much heat
needed air conditioning
very large machines
unreliable
limited storage
language-translator programs
<u>Second Generation</u>
used transistors
created less heat
smaller machines
faster, more reliable computers
better storage
tapes and disks
real-time computing
<u>Third Generation</u>
silicon chips and integrated circuits
computers much faster, smaller, more reliable
minicomputers
remote terminals
software industry emerged
<u>Fourth Generation</u>
miniaturization by large-scale integration
microprocessor
microcomputer
even smaller circuitry by very large-scale integration

TEACHING RESOURCES
(continued)

Worksheet 7-4 RETEACH. Four Technologies:
Students fill in the blanks with words or phrases
and answer a question about trends in technology.
This activity begins with three paragraphs summa-
rizing the four generations of computers. May be
used as reteach or review at the end of the chapter.
Answers:
Fill-in-the Blanks
vacuum tubes
generation
smaller
speed
reliability
large-scale integration
Accept reasonable answers to the question concerning trends in computer technology.
Worksheet 7-5 ENRICHMENT. Even More:
Additional people and developments are included in
this worksheet on computer history. This is good for
students who are particularly interested in computing and its history. Any of these thirteen topics
would make an interesting report for a student to
give to the class. The report should be word
processed before giving it orally.
**Transparency Master 7A . Chief Characteristic
of Each Generation:** Lists the four generations and
one important characteristic of each. Use as an
opening for this lesson or as a review at the end of
the lesson.

 LEARNING CHECK 7-3 ANSWERS

1. UNIVAC I
2. Mauchly and Eckert
3. words, symbols
4. a
5. integrated circuits on chips
6. microprocessors
7. Answers will vary; however responses may
include ideas such as freedom of experimentation,
openness to new ideas, etc.

SKILLS TEST 7 ANSWERS

1. To add or delete a field, to change to a more
exact name.

The Test7 report will look like this when printed.

Inventor	Male/Female	Invention	Date
Blaise Pascal	M	La Pascaline	1642
Gottfried Wilhelm von Leibniz	M	Leibniz Calculator	1673
Joseph Marie Jacquard	M	Jacquard Loom	1801
Charles Babbage	M	Plans for Analytical E	1834
Augusta Ada Byron	F	Program	1842
Herman Hollerith	M	Tabulating Machine	1887
Howard Aiken	M	Mark I	1944
John Vincent Atanasoff	M	ABC	1939
John Mauchly and J. Presper Ec	M	ENIAC	1946
John von Neumann	M	Stored-program idea	1944
John Mauchly and J. Presper Ec	M	UNIVAC I	1951

● Chapter 7 Summary

SUMMARY POINTS

● Early devices used for counting and problem solving include the abacus, La Pascaline, and the Leibniz Calculator.

● The first "programmable" machine was a weaving loom, with punched cards to guide the loom. Hollerith also used punched cards in his Tabulating Machine that handled census data.

● Charles Babbage was called the Father of Computers because his plans for an Analytical Engine outlined ideas important in the design of computers. The first automatic calculator, the Mark I, used many of these ideas, but the first actual computers were the ABC and the ENIAC.

● Von Neumann outlined the stored-program concept, an idea for storing programs in computer memory rather than resetting switches and wires. The idea was used in the EDVAC.

● Electronic computers first used vacuum tubes for their circuits. These first-generation machines were huge, slow, and unreliable. The invention of transistors led to faster smaller second-generation computers. The use of silicon chips led to even faster and smaller third- and fourth-generation computers. Today's computers rely on large-scale integrated circuits and very-large-scale integrated circuits.

DISCUSSION QUESTIONS

1. People probably like the idea of machines that would do routine work quickly and accurately. Expense, unfamiliarity, skepticism, fear, repair and maintenance problems, space, and special structural adaptations might have prevented many businesses from buying computers.

2. Women commonly avoided science and math careers and were not involved in military jobs.

DISCUSSION QUESTIONS
(continued)

3. Pascal needed help figuring taxes. Babbage was frustrated with the inaccurate math tables of his time. Hollerith tried to solve the problem of slow speeds in compiling census data. Von Neumann recognized the problems in accuracy and speed in manually loading computer programs. Hopper knew there must be a short cut to machine language and a way to prevent many of the errors that were sure to happen in using machine language.

ACTIVITIES

1. Perhaps short articles could be pasted onto the time line.

2. Which needs involved math? In which country have the most developments originated? Which needs involved war? The file contains nothing about general acceptance and other developments by the inventors, for example. Fields for these might be interesting, as well as fields for costs, developments or ideas that triggered each invention (an earlier invention perhaps), actual use of the machine, and so on.

Enrichment Activities.

1. The word automation is in the glossary. Accept headings such as machines, manual job, effect on worker, and so on.

2. See enrichment sheet 7-5 for further direction.

Vocabulary

1. a
2. d
3. b
4. c
5. d
6. b
7. d
8. a

Questions

1. They had the advantage of electricity, better manufacturing methods, and improved adding machines.

2. Hollerith used punched cards extensively. Atanasoff used vacuum tubes and binary codes. Hoff made a general-purpose microprocessor all on one chip.

3. The stored-program concept describes the technology that enabled programmers to put instructions into primary memory using tapes or cards rather than changing circuits manually. The method improved speed and accuracy.

4. They reduced heat, size, and problems related to hunting for burned out tubes.

5. First generation: vacuum tubes; second generation: transistors; third generation: integrated circuits; fourth generation: large-scale and very large-scale integration—that is, miniaturization of circuits.

Chapter 8

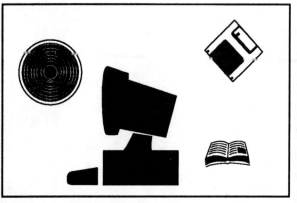

COMPUTER HARDWARE

DESCRIPTION: Length 4:13. In this program, a novice computer user ventures into the Hi-Tech computer store and is shown a variety of computer systems including IBM PS/2, Macintosh, and Apple IIgs computers. Basic computer terms are introduced, and a variety of peripherals and computers are shown.

Search to Chapter 8........Play

Suggested Additional Resources

● <u>Understanding Computers</u>, Third Edition, by Grace Murray Hopper and Steven L. Mandell, West Publishing Co.
● Computer magazines

PROJECTED LEARNING OUTCOMES

After studying the concepts and practicing the skills in this chapter, students should be able to:
● Explain what distinguishes digital computers from analog computers.
● List the functions of the central processing unit.
● Describe types of primary and secondary storage.
● Distinguish between the four classifications of digital computers.
● Describe the various input devices used today.
● Distinguish between the types of monitors.
● Detail the differences between impact and nonimpact printers, and give examples of each.
● Give examples of some special-purpose output devices.

VOCABULARY TERMS

Analog computer	Back up
Digital computer	Sequential-access storage
Binary number system	Format
	Direct-access storage
Bit	Hard disk
Byte	Optical disk
Central processing unit (CPU)	Video display terminal (VDT)
Control unit	Joystick
Arithmetic/logic unit	Mouse
Primary memory	Track ball
Processor	Graphics tablet
Read-only memory (ROM)	Light pen
	Scanner
Read	Touch screen
Write	Voice-recognition unit
Random-access memory	Monochrome monitor
	Resolution
Megabytes	Flat panel display
Gigabyte	Impact printer
Mainframe	Dot-matrix impact printer
Supercomputer	Daisy-wheel printer
Secondary storage media	Letter-quality
	Nonimpact printer
Magnetic tape	Plotter
Tape drive	Voice-response unit
Read/write head	Voice synthesizer

Examining Hardware

CHAPTER OVERVIEW

- Digital computers run in units of "on" and "off." Analog computers, on the other hand, measure changes, such as temperature, in flow rather than in units.
- Data for a computer is represented by binary digits (bits)—0 (zero) and 1 (one). This system suits the computer because it matches the on/off states of electricity. Bits are often grouped in eights. Each group of eight bits is called a byte. A code based on eight bits allows 256 choices, enough for all of the characters on the keyboard and special functions such as Space Bar, Delete, and so on.
- The central processing unit (CPU) is the "brain" of the computer. It has three parts: the control unit controls the computer's activities, the ALU does arithmetic and logic jobs, and primary memory holds items needed for processing.
- Read-only memory (ROM) is a form of primary memory that is built into chips at the factory. Items in ROM can be read over and over again, but they cannot be changed by normal input methods. Random-access memory (RAM) is a form of primary memory into which items can be read, written, or erased. Items in RAM such as programs and input can be used over and over again until they are erased or replaced. When the computer is turned off, the items in RAM vanish.
- The four types of digital computers are supercomputers, mainframes, minicomputers, and microcomputers. The main differences are speed, cost, and amount of memory.
- Secondary storage is located outside the computer. Magnetic tapes are sequential-access storage: a tape is read from the beginning until an item is found. Disks are direct-access storage in which data can be found in any order.
- To communicate with the computer, input and output devices are needed. Input devices include the keyboard, tape or disk drives, joysticks, mice, graphics tablets, track balls, light pens, scanners, touch screens, and voice recognition systems.
- Output can be printed in soft copy on a monitor or as hard copy on paper with an impact (striking) or nonimpact printer. Common impact printers are

CHAPTER OVERVIEW
(continued)

dot-matrix impact printers and daisy-wheel printers. Nonimpact printers include thermal printers, ink-jet printers, and laser printers. Plotters also provide hard copy output. Voice response units and voice synthesizers give spoken output. Output can also be recorded on disks or tapes.

TEACHING RESOURCES

Practicing Computer Skills 8-1: Figuring Bytes Students will use a spreadsheet to figure out the number of bytes to store the spreadsheet.

Worksheet 8-1 ACTIVITY. Related Terms: Students circle three terms most closely related in a group of terms.

Worksheet 8-2 ACTIVITY. Four Groups of Computers: Students write the characteristics of each of the four classifications of computers: supercomputers, mainframes, minicomputers, and microcomputers.

Worksheet 8-3 ACTIVITY. Buy A Printer: Students "shop" for printers that are compatible with the school's computers in magazines and fill out the worksheet.

Worksheet 8-4 RETEACH. Computer Codes: Students work through a two digit system (0 and 1) and discover the number of codes available in blocks of eight bits.

Worksheet 8-5 RETEACH. In Your Own Words: Students respond to questions as they read the section Classifications of Digital Computers.

Worksheet 8-6 RETEACH. Give an Example: Twelve input and output devices are listed for students to give examples of each.

Worksheet 8-7 ENRICHMENT. Binary to Decimal: Interested students can figure out how to convert an ASCII code into a decimal number.

Transparency Master 8A. Jobs of the CPU: A fill-in-the blank outline of the three parts of the CPU: the control unit, the arithmetic/logic unit, and the primary memory.

TEACHING RESOURCES
(continued)

Assessment:
HyperCard Stack. Parts of a Computer: Gives information about the parts of the computer that allow you to give input and receive output. Processing hardware and storage terms are also covered.
HyperCard Stack. Memory: Defines memory, types of memory, and measurement of memory.
HyperCard Worksheet. The Parts of a Computer System: Students will describe what pieces of hardware do and tell if they are used for input, processing and storage, or output.
HyperCard Worksheet. Computer Memory: Students will define memory, types of memory, and measurement of memory.

Test 8-A

Test 8-B

Portfolio 8: Examining Hardware: Students will cut and paste pictures of computers, respond to a question about computer memory, design a house for the year 2020, and create a concept map about the classification of computers.

Skills Test 8. Students design the "perfect" computer and list its components. They write a paper describing each part of the "perfect" computer using the Microsoft Works word processor, and print it on a printer.

TEACHING STRATEGIES

Opening. Concrete objects can be used to introduce the differences between the two types of computers. Even items as simple as a digital watch and a gear-driven watch can be used to demonstrate the difference between the flow measurements of analog devices and the counting measurements of digital devices. Other analog devices such as meters and thermometers can be used to show the flow measurements. The analog device shows an approximate measurement and the digital device shows a numerical read-out that should be a precise value.

Teaching Tips. Analogies are useful for this lesson. RAM can be called the working area, or chalkboard, of processing. When items in RAM are no longer needed, they are discarded either by writing something else to RAM or by turning off the machine. The same principle occurs on a chalkboard. The chalk marks are erased to make room for the next data. ROM is the area that resembles a textbook that you do not write on. The data is stored permanently, but the computer can use what is written there for processing. The actual storage places can be compared to mail boxes, but students should realize that each "mail box" contains only one "letter."
An analogy can also be used for the pathways that the coded data take in traveling from place to place. The pathways are like multiple-lane highways. If there are eight cars (the byte) traveling down eight lanes going one direction, the cars actually end up in eight different garages (that is, eight different RAM chips) rather than in the same garage. In most computers today, the chips are measured in kilobits rather than kilobytes because each chip holds only one bit of each byte.
Collect samples of output from different types of printers. Perhaps parents who use computers at work or in home offices would be willing to provide some copies. Compare the fully-formed characters and the dot-matrix characters. Try to find copies of output from at least one of each kind of printer mentioned in the text.

TEACHING STRATEGIES
(continued)

When & How.

1. Open the chapter with the videodisc clip to get students' attention. Discuss the many items that could be included with a computer.

2. Before beginning, you may want to review the three stages of the data processing flow: input, processing, and output.

3. The principles of binary data representation and the two states of electricity are not as simple as they sound. We have reduced the description to simple on and off states, but in reality, the states are always on: there is just more power or less power. There is a great deal of detail involved in explaining how electricity works in a digital computer. It is sufficient for this text that students understand that the codes used to handle data match the two states of electricity in the computer.

4. At one time, there were only mainframe computers. Technology has advanced so fast in just a few decades that the microcomputers of today are more powerful than the very large first computers. Describing the classifications of computers without telling about ranges of technical characteristics seems somewhat nebulous, but students can get an idea of the different computers by the uses of each. The differences are generally based on price, amount of primary memory, size, amount of data that can be handled at one time, speeds, the amount of peripheral devices the computer can handle, and functions. In the cases of some supercomputers, even the architecture—or the way the computer handles the data—is different.

5. The concepts of sequential-access and direct-access storage are very important. Students should be able to explain the difference and judge when one type would be preferred over the other. Teachers can mention that tapes are inexpensive, that disks are generally more reliable, and that laser disks are used for read-only material because most current inexpensive optical disks can be written to only once, but read many times (WORM - write once, read many). Tapes are often used for backup copies.

6. Any input or output device used in the classroom or school should be identified, and the ease of use explored. For instance, to enter data by keyboard, students can work faster if they know how to type. To see data on a monitor, students must know how to get the screen to scroll. Students should try as many input and output devices as they can.

TEACHING STRATEGIES
(continued)

7. Use the HyperCard stacks "Parts of a Computer," and "Memory" aalong with their worksheets for assessmant, review, or to introduce terms and ideas.

Computer Demonstration. Find out if any people in your school or town are using special computerized equipment that help them overcome disabilities. Invite them to speak to your classes.

Writing Activity. Instruct students to find magazine articles about the competition between the United States and Japan in supercomputer technology and the Fifth Generation of computers. Then, word process a report or summary of the article. Discuss how the latest technology in large computers will trickle down to microcomputers.

Trouble shooting. Discuss with students good trouble shooting techniques for discovering problems with input and output devices on computers. For example, if a monitor is not working, try another monitor on that computer and see if it works. If it does not, then the original monitor was not at fault. Trade cables or CPUs with working computers to isolate the faulty piece of hardware. If a mouse is not working properly, check that the ball is clean and properly in place.

Closing. Ask students to produce posters or mobiles with drawings or pictures from magazines of input and output devices. All pictures should be labeled "input" or "output" and properly named.

Lesson 8 - 1

p.146 - p.151

 ## PROJECTED LEARNING OUTCOMES

After studying the concepts and practicing the skills in this lesson, students should be able to:

- Explain what distinguishes digital computers from analog computers.
- List the parts of the central processing unit and their functions.
- Describe the kinds of primary storage.

 ## VOCABULARY TERMS

Analog computer	Primary memory
Digital computer	Processor
Binary number system	Read-only memory
Bit	(ROM)
Byte	Read
Central processing unit	Write
(CPU)	Random-access
Control unit	memory
Arithmetic/logic unit	

LESSON OVERVIEW

- Digital computers run in units of "on" and "off." Analog computers, on the other hand, measure changes, such as temperature, in flow rather than in units.
- Data for a computer is represented by binary digits (bits)—0 (zero) and 1 (one). This system suits the computer because it matches the on/off states of electricity. Bits are often grouped in eights. Each group of eight bits is called a byte. A code based on eight bits allows 256 choices, enough for all of the characters on the keyboard and special functions such as Space Bar, Delete, and so on.
- The central processing unit (CPU) is the "brain" of the computer. It has three parts: the control unit controls the computer's activities, the ALU does arithmetic and logic jobs, and primary memory holds items needed for processing.

LESSON OVERVIEW
(continued)

- Read-only memory (ROM) is a form of primary memory that is built into chips at the factory. Items in ROM can be read over and over again, but they cannot be changed by normal input methods. Random-access memory (RAM) is a form of primary memory into which items can be read, written, or erased. Items in RAM such as programs and input can be used over and over again until they are erased or replaced. When the computer is turned off, the items in RAM vanish.

 ## TEACHING RESOURCES

Practicing Computer Skills 8-1: Figuring Bytes
Students will use a spreadsheet to figure out the number of bytes in their computer.

Worksheet 8-1 ACTIVITY. Related Terms:
Students circle three terms most closely related in a group of terms. This will help students organize the meanings and relationships among the terms in this section.
Answers:
1. hardware, peripherals, central processing unit
2. RAM, ROM, primary memory
3. kilobytes, bits, bytes
4. circuits, silicon chips, microprocessor
5. ROM, firmware, programs
6. primary memory, ALU, control unit
7. bit, ASCII, byte
8. binary numbers, codes, 1001100
9. equal to, less than, not equal to
10. memory, address, store

Worksheet 8-4 RETEACH. Computer Codes:
Students work through a two digit system (0 and 1) and discover the number of codes available in blocks of eight bits. Helps students review the way binary digits are used to encode data.
Answers:
4
00, 01, 10, 11
4

codes
000, 001, 010, 011, 100, 101, 110, 111
8

TEACHING RESOURCES ———

(continued)

0000, 0001, 0010, 0100, 0011, 0101, 0110, 0111,
1000, 1001, 1010, 1011, 1100, 1101, 1110, 1111
32
64
128, 256
512

byte
ASCII

Worksheet 8-7 ENRICHMENT. Binary to Decimal: Interested students can figure out how to convert an ASCII code into a decimal number. See Enrichment Activity #1 for more in this area.
Answers:
sixty-fours place
8
16
57
72
87
38
1011101

Transparency Master 8A. Jobs of the CPU: A fill-in-the blank outline of the three parts of the CPU: the control unit, the arithmetic/logic unit, and the primary memory. Ask students to help suggest terms for the blanks.
Answers:
<u>The control unit</u>
1. order; operations
2. input; output
3. storage
<u>The arithmetic/logic unit</u>
1. arithmetic
2. a. =; b. ≠; c. <, d. >, e. <=, f. >=
<u>Primary memory</u>
1. instructions
2. intermediate; final
3. erased, output, stored

 ## LEARNING CHECK 8-1 ANSWERS ———

1. 2
2. byte
3. central processing unit
4. the ALU (arithmetic/logic unit)
5. the control unit
6. b, c
7. Answers will vary; however the better choice is RAM since it can be constantly changed and updated to fit new information.

 # PRACTICING COMPUTER SKILLS ———

8-1: Figuring Bytes

Bytes of Primary Storage

32K means	32768
128K means	131072
256K means	262144
2M means	2097152

The Bytes file should also show the number of bytes for your computer if the students have entered the correct information.

Lesson 8 - 2

p.151 - p.156

 PROJECTED LEARNING OUTCOMES

After studying the concepts and practicing the skills in this lesson, students should be able to:

● Distinguish between the four classifications of digital computers.

 VOCABULARY TERMS

Megabytes
Gigabyte
Mainframe
Supercomputer

 **LESSON OVERVIEW**

● The four types of digital computers are supercomputers, mainframes, minicomputers, and microcomputers. The main differences are speed, cost, and amount of memory.

 TEACHING RESOURCES

Worksheet 8-2 ACTIVITY. Four Groups of Computers: Students write the characteristics of each of the four classifications of computers: supercomputers, mainframes, minicomputers, and microcomputers. This will help students visualize the differences in the computers.

Answers:

<u>Supercomputers</u>
fast, efficient, expensive
densely packed circuitry may need special liquid coolant
very complex uses

<u>Mainframes</u>
support many peripherals
may need special wiring, cooling, platforms, security
used by groups that process a lot of data

<u>Minicomputers</u>
small versions of mainframes
cheaper than mainframes
can be linked to large computers
easier to install than mainframes
store less data and work more slowly than mainframes

<u>Microcomputers</u>
small enough to fit on a desk
can be linked to large computers
most are single-user machines

Worksheet 8-5 RETEACH. In Your Own Words: Students respond to questions on the section Classifications of Digital Computers. This could be used as reteach, review or filled out as they read the section.

Answers:
1. The 16-bit computer can handle a larger chunk of data at a time—16 bits—than an 8-bit computer that handles 8 bits at a time.
2. RAM is measured in kilobytes, megabytes, and gigabytes. Large RAMs can hold more instructions and data at one time, which allows larger computation and other work.
3. Know how you want to use the computer, how much speed you need, how much memory you need for the software you want to use, how many peripheral devices you want the computer to handle, and how much money you want to spend.

4. Minicomputers, mainframes, microcomputers, and supercomputers are available. There is an affordable microcomputer for almost everyone. Minicomputers are more limited to at least small businesses, schools, small offices, and professional people, although large businesses use minicomputers, too. Mainframes are used by large organizations that have large data processing needs and many people using the computer. These may include hospitals, large manufacturers, banks, and universities, for example. Supercomputers are primarily used for vey large complex problems and research. They are expensive and so are limited to problems that are too large for smaller, less expensive computers. Expense and facilities for keeping the computer are primary considerations in who uses which classification.

LEARNING CHECK 8-2 ANSWERS

1. microcomputer, minicomputer, mainframe, supercomputer
2. Air conditioning, platforms, and special wiring need to be added.
3. how you want to use the computer, how fast the computer is, cost, etc.
4. smaller or minimal
5. b
6. energy studies (answers may vary)
7. Answers will vary

Lesson 8 - 3, 4

p.156 - p.166

 ## PROJECTED LEARNING OUTCOMES

After studying the concepts and practicing the skills in these lessons, students should be able to:

● Identify the types of secondary storage and characteristics of each.
● Describe the various input devices used today.

 ## VOCABULARY TERMS

Secondary storage
  media
Magnetic tape
Tape drive
Read/write head
Back up
Sequential-access storage
Format
Direct-access storage
Hard disk
Optical disk

Video display terminal
  (VDT)
Joystick
Mouse
Track Ball
Graphics tablet
Light pen
Scanner
Touch screen
Voice-recognition unit

 ## LESSON OVERVIEW

● Secondary storage is located outside the computer. Magnetic tapes are sequential-access storage: a tape is read from the beginning until an item is found. Disks are direct-access storage in which data can be found in any order.
● To communicate with the computer, input and output devices are needed. Input devices include the keyboard, tape or disk drives, joysticks, mice, graphics tablets, track balls, light pens, scanners, touch screens, and voice recognition systems.

 ## LEARNING CHECK 8-3 ANSWERS

1. secondary storage
2. computers cannot hold all necessary data in RAM
3. a
4. Magnetic tape
5. floppy disk or magnetic disk
6. optical disks; CD-ROM
7. both are difficult to change information on
8. holds more information, holds pictures, holds sound, etc.

 ## LEARNING CHECK 8-4 ANSWERS

1. video display terminal
2. joystick and mouse (answers will vary)
3. d
4. scanner (or digitizer)
5. joystick or mouse
6. Answers will vary; however ideas such as accents, using colloquial expressions or slurring words together may be mentioned.

NOTES ——————————————— **NOTES** ———————————————

 # Lesson 8 - 5

p.166 - p.171

 PROJECTED LEARNING OUTCOMES

After studying the concepts and practicing the skills in this lesson, students should be able to:

● Distinguish between the types of monitors.
● Detail the differences between impact and nonimpact printers, and give examples of each.
● Give examples of some special-purpose output devices.

 VOCABULARY TERMS

Monochrome monitor	Letter-quality
Resolution	Nonimpact printer
Flat-panel display	Plotter
Impact printer	Voice-response unit
Dot-matrix impact printer	Voice synthesizer
Daisy-wheel printer	

LESSON OVERVIEW

● Output can be printed in soft copy on a monitor or as hard copy on paper with an impact (striking) or nonimpact printer. Common impact printers are dot-matrix impact printers and daisy-wheel printers. Nonimpact printers include thermal printers, ink-jet printers, and laser printers. Plotters also provide hard copy output. Voice response units and voice synthesizers give spoken output. Output can also be recorded on disks or tapes.

 **TEACHING RESOURCES**

Worksheet 8-3 ACTIVITY. Buy A Printer: Students "shop" for printers that are compatible with the school's computers in magazines or newspapers and fill out the worksheet. These factors should be considered when buying printers: cost, compatibility with existing equipment, quality of output, use, noise, size, service needed, ease of use, cost of accessories such as special paper or cartridges, and known problems such as clogging on ink-jet printers.
Answers:
<u>Daisy-Wheel Printer</u>
Advantages: makes fully-formed characters; you can change fonts by installing a different wheel; it uses ordinary paper.
Disadvantages: noisy; slow; you cannot change fonts during printing; the machine will not print graphics.
<u>Dot-Matrix Printer</u>
Advantages: produces graphics; you can change fonts during printing; it is generally faster than a daisy-wheel; inexpensive.
Disadvantages: lower print quality; noisy.
<u>Ink-Jet Printer</u>
Advantages: high-quality dot-matrix print and graphics; uses colors; quiet; fast.
Disadvantages: ink jets may clog; sometimes requires special paper to prevent ink spread and running ink.
<u>Laser Printer</u>
Advantages: quiet; prints graphics; fast; makes high-quality images; prints different fonts on the same page.
Disadvantages: cost; needs toner cartridges, font modules, and drums; uses more power.

TEACHING RESOURCES
(continued)

Worksheet 8-6 RETEACH. Give an Example:
Twelve input and output devices are listed for students to give examples of each. This can be used for reteach or review.
Answers:
1. membrane, QWERTY, numeric keypad
2. joystick, track ball
3. graphics tablet
4. image scanner
5. monitor
6. printer
7. monochrome, RGB, flat panel
8. dot-matrix impact, daisy-wheel
9. daisy-wheel
10. laser, thermal, ink-jet
11. drum, flatbed
12. voice-response unit, voice synthesizer

LEARNING CHECK 8-5 ANSWERS

1. monochrome
2. impact and nonimpact
3. nonimpact
4. b
5. resolution
6. flatbed and drum
7. Answers will vary

SKILLS TEST 8 ANSWERS

Students' papers will vary, since each student will have his/her own concept of what a "perfect" computer is.

● Chapter 8 Summary

SUMMARY POINTS

● Digital computers run in units of "on" and "off." Analog computers measure changes, such as temperature, in flow rather than in units.

● Data for a computer is represented by binary digits (bits)—0 (zero) and 1 (one) which matches the on/off states of electricity. Bits are often grouped in eights; each group of eight bits is called a byte. A code based on eight bits allows 256 choices, enough for all of the characters on the keyboard and special functions such as Space Bar, Delete.

● The central processing unit (CPU) is the "brain" of the computer. It has three parts: the control unit controls the computer's activities, the ALU does arithmetic and logic jobs, and primary memory holds items needed for processing.

● Read-only memory (ROM) is a form of primary memory that is built into chips at the factory. Items in ROM can be read over and over again, but cannot be changed by normal input methods. Random-access memory (RAM) is a form of primary memory into which items can be read, written, or erased. Items in RAM such as programs and input can be used over and over again until they are erased or replaced. When the computer is turned off, the items in RAM vanish.

● The four types of digital computers are supercomputers, mainframes, minicomputers, and microcomputers. The main differences are speed, cost, and amount of memory.

● Disks are direct-access storage in which data can be found in any order.

● Input devices include the keyboard, tape or disk drives, joysticks, mice, graphics tablets, track balls, light pens, scanners, touch screens, and voice recognition systems.

● Output can be printed in soft copy on a monitor or as hard copy on paper with an impact (striking) or nonimpact printer. Common impact printers are dot-matrix impact printers and daisy-wheel printers. Nonimpact printers include thermal printers, ink-jet printers, and laser printers. Plotters also provide hard copy output. Voice response units and voice synthesizers give spoken output.

DISCUSSION QUESTIONS

1. Programs are coded into binary codes and read into RAM, thereby being stored temporarily until changed by other coded programs. The circuits do not have to be changed. Only the bit patterns are changed. ROM is hard to change without special machines, and therefore can hold programs that software companies want to guard from piracy. Programs on disks, on the other hand, can be copied using special copying programs that break the protection devices some manufacturers use to prevent piracy.

2. The human brain seems a suitable analogy, without using other computerized devices to describe what the CPU does. The human analogies, however, disregard the fact that computers are still very limited in what they can do compared with the human brain.

3. Students may all wish for the best system possible, but for purposes of the discussion, they should justify it with a valid use.

4. Students may answer this question on prior experience or on classroom work. Accept valid reasons for each device named.

5. Punched cards are unhandy to use and keep track of. They take up a lot of space. The methods needed to punch the data are time-consuming, and the cards can be easily bent and rendered useless.

6. The touch screen and mouse use familiar motions, but the keyboard requires people to know what each key means. Often, the screen layouts that accompany these tools look "user-friendly."

ACTIVITIES

1. Use Figure 8-1 to check the work. These codes are for upper-case letters, and students who wish to use lower-case letters also might want to see a copy of the entire ASCII code in Appendix E.

2. Some articles may be business or technically oriented, and students may find them hard to understand. Ask students to find articles that they can at least partially understand.

3. Use Worksheet 8-3, Buy a Printer, with this activity.

Enrichment Activities.

1. Enrichment sheet 8-7, Binary to Decimal, can get students started on this activity. Some students may want to carry the concept further, working with the powers of two. Some students may wish to learn to count (say, from 1 to 20) in binary numbers.
2. The information students offer will describe the primary memory capacity and speed of the computer.
3. The term "open" means that the computer can easily be opened and add-on cards or boards can be installed by the user or owner. The term "closed" means that the owner should take the computer to the store to have equipment added. Some closed systems have very little room for extra cards. Owners who know a lot about computer technology and wish to buy equipment by mail-order find the open systems suit their needs. On the other hand, closed systems discourage the owner from tinkering and perhaps even invalidating warranties by making inappropriate adjustments to the computer.
4. This activity may be preceded by studying computer magazines that specialize in the system being used.
5. Television sets have lower resolution and do not show characters with as much clarity as monitors made for text output. The text may be blurred enough to make the eyes tired.

CHAPTER REVIEW ——————————

Vocabulary

1. primary memory
2. bit
3. processes
4. digital
5. read-only memory

1. disk, input, read/write head
2. optical disk, CD-ROM, laser disk
3. joystick, mouse, graphics tablet
4. monochrome, RGB, flat panel
5. daisy wheel, solid font, petal
6. monitor, printer, disk drive

Questions

1. It matches the states of electricity and circuits.
2. Use several positions, or places, that can hold two choices each. The principle works the same way that you use nine digits (0-9) to build numbers in the millions and billions.
3. The control unit keeps order and manages the activity in the CPU. It communicated with input and output devices, too. The ALU does arithmetic and makes comparisons. Primary memory stores the instructions and data needed immediately for processing.
4. RAM holds data that can be read when the program needs it, but it can also be erased and new data can be written into it.
5. Cost, size, and the limited use it would receive in your home.
6. A disk is usually more reliable and can be accessed directly.
7. graphics tablet, joystick, mouse
8. You can write on it and use it without a computer.
9. cost, noise, cost of maintaining, cost of extra materials, use

Chapter 9

USING COMPUTERS RESPONSIBLY

DESCRIPTION: (2:29) This program encourages responsible computer use. Software piracy, computer viruses, and hacking are discussed. Common security measures, including passwords, locks, and security cameras are shown.

Search Chapter 9 .... Play

Suggested Additional Resources

● <u>Understanding Computers</u>, Third Edition, by Grace Murray Hopper and Steven L. Mandell, West Educational Publishing Co.

● "Cracking Down on Software Pirates," by Peter H. Lewis, 1989 -- The New York Times Company.

● Newspapers - computer section (if there is one), computer magazines -- <u>Byte</u>, <u>MacUser</u>, <u>PCWorld</u>, <u>Electronic Learning</u>, etc., and electronic bulletin boards.

PROJECTED LEARNING OUTCOMES

After studying the concepts and practicing the skills in this chapter, students should be able to:

● Discuss the ethics involved in using computers, databases, and software.

● Discuss federal legislation enacted for computer crimes.

● Discuss security problems dealing with computers.

● Be able to use the integrated features of the applications program to move a data base report into a word processor file.

VOCABULARY TERMS

Computer Ethics	Piracy
Computer Crime	Integrated Software
Download	Artificial Intelligence (AI)
Privacy	Natural Language

Using Computers Responsibly

CHAPTER OVERVIEW

● Computer ethics are standards by which we judge the correct use of computers. Because computers are impersonal machines, people may use them to do things they would never consider doing to, or in front of, other people.

● Four major categories of computer crime:
1) sabotage;
2) theft of services;
3) financial crimes; and
4) property crimes.

● Telecommunications. Many people are using on-line information services. Problems occur when people don't pay for their services. Bulletin boards are easily misused.

● Major privacy concerns include:
1 too much personal information is collected;
2) organizations make decisions on the bases of these files;
3) irrelevant information is given and used;
4) accuracy, completeness, and currentness of data may be unacceptably low; and
5) data security is a problem.

● Computers have made the collection and storage of data easy, and often too much data is collected.

● Privacy Laws passed:
1) Freedom of Information Act (1966);
2) The Fair Credit Reporting Act of 1970;
3) Privacy Act of 1974;
4) Right to Financial Privacy Act;
5) Family Education Rights; and
6) Comprehensive Crime Control Act of 1984.

● Many state privacy laws are patterned after the Privacy Act of 1974.

● Software piracy is the illegal copying of copyrighted software. Software is protected by the U.S. Copyright Act of 1978. Many companies do not rely soley on the copyright law.

● Voice recognition can help with security. Natural languages let people ask questions in their normal speech patterns. Machines that recognize "voice prints" of authorized users could prevent outsiders from illegal access.

● Most security problems are accidents.

● A virus program can enter and attack a computer system like a virus infects a human being.

TEACHING RESOURCES

Practicing Computer Skills 9-1. "Using the Integrated Feature of Microsoft Works" Uses some integrated features of Microsoft Works. Students will move some data from the database file about sources into a letter created in the word processor.

Practicing Computer Skills 9-2. "Moving the Database Report" Students move their Ethics report to the clipboard and print it in the letter.

Worksheet 9-1   ACTIVITY. Benefit or Problem? Use this activity sheet to summarize the benefits and problems of data bases, telecommunications, and automation.

Worksheet 9-2   RETEACHING. Summing Up. Have students use their text to insert their answers to this worksheet.

Worksheet 9-3   VOCABULARY. Matching. Students are asked to match the term it best describes.

Transparency Master 9A. Computer Crimes. Gives the four major categories of computer crimes.

Transparency Master 9B. Abuse of Data, shows the major problems related to data bases.

Transparency Master 9C. Federal Privacy Legislation, shows the main privacy laws and their provisions.

TEACHING RESOURCES ——————

(continued)

Assessment:

Test 9-A
Test 9-B

Portfolio 9 Computers and Responsibility Use the four activities to help students recognize the responsibility that is attached to owning or operating a computer.

1.   You could also use telecommunication networks to locate information about computer crimes.

2.   Students should point out that it is illegal for Julio to copy his office program for home use. Students should quote the Copyright Law. This activity should be done after reading the section on Copywrights.

3.   This can be used as a creative activity to make students more aware of existing computer crimes.

4.   Junk mail is a problem that society is having to deal with more frequently every day. It is a good activity that students can relate to their own home environment. It can also make them aware of the problem, if they were not already aware of it.

 TEACHING STRATEGIES ——————

Opening. Students need to relate the abstract meanings of privacy, security, and ethical behavior to things that may occur in school. Talk about problems with locking up all personal belongings, having items stolen from desks, contending with teammates who cheat in sports or exams, dealing with peers who try to talk students into doing things they would rather not do, or working on projects only to have ideas stolen by someone entrusted with information about the projects.

Teaching Tips. Discuss the fact that the behaviors listed affect people directly, but similar behaviors done through computers seem impersonal because computers are just machines. Students need to see these correlations. Students can talk about the fact that any information that can be accessed by computers has been entered by humans, affects humans, and probably costs money, as well. Discuss whether companies should beef up their security systems in order to prevent damage, making humans even less responsible for their own behaviors.

When & How. Suggestions . . .
1. Open the lesson with the clip from the video lesson. Discuss the stills with the students.
2. Have students read the lesson.
3. Have students do the Practicing Computer Skills associated with the second lesson.
4. Discuss the issues in each lesson, using the transparencies provided and the videodisc stills.
5. Check for understanding orally or have students write out the answers to the learning checks. You could also have students print out their answers, using their word processor.
6. End of Chapter.
. Use **Worksheet 9-1, Benefit or Problem?**, to summarize the benefits and problems.
. Orally talk about the "discussion questions."
. Assign the activities and enrichment activities as group activities -- with groups of two to five students.
. Do the "Chapter Review" together with the class or in cooperative groups.
7. Use the Portfolio activities associated with each lesson. Use this assessment method to evaluate student's understanding of the concepts presented in this chapter.
8. Use Test 9-A,B to evaluate student understanding.

TEACHING STRATEGIES

(continued)

Cooperative Learning. Have students work in groups of two to five to do the activities and enrichment activities, and then have students share their results with the whole class. In each group, someone will need to be the scribe -- the note taker. A leader should also be selected -- a different leader from previous activities, so that each student will have an opportunity to become a leader. The group presentation to the class should involve all participants in the group in some way -- one student may present the opening, one student may show and explain a chart, one student might do the closing, etc. Again, these responsibilities should be done by different students each time, so that one student isn't doing the same task every time.

Writing Activity. Some people predict that highways or cars will be computerized to prevent tailgating, speeding, dangerous passing, and so on. Have students write a discussion, using their word processor, about the implications of this and its effects on safety and personal freedom.

Computer Demonstration. Show students how to bring information from the database into the word processor before doing the Practicing Computer Skills.

Reteaching. Use **Worksheet 9-2: Summing Up**, and **Worksheet 9-3: Vocabulary. Matching**.

Interdisciplinary Learning. Connecting with social studies . . . Have each student find an example of a computer crime committed, including where it was committed. Have students list the cities and states where these computer crimes happened. Locate these on a map.
Open-Ended Discussion. . . Discuss with the class the results: is there a correlation between computer crimes and locations, are more computer crimes committed in large cities versus small towns, are different parts of the United States affected more than others?

Closing. Relate progress in automation and artificial intelligence to the discussion of issues and ethics from the standpoint of increased impersonal events.

NOTES

Lesson 9 - 1

p.176 - p.181

 ## PROJECTED LEARNING OUTCOMES

After studying the concepts and practicing the skills in this lesson, students should be able to:

● Discuss the ethics involved in using computers, data bases, and software.

● Use the integrated features of AppleWorks to move a data base report into a word processor file.

 ## VOCABULARY TERMS

Computer
Ethics
Computer Crime
Download

 ## LESSON OVERVIEW

● Computers have already become entrenched in our daily lives. We cannot perform transactions at banks, travel agencies, or many stores without them. Our tax returns, school records, health records, utility bills, and magazine and newspaper subscriptions are processed through computers.
● Computer-related crime is more of a problem than most people realize. Many computer crimes are committed by professionals, and they're often called "white-collar" crimes. Only about 15% of computer crimes are reported to the police.
● Major categories of computer crimes:
1) sabotage -- destruction or damage of computer hardware;
2) theft of services -- company computers used for private services;
3) financial crimes -- stealing or altering accounts with a computer; and
4) property crimes -- loss or gain of property (usually monetary) with the use of a computer.
● Concern exists that computer systems will become the target for terrorists.
● Accessing an on-line information service without paying the fees is a problem. People misuse information from on-line information services and electronic bulletin boards.

 ## TEACHING RESOURCES

Practicing Computer Skills 9-1. Using the Integrated Features of Microsoft Works.
  Integrated software usually:
. is made up of separate application packages;
. provides movement of data between the packages; and
. uses a common group of commands or menus.

Data can be moved from an Microsoft Works database file into a word processing file. This activity moves information from SOURCES to the LETTER file and names the new report "Ethics."

Transparency Master 9A. Computer Crimes.
  The four major categories of computer crimes:
. sabotage;
. theft of services;
. financial crimes; and
. property crimes.

1. ethics
2. a.-- with a computer
3. misuse of information
4. sabotage, theft of services, financial crimes, and property crimes.
5. a criminal act that is done through the use of a computer or that causes a threat to those who use computers.
6. possible answers: stealing of a software program; changing or stealing data; unauthorized computer time; or a virus put on a computer system.
7. damage to computer hardware, destroying or rearranging a computer keyboard.
8. a secretary using her/his computer to do work for another company -- for private gains.
9. an employee who enters into the company's computer illegal entries -- adding illegal deposits to his/her account.
10. yes. Even though computer crimes may not seem as serious as other crimes, they can affect the profit and loss of both companies and individuals. Misuse of computers affects our economy, which in turn affects all of us.

 PRACTICING COMPUTER SKILLS

9 - 1 Title: Using the Integrated Features of Microsoft Works.

```
167 Mulberry Street
Bryan, OH
February 12, 1995

Dear Roger,
 Yesterday in computer class, we talked about ethics and
computers.  What a coincidence!  In your last letter, you
said that you were writing a paper on computer issues.
Thought you might be interested in some sources that
we used in our Microsoft Works database file.  Here they
are:

Periodical                  Date         Volume    Pages
--------------------------------------------------------
Compute!                    Dec  1, 1988   10          7
Business Week               Mar  6, 1989              30
Parents                     Sep  1, 1985   60        158
Time                        May 19, 1986  127        104
U.S. News and World Report  May  1, 1989  106        52+
Classroom Computer Learning Feb  1, 1988    8      58-60
The Education Digest        Feb  1, 1987   52      34-35
Newsweek                    Jan 14, 1985  105         76
```

Discussion: The final screen may look like the one shown above.

Lesson 9 - 2

p.181 - p.191

 ## PROJECTED LEARNING OUTCOMES

After studying the concepts and practicing the skills in this lesson, students should be able to:

● Discuss federal legislation enacted for computer crimes.

● Discuss security problems dealing with computers.

 ## VOCABULARY TERMS

Privacy
Piracy
Artificial Intelligence (AI)
Natural Languages

LESSON OVERVIEW

● Besides crime, a number of other issues are making people think about how computers are used. The issue of privacy deals with the use of computerized databases that hold personal data about all of us. The issue of piracy concerns copying copyrighted software for purposes other than having a backup copy.
● Computers are the main means by which information is stored about people.
● Databases. The federal government is the largest collector of data. Other organizations such as schools, banks, and hospitals also collect data. Information retrieved about an individual is often embarrassing, harmful, or incorrect.
● The most sweeping federal legislation is the Privacy Act of 1974.
● Very few cases regarding information-privacy violations have been litigated; many people are not aware when their privacy has been violated.
● Copyright laws do not provide an exclusive monopoly for protected work. Patents should be considered.
● Security really depends on the ethics of the individuals who have access to computer systems.

 ## TEACHING RESOURCES

Practicing Computer Skills 9-2. Moving the Data Base Report. This exercise involves moving the "Ethics" report to the clipboard and printing it in a letter. Students use the SOURCES file, and they delete all of the new information from the "File: SOURCES" down to the word PERIODICAL.

Worksheet 9-1 ACTIVITY. Benefit or Problem? Use this activity sheet to summarize the benefits and problems of data bases, telecommunications, and automation.
Answers may include:

Benefits	Problems
Large Data Bases: . Quick access to large amounts of data . Puts data in central place . Gets answers from cross-referenced files	. Easy to store too much data . May be easy to access by telephone
Telecommunications: . Quick access over long distances . Allows current information . Can let people work at home	. May allow unauthorized access to data . Reduces human contact
Automation: . Increases number of tasks done . May free humans to do more creative work	. May reduce well-paying jobs . May make workers feel that their jobs are less valuable than before automation

Worksheet 9-2 RETEACHING. Summing Up.
Have students use their text to insert their answers to this worksheet. Some possible answers:
1. ethics (computer ethics); impersonal; illegal; white-collar;
2. privacy; Privacy; federal government;
3. piracy; illegal; ©;
4. defining; passwords; locking; scrambling; and
5. automation; artificial intelligence.

TEACHING RESOURCES

(continued)

Worksheet 9-3 VOCABULARY. Matching.
Students are asked to match the term it best describes.
Answers:

1. g	5. c	9. e
2. d	6. h	10. l
3. l	7. f	11. a
4. k	8. j	12. b

Transparency Master 9B. Abuse of Data.
Shows some major problems of data bases. Remind students that many organizations (namely the federal government) handle so much data that computerization seems to be the only efficient way to handle the data.

Transparency Master 9C. Federal Privacy Legislation This chart shows the main privacy laws and their provisions. Examining the chart with students can lead to some "open-ended" discussions about the effectiveness of the listed legislation.

LEARNING CHECK 9-2 ANSWERS

1. They make it easy to get information.
2. both "a" and "b" are correct
3. Possible answers include:
   . using and changing passwords;
   . watching for careless behavior;
   . locking the computer rooms;
   . set hiring and training standards;
   . scramble data so only authorized personnel can have access;
   . use dial-back measure to guard access;
   . store up-to-date backup copies in a different location than the business.
4. the federal government
5. see Federal Privacy Legislation Transparency
6. unauthorized copying of copyrighted software
7. U.S. Copyright Act of 1978
8. A patent protects novel ideas and processes.
9. see the answers to question 3, you might ask for more expanded responses in this question.

LEARNING CHECK 9-2 ANSWERS

(continued)

10. possible answers include:
    . too much personal information is collected;
    . decisions are made solely on data collected;
    . accuracy and currency of data is

PRACTICING COMPUTER SKILLS

9- 2 Title: Moving the Data Base Report.

```
167 Mulberry Street
Bryan, OH
February 12, 1995

Dear Roger,
  Yesterday in computer class, we talked about ethics and
computers.  What a coincidence!  In your last letter, you
said that you were writing a paper on computer issues.
Thought you might be interested in some sources that
we used in our Microsoft Works database file.  Here they
are:

Periodical                    Date        Volume   Pages
-----------------------------------------------------------
Compute!                      Dec  1, 1988    10        7
Business Week                 Mar  6, 1989              30
Parents                       Sep  1, 1985    60      158
Time                          May 19, 1986   127      104
U.S. News and World Report May  1, 1989   106      52+
Classroom Computer LearningFeb  1, 1988     8    58-60
The Education Digest          Feb  1, 1987    52    34-35
Newsweek                      Jan 14, 1985   105       76

  I'm not sure that you can get them at your library, but
most libraries have an exchange program.  Through an
exchange program, you might be able to order copies from
another library.  Hope these sources help you write your
paper for your computer class!
  See you during spring vacation!

Til then.
Mark
```

● Chapter 9 Summary

SUMMARY POINTS

● Because computers are impersonal machines, people may use them to do things they would never consider doing to other people.

● Relatively few cases regarding information-privacy violations have been litigated.

● Security really depends on the ethics of the individual.

DISCUSSION QUESTIONS

1. Perhaps the question should be "Can computers be banned?" Most organizations use computers to their benefit and do not abuse them.
2. A universal credit card would eliminate cash, which can be counterfeit, and checks, which can bounce. The store would have a method to check on whether the customer can actually pay for merchandise. The card would remove some individual freedom in that people would no longer have a choice of payment methods and would be open to abuses of data collected about their spending habits.
3. Answers will vary depending upon the existing code of ethics and the importance of ethical behavior to the students.
4. Such exams might benefit the people who have to deal with the person being examined, but that person's privacy would be invaded. Discuss whether the benefits to society are greater than individual freedom.
5. A possible answer might have a system that includes extensive restraints on computer access, or even access to the computer room. Voice recognition and artificial intelligence could certainly be an integral part. Encourage students to use creative solutions.

DISCUSSION QUESTIONS

(contunued)

6. Discussion could relate back to students' own choices in their every day decisions on cheating.
7. Encourage open-ended discussions. Include prompts that discuss the ramifications of both pros and cons of each
8. Some answers may include: your school, doctor, the federal government (using your social security number), and other organizations.
9. answers will vary according to groups
10. Laws may include more information available to individual about their information in data bases.

ACTIVITIES

1. Answers will vary according to how personal the questions are. Make students aware that real evidence to support an answer is important.
2. The data base should include all of the legislation from the transparency: Federal Privacy Legislation. Encourage students to also include any State legislation they can find.
3. Answers will vary.

ENRICHMENT ACTIVITIES

1. Encourage students to be creative. If you have desktop publishing software, have students either draw a visual to go with their story or paste in a relevant clip art.
2. Answers will vary according to your school.
3. Answers will vary.

CHAPTER REVIEW

Vocabulary

1. Privacy is the right of people to decide what, when, and how personal data is shared with others.
2. Piracy is unauthorized copying of copyrighted software.
3. Computer ethics are behavior and beliefs that conform to a standard for correct uses of computers.
4. Voice recognition is the ability of a computer to recognize "voice prints" of an individual.
5. Security is the protection against computer crime -- such as theft, privacy, and piracy.

Questions

1. d -- beliefs about personal behavior around computers
2. use a computer program to steal money or merchandise from a company or bank
3. scramble data; be sure procedures that limit access to a computer actually work
4. d -- all of the above
5. federal government
6. c -- privacy
7. b -- to make one backup copy
8. artificial intelligence
9. Answers should include provisions from Transparency 9C.
10. Answers should include:
    . allowing people to ask questions in normal speech patterns;
    . allowing handicapped people to do things they couldn't do before; and
    . providing improved security.

● Chapter 10

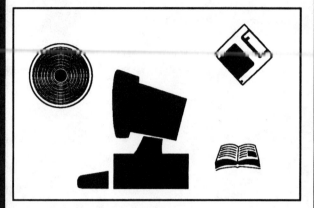

◉ COMPUTERS IN THE WORLD

DESCRIPTION: (3:00) The prevalence of computers in the world of work and play is shown. Common ways that we all interact with computers such as bank teller machines, video games, and grocery scanners are shown. Issues in the way that computers influence our lives are raised.

Search Chapter 10 .... Play

Suggested Additional Resources

● Newspapers: employment section.

● <u>Time</u>, <u>Newsweek</u>, T<u>he Wall Street Journal</u>'s Technology section.

● The evening news on TV - sometimes. "Technology and Science" on CNN.

● Computer magazines -- <u>BYTE</u>.

➡ PROJECTED LEARNING OUTCOMES

After studying the concepts and practicing the skills in this chapter, students should be able to:

● Define source-data automation and give examples of it.

● Give examples of how computers have helped automate factories, banks, stores, and offices.

● Describe special uses of computers in the government, science, health care, and the entertainment industry.

VOCABULARY TERMS

Automation
Source-data Automation
Electronic Funds Transfer (EFT)
Point-of-Sale Terminal (POS)
Optical Recognition Device
Bar Code
Electronic Mail (E-Mail)
DIP
Information Retrieval
Teleconference
Materials Requirement Planning (MRP)
Computer-aided Design (CAD)
Computer-aided Manufacturing (CAM)
Computerized Axial Tomography (CAT scan)

Finding Computers in the World Around You

CHAPTER OVERVIEW

● This chapter outlines some of the many ways that computers are used in industry, government, science, medicine, and the entertainment industry.

● Included are general descriptions of computer-aided design, computer-aided manufacturing, robots, medical testing, and computer graphics.

● Banks use electronic funds transfer, ATM machines, to accurately transfer funds.

● Retail stores use remote terminals to get source data to record sales and act as a cash register.

● E-mail is widely used by companies to transmit data and messages over phone lines.

● Video teleconferences are used by business to show and hear the speakers.

● Robots are used to do unsafe jobs, and they have saved factories money by continuously working.

● The federal government is the largest user of computers. The FBI and police departments use computers to track criminals. The military uses computers to simulate wars. Weather services use computers to track weather.

● Scientists use computers to handle large amounts of data.

● Computers offer graphics sound, editing, word processing, and data-handling powers to the entertainment business.

TEACHING RESOURCES

Practicing Computer Skills 10-1. "Starting the Home Banking Simulation." A simulation that initiates "home banking." It allows eight transactions using the WestSoft program.
Practicing Computer Skills 10-2. "Transferring Money." Uses the WestSoft program to simulate a banking transaction: transferring funds.
Practicing Computer Skills 10-3. "Doing More Banking." Uses the WestSoft Home Banking System to simulate "paying a bill."
Practicing Computer Skills 10-4. "Checking a Statement". Uses the WestSoft Home Banking System to simulate "checking a statement."

Worksheet 10-1 ACTIVITY. Computer Graphics. Use this worksheet to help students identify graphical uses of computers in business, engineering, medicine, sports and entertainment. Use sources other than the text.
Worksheet 10-2 ACTIVITY. Classify It. This worksheet can help classify computer jobs into four categories.

Worksheet 10-3 RETEACH. Complete the Sentence. Students are asked to complete each sentence with associated concepts from this chapter.

Transparency Master 10A. Computers at Work and Play. Shows examples of computers used. This could be used as part of the lesson opener.
Transparency Master 10B. Computers in the Government. Shows examples of computers used in government.

TEACHING RESOURCES ——————
(continued)

Assessment:

Test 10-A
Test 10-B

Portfolio 10. Students are asked to respond to a question about computer usage, cut and paste pictures of different ways computers are being used, and design their own graphic design or music. They are also asked to create a concept map. A possible solution follows:

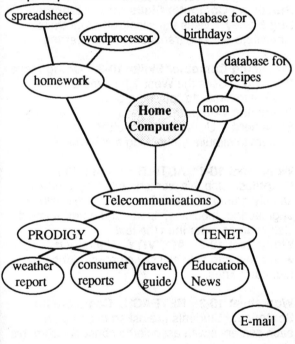

The other three exercises in Portfolio 10 should be used to help students gain a visual understanding of how computers can be used for work and in the world around us.

 TEACHING STRATEGIES ——————

Opening. Introduce the chapter with examples from the videodisc. Students will be able to visualize more of the activities if they have actually seen computers do some of the work. They may also realize how some of the various uses overlap in different fields.

Teaching Tips. A field trip could help students see how computers are actually used in one specific workplace -- could even be the administration building of your school system. Objectives should be set so that students are looking for computer use in industry or an automated office.

When & How.
1. Open the lesson with the video clip. Discuss the stills with the class.
2. Have students read the text for each lesson, do the associated Practicing Computer Skills using the WestSoft Home B anking System Simulation program.
3. Discuss the contents of each lesson, and use the transparencies associated with it. Use additional videodisc stills to enhance your visual presentation.
4. Check for understanding orally, or have students use their word processor to print out their answers.
5. End of Chapter.
   . Use Worksheet 10-3 for reteaching.
   . Orally talk about the discussion questions.
   . Assign the Activities and Enrichment Activities -- you may want to choose one or more of these or divide into groups.
6. Do the Chapter Review together to summarize the contents of the chapter.
7. Use the Portfolio to help monitor student understanding and progress.
8. Use Test 10-A or 10-B to evaluate.

Computer Demonstration. Demonstrate the use of the WestSoft Home Banking program before students do their Practicing Computer Skills in this chapter.

Classroom Management. Using group activities for this chapter could cut down the time needed for the chapter, and it could make the contents more interesting.

TEACHING STRATEGIES ———
(continued)

Cooperative Learning. Teams of students could work on the different sections of the chapter separately, finding information from outside sources as well as reporting to the group. The size of each team, group, is important. Each group should not be more than five, nor less than two. Each group should be mixed both socially and by learning abilities to achieve maximum levels of critical thinking.

Reteaching. Use worksheet 10-3 for reteaching. You could also use the worksheet 10-2, **Classify It**, for reteaching.

Interdisciplinary Learning. Connecting with science . . . Have students find out as many jobs as they can that use computers in science. Also, have students identify the types of technology used along with its functions.
Connecting with music . . . Have students listen to some computer-generated music -- could use recordings of the MOOG synthesizer and progressing to more modern recordings of popular groups. A film, Discovering Electronic Music (from Barr Films, by Bernard Wilets), may help students understand synthesizers.

Writing Activity. Have students compile a book of interviews with computer users (could be fictional). Use photos to enhance the product -- use a scanner or graphics if available.

Closing. Help students to understand the impact of computers on today's job market, and promote discussion of what kinds of skills they will need to find a job in tomorrow's job market.

NOTES ———

Lesson 10 - 1

p.196 - p. 203

 PROJECTED LEARNING OUTCOMES

After studying the concepts and practicing the skills in this lesson, students should be able to:

● Define source-data automation and give examples of it.

● Give examples of how computers have helped automate factories, banks, stores, and offices.

 VOCABULARY TERMS

Automation
Source-data Automation
Electronic Funds Transfer (EFT)
Point-of-sale (POS)
Optical Recognition Device
Bar Code
Electronic Mail (E-Mail)
DIP
Information Retrieval
Teleconference
Materials Requirement Planning (MRP)
Computer-aided design (CAD)
Computer-aided manufacturing (CAM)

 LESSON OVERVIEW

● The government uses large databases with computers to collect taxes and record information, military planning and modeling, weather forecasting from data collected, and tracking criminals.
● Computers in health care can help diagnose illnesses and test and monitor patients.
● Scientists use computers to help monitor experiments and events.
● Computers are used in sports to figure statistics, schedule events, judge athletic performance, and compare teams.
● The entertainment industry uses computers to create special effects, graphics, and cartoons.

TEACHING RESOURCES

Practicing Computer Skills 10-1. Starting the Home Banking Simulation. Uses the WestSoft Home Banking System as a simulation. Shows students "password" entry into a program.
Practicing Computer Skills 10-2. Transferring Money. Simulates transferring funds ($300.00) from savings to a charge account.
Practicing Computer Skills 10-3. Doing More Banking. Students are to write the answers on paper, after analyzing each computer activity.
Answers:
(1) 3, account balances;
(2) 1;
(3) $1472.21;
(4) Press return, then press 4
(5) no written answer;
(6) Press 4 for phone, type an amount (for example, 112.37), choose an account (for ex ample, checking), and then type Y if the summary is correct;
(7) $1359.84
Practicing Computer Skills 10-4. Checking a Statement. Students use the banking program and answer the questions on paper.
Answers:
(1) At the Bank menu, press 1 for account statements, then 1 for checking;
(2) No; 4
(3) Type N;
(4) no written answer;
(5) $5281.91; and
(6) $1409.84

Transparency Master 10A. Computers at Work and Play Shows examples of computers used.

LEARNING CHECK 10-1 ANSWERS —————

1. automated teller machine (ATM).
2. c -- bar code.
3. a -- painting cars; b -- welding bolts;
4. CAD
5. a remote terminal that acts as a cash register and also records sales information.
6. bar codes or UPCs.
7. lets factory owners find out when they need what raw materials in order to deliver a finished product on time.
8. CAD lets an engineer design a product by computer. The computer model can be tested for strengths and weaknesses before a sample is even built. CAM simulates, or models, what could happen on an assembly line, helping engineers to spot and correct problems beforehand.
9. Robots have performed many skills that were humanly unsafe. They also can work 24-hour days.
10. Possible answers include:
    (1) taking jobs away from humans; and
    (2) requiring more highly skilled workers to program robots.

 PRACTICING COMPUTER SKILLS —————

10 - 1 Title: Starting the Banking Simulation.

```
Home Banking
------------------------------------------------

Welcome to the WestSoft Home Banking System

Enter password and press [return]: ABC
```

Discussion: The above screen should be displayed. Notice that the password is shown on the screen. You might want to point out to students that passwords are not usually displayed on the screen.

 PRACTICING COMPUTER SKILLS —————
(continued)

10 - 2 Title: Transferring Money

```
Transaction Summary
--------------------------------


Date: 05/15
Transfer from: Savings
Transfer to: Charge
Amount: $   300.00
--------------------------------

Is this correct? (Y/N): y
```

Discussion: The above screen should be displayed.

10 - 3 Title: Doing More Banking.

```
Current balance of Checking accoutn is:
$ 1359.84
Press [return] to continue
```

Discussion: Transaction summary shown.

10 - 4 Title: Checking a Statement.

```
Current balance of Checking accoutn is:
$ 1409.84
Press [return] to continue
```

Discussion: The amounts shown could change if these Practicing Computer Skills are done in different sessions. The balance of the savings account is $5281.91.

Lesson 10 - 2

p.204 - p.215

 PROJECTED LEARNING OUTCOMES

After studying the concepts and practicing the skills in this lesson, students should be able to:

● Describe special uses of computers in government, science, health care, and entertainment.

● Give examples of how computers have helped automate factories, banks, stores, and offices.

VOCABULARY TERMS

Computerized Axial Tomography (CAT scan)

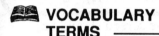 **LESSON OVERVIEW**

● The government uses large databases with computers to collect taxes and record information, military planning and modeling, weather forecasting from data collected, and tracking criminals.

● Computers in health care can help diagnose illnesses and test and monitor patients.

● Scientists use computers to help monitor experiments and events.

● Computers are used in sports to figure statistics, schedule events, judge athletic performance, and compare teams.

● The entertainment industry uses computers to create special effects, graphics, and cartoons.

 TEACHING RESOURCES

Worksheet 10-1   ACTIVITY. Computer Graphics. Use this worksheet to help students identify graphical uses of computers in business, engineering, medicine, sports and entertainment. Use sources other than the text.

Worksheet 10-2   ACTIVITY. Classify It. This worksheet can help classify computer jobs into four categories.
Answers could include:
<u>Simulation:</u> playing war games, computer-aided manufacturing, simulation of emergency room procedures.
<u>Graphics:</u> computer-aided design, CAT scans, animation.
<u>Monitoring:</u> monitor patients on life-support systems; monitor chemical plants; monitor weather, environment, and crime.
<u>Automation:</u> robots, EFT, ATM, optical recognition.

Worksheet 10-3   RETEACH. Complete the Sentence.
Some possible answers:
1. optical recognition
2. source-data automation
3. automatic teller machine
4. bar code
5. word processing, database management, using a spreadsheet, or teleconferencing
6. computer-aided manufacturing
7. handle hot materials, welding, painting
8. process tax returns; identify problem returns
9. oxygen
10. monitor patients
11. identify problems with performance, compile statistics
12. sound effects, making background scenery

Transparency Master 10B. Computers in the Government. Use this to show a visual example of some computers used in the government. Ask students if they know of other uses of computers in the government -- legislature, public information office, etc.

LEARNING CHECK 10-2
ANSWERS ——————————

1. b -- database
2. computerized axial tomography (CAT scan)
3. answers may include:
   background art, sound effects, special effects.
4. c -- ways to study individual performance
5. many studio musicians are replaced by computer-controlled instruments. Musicians are learning to play synthesizers.
6. answers may include:
   They can help an athlete prepare for competition. They can help monitor oxygen and muscles. They can help an athlete study his/her form.
7. answers may include:
   Computers are used for animation, special effects, and imitation of sounds.
8. Answers will vary: Information on property all over the country can be obtained from the FBI.
9. Data from weather stations and satellites about air pressure, wind speed, and humidity can be processed to predict weather patterns.
10. Answers will vary. One example may be McDonalds -- it uses a computer as a cash register and inventories products used.

NOTES ——————————

● Chapter 10 Summary

SUMMARY POINTS

● Almost every office function can be done electronically.
● Manufacturers have benefited from computers from the designing stage to the implementation stage.
● Computers help people in medicine to diagnose illnesses, test patients, and monitor patients.
● Sports use computers to figure statistics, schedule events, and judge athletic performance.
● Computers help the fine arts do routine work that could have taken a lot of time.

DISCUSSION QUESTIONS

1. The word source means the place of origin. The word data means the raw facts. The word automations means any method in which things such as self-operating machines or electronic devices are used to replace human workers. Thus, data is collected automatically at its source. Examples of source-data automation:
. POS terminals;
. EFT;
. life-support systems,
. monitoring systems in chemical plants; and
. ATMs.
2. Inventory control is the biggest advantage, because stores can restock easily and also can pinpoint popular and unpopular products.
3. The POS terminal is programmed for particular products, with no breakdown in costs for individual items such as lettuce and tomato, for example.
4. Workers could enter data into the system that could benefit themselves, but not the banks. ATMs may be located in busy, dangerous places.
5. Discuss this question from the standpoint of making decisions based on numerical information, rather than on experience or intuition.
6. Discussions might include the misuse of information -- like credit reports. Wrong information might also be discussed -- diagnosis of a wrong ailment.

ACTIVITIES

1. Accept well-thought out answers and reports for this activity.
2. Sample:

Scanner	Plotter	flat-panel display	Color Monitor
graphics	CAD	special effects	animation

3. Databases should contain a variety of uses. Encourage students to use sources outside of the ones given in the text.

Enrichment Activities.
1. Students should use or demonstrate available software for microcomputers in the fields of music and graphics.
2. Look for model computerized homes in current magazines. Advise student to become aware of computer usage in their school: grade and attendance reporting, report cards, test questions, analysis of test data for parents (from standardized tests), etc.
3 - 5. Students should be encouraged to write their stories with examples found from sources outside of the text. These stories should be creative, but based on some plausible projections.

CHAPTER REVIEW ———————

Vocabulary

1. EFT
2. POS
3. robots
4. CAD
5. computerized axial tomography (CAT scan)

Questions

1. to diagnose and monitor problems
2. designing cars, airplanes, cards, machines, etc.
3. having a meeting with people from different parts of the country.
4. They can save factories money and risk of hurting human employees.
5. It is used to keep track of inventory, see which products are popular, and to accurately enter prices at a check-out stand.
6. take pictures of a person's insides
7. word processing, database management
8. Possible answer: takes away human jobs.
9. It can let factory owners find out when they need specific raw materials in order to deliver a finished product on time.
10. to track criminals, to forecast the weather, to collect information for taxes, etc.

● Chapter 11

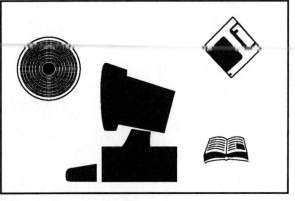

● CAREERS IN COMPUTING

DESCRIPTION: Length 3:30. This program presents various ways in which computers are used in the workplace. The importance of computer skills in obtaining good jobs is emphasized. Scenes depicting office operations, commercial art, airline operations, newspaper publishing, and commercial shipping are included.

Search to Chapter 11........Play

Suggested Additional Resources

● <u>Understanding Computers</u>, Third Edition, by Grace Murray Hopper and Steven L. Mandell, West Publishing Co.
● Computer magazines
● Telecommunications networks and bulletin boards - CREN, TENET, DIALOG, PRODIGY, or a local bulletin board for your city/state.
● <u>Exploring Business and Computer Careers</u>, by June Atkinson and Grady Kimbrell, West Publishing Co.

➡ PROJECTED LEARNING OUTCOMES

After studying the concepts and practicing the skills in this chapter, students should be able to:

● Describe jobs in computer operations.
● Describe careers dealing specifically with system development and programming.
● Describe careers related to the computer industry, such as engineering, sales, and documentation.
● Create letters using merged information from a database with Microsoft Works.

📖 VOCABULARY TERMS

Data processing librarian	System analyst
Data entry operator	Database analyst
Computer operator	Computer consultant
Application programmer	Computer engineer
System programmer	Technical writer
Maintenance programmer	Computer technician
	Security specialist

Investigating Careers

CHAPTER OVERVIEW

● While many people will need to know how to use computers on their jobs, some people will be directly responsible for computer operations at a business or manufacturer. Some of these people will be employed in computer operations, acting as data-processing librarians, data-entry operators, and computer operators.

● A career in systems development and programming involves designing the flow of information. Jobs in this area include systems analysts, database analysts, and programmers. Computer consultants work independently to do many of the same jobs as programmers and system analysts: they help a business decide how to use computers.

● Companies who make computers may need a variety of technical and assembly people: engineers, assemblers, inspectors, machinists, sales and marketing people. They may also use a variety of support people who train other people how to use their machines and write documentation that explains their machines.

● Technicians and security specialists may work for a company, a manufacturer, or themselves. Technicians install, repair, and maintain computers, and security specialists set up methods to prevent losing data or machines.

TEACHING RESOURCES

Practicing Computer Skills 11-1: Creating a Database for a Merged Letter
In Chapter 4, students learned how to create a database. In this exercise, students will make a database that will be merged with a form letter in a later exercise.

Practicing Computer Skills 11-2: Creating a Letter to Request Information.
In this exercise, students will create a form letter that will be merged later with the database created in the previous exercise.

Practicing Computer Skills 11-3: Merging a Database Into a Word Processor Document.
In this exercise, students merge the Jobs database into the Form letter.

Worksheet 11-1 ACTIVITY. How Computers Have Changed Work: Sheet to fill out while interviewing a person concerning current computer usage. See Cooperative Learning strategy.
Worksheet 11-2 RETEACH. Summing Up: Fill-in-the blank questions reviewing this chapter.
Worksheet 11-3 ENRICHMENT. Analyze Your System: Sheet to use while role-playing the job of system analyst. See When & How strategy.

Transparency Master 11A. Careers and Computers: Lists some computer careers in hardware, software, and support personnel.

TEACHING RESOURCES
(continued)

Assessment:
Test 11-A

Test 11-B

Portfolio 11. Investigating Careers: Students will answer a question about using computers in a certain career field, cut and paste pictures showing careers in computer technology, and create a concept map about careers in manufacturing and technical support.

Skills Test 11. Students use the Skills Test 11 sheet to create and print two thank-you letters to parents by merging the Thanks word processor document and the Parents database.

TEACHING STRATEGIES

Opening. After watching someone who works with computers or seeing a film about computer-related careers, students might want to discuss how personality traits affect job choices. They could offer suggestions about the skills needed to do detailed work, sales work, or repair and engineering work. Students may also volunteer how they expect future education and job plans to be influenced by computers.

Teaching Tips. Arrange a field trip to one company that would give a good overview of most careers mentioned in this chapter. Limit the object of the trip to those jobs that have a direct relationship to computers: computer operators, system analysts, technicians, librarians, programmers, and data-entry operators, for example.
Use the Microsoft Works database module to create a database file about computer careers. Categories may include education, job experience, starting pay, current pay scales, possible employers, and so on.

When & How.
1. Before any discussion of computing careers, ask students to quickly write down the first ten jobs or occupations that they think about. Then, ask them to mark any job that might involve computers. Discuss.
2. Show the videodisc clip to further interest students in computing careers. Use ideas from the Opening strategy to continue discussion.
3. Arrange a field trip or a speaker for your classes. Use a variety of activities each class period so that this chapter will not involve just reading and answering questions.
4. Set up a simulation for a system analyst to upgrade a system for teachers to use in classrooms. Uses include averaging grades, preparing memos to send to parents, and helping students in school work. Use enrichment worksheet 11-3 to prepare the questions that the "system analyst" will ask the teachers and perhaps the principal to determine what system would be useful.

TEACHING STRATEGIES
(continued)

Cooperative Learning. In teams, have students pick a field, such as law, insurance, medicine, secretarial work, real estate, or teaching about office practices, and find out how that field has changed with the introduction of computers. Students may use Worksheet 11-1, How Computers Have Changed Work, as a guide to research. They should find an interview subject who has worked with both old and new methods.

Writing Activity. Write about the importance of computer literacy, keyboarding, and reading to any job in the future.

Interdisciplinary Learning.
1. Ask students to find and list one way that computers are used by teachers, school administrators, librarians, secretaries, bank tellers, accountants, lawyers, real estate salesmen, and police. Compare the answers. What is the most common use? Students should word process a report on their findings.
2. Look through the Sunday newspaper from a large city to find advertisements for classes, seminars, book reviews, and other aids to learning about computers. Post the ads. They might include classes offered through community colleges, high schools, the YMCA, scouting programs, and private sources.

Closing. Using the same newspaper, find want ads for jobs listed in this chapter. Mark any characteristics or requirements listed in the ads. Record the jobs, companies, and requirements on a large chart or Microsoft Works database file.

NOTES

Lesson 11 - 1

p.220 - p.226

 PROJECTED LEARNING OUTCOMES

After studying the concepts and practicing the skills in this lesson, students should be able to:

- Describe jobs in computer operations.
- Describe careers dealing specifically with system development and programming.

 VOCABULARY TERMS

Data processing librarian	System programmer
Data entry operator	Maintenance programmer
Computer operator	System analyst
Application programmer	Database analyst
	Computer consultant

 **LESSON OVERVIEW**

- While many people will need to know how to use computers on their jobs, some people will be directly responsible for computer operations at a business or manufacturer. Some of these people will be employed in computer operations, acting as data-processing librarians, data-entry operators, and computer operators.
- A career in systems development and programming involves designing the flow of information. Jobs in this area include systems analysts, database analysts, and programmers. Computer consultants work independently to do many of the same jobs as programmers and system analysts: they help a business decide how to use computers.

 **TEACHING RESOURCES**

Practicing Computer Skills 11-1: Creating a Database for a Merged Letter
In Chapter 4, students learned how to create a database. In this exercise, students will make a database that will be merged with a form letter in a later exercise.

Practicing Computer Skills 11-2. Creating a Letter to Request Information.
In this exercise, students will create a form letter that will be merged later with the database created in the previous exercise.

Worksheet 11-1 ACTIVITY. How Computers Have Changed Work: Sheet for students to fill out while interviewing a person concerning current computer usage. See Cooperative Learning strategy at the beginning of this chapter.

Worksheet 11-3 ENRICHMENT. Analyze Your System: Sheet for students to use while role-playing the job of system analyst. See When & How strategy at the beginning of this chapter.
Answers:
Examples of questions about current system:
1. What equipment is used to average and record student grades?
2. How are parents notified about the grades?
3. How much time is consumed in figuring grades?
Examples of questions about problems and advantages of the current system:
1. What features of the current system would you retain?
2. Do problems occur with parents understanding grades?
3. What problem seems to be the greatest in the current system?
Examples of questions about expected output and changes that are needed:
1. What type of report to parents do you favor?
2. What hard copy or output would you like to see implemented?
3. What would you report on a report card that you do not report now because of the time element?
4. What could be dropped in a new or upgraded reporting system?

1. files, disks, tapes
2. b
3. Computer operators
4. The field in which they are working, such as business or science.
5. d
6. Answers will vary, but can include items like automobile guidance, and electronic secretary.

Lesson 11 - 2

p.226 - p.231

 ## PROJECTED LEARNING OUTCOMES

After studying the concepts and practicing the skills in this lesson, students should be able to:

● Describe careers related to the computer industry, such as engineering, sales, and documentation.
● Create letters using merged information from a database with Microsoft Works.

 ## VOCABULARY TERMS

Computer engineer
Technical writer
Computer technician
Security specialist

 ## LESSON OVERVIEW

● A database file can be the basis for a report. A report format, or plan, includes only the categories and records needed, in the order desired. Options for the appearance of the page can be picked, too. The report format can be saved so that it can be used again.

 ## TEACHING RESOURCES

Practicing Computer Skills 11-3: Merging a Database Into a Word Processor Document. In this exercise, students merge the Jobs database into the Form letter.

Worksheet 11-2 RETEACH. Summing Up: Fill-in-the blank questions reviewing this chapter.
Answers:
data-processing librarian
data-entry operator
typing or keyboarding
source-data automation or optical recognition devices
computer operator
human
system
upgrades or updates programs
know a lot about a company's business and work well with people
database
engineers
assemblers
machinists
inspectors
computer technicians
training personnel
technical writers
security specialists

Transparency Master 11A. Careers and Computers: Lists some computer careers in hardware, software, and support personnel. This categorizes careers by one criterion, the type of job. The categories vary slightly from those in the chapter. Students may suggest and categorize careers by other criteria, including education required, personality traits required, and so on.

 ## LEARNING CHECK 11-2 ANSWERS

1. documentation
2. c
3. security specialist
4. Technicians
5. time, money
6. answers will vary

![icon] PRACTICING COMPUTER SKILLS

Practicing Computer Skills 11-3: Merging a Database Into a Word Processor Document.

Student's Name

Student's Address

Student's City, State and Zip Code

Joan Swift

Inventive Technologies, Inc.

2325 Orchard Lane

El Paso, TX 79986

Dear Ms. Swift:

I am a student in the Computer Literacy class at Mill Valley

Secondary School. Our teacher, Mr. Higgins, has given us an

assignment to find out about the jobs that use computers in

your company. If you could send some information about

these jobs, it will be very helpful to our class.

Sincerely,

Student's Name

The first of three Form letters is printed out as shown.

SKILLS TEST 11 ANSWERS

TO: Carol Fleece

FROM: Student's Name

DATE: Current Date

On behalf of the Computer Literacy class I want to thank you
for volunteering to serve as a Tutor. Your help
on Saturday will make it possible for more students
to participate in the activities.

We appreciate the extra time you are donating to our school.

TO: Jose Martinez

FROM: Student's Name

DATE: Current Date

On behalf of the Computer Literacy class I want to thank you
for volunteering to serve as a Lab Manager. Your help
on Monday will make it possible for more students
to participate in the activities.

We appreciate the extra time you are donating to our school.

These are the two Thanks letters printed out.

● Chapter 11
Summary

SUMMARY POINTS

● While many people will need to know how to use computers on their jobs, some people will be directly responsible for computer operations at a business or manufacturer. Some of these people will be data-processing librarians, data-entry operators, and computer operators.

● A career in systems development and programming involves designing the flow of information. Jobs in this area include systems analysts, database analysts, and programmers. Computer consultants work independently to do many of the same jobs as programmers and system analysts.

● Companies who make computers may need a variety of engineers, assemblers, inspectors, machinists, sales and marketing people. They may also use a variety of support people who train other people how to use their machines and write documentation that explains their machines.

● Technicians install, repair, and maintain computers, and security specialists set up methods to prevent losing data or machines.

DISCUSSION QUESTIONS

1. Students may suggest jobs in the arts, such as dancing, drawing and painting, and playing a musical instrument. Other jobs might include furniture making, house painting, and other crafts.
2. Relate the importance of computer skills as compared with other skills such as reading.
3. Again, students may have several suggestions, among them willingness to try new things and good background in reading, mathematics, and evaluating and thinking skills.

ACTIVITIES

1. This activity can be used with the Writing Activity strategy at the beginning of the chapter.
2. This is a shorter version of one part of the Writing Activity. The ads may be more or less specific, depending on how many employees a company has and needs depending upon the extensiveness of the job within the company.
3. Some extra research may be needed for this activity.

Enrichment Activities.

1. Answers will vary depending on what manual has been chosen and how technical the subject is.
2. This activity is related to other activities, and can be part of a larger project or self-contained.

CHAPTER REVIEW ————————

Vocabulary

1. A computer operator sets up equipment for the day's use and may do some minor repair and maintenance work.
2. The application programmer writes computer instructions for programs that help a user accomplish a user-oriented job.
3. A system analyst studies a company's needs, and then designs and suggests computer systems to fill the needs.
4. A technical writer prepares documentation for computer hardware and software.
5. The security specialist is responsible for keeping computer equipment and data files safe from disasters and unauthorized people.

Questions

1. The data processing librarian catalogs and maintains the tapes and disks that hold computer files and programs.
2. Scanners and other optical-recognition devices may make it possible for almost all data to enter the computer system by automated methods. The data entry operator may need to learn how to use the machines, or may need to learn an entirely new job.
3. The application programmer writes programs for user-oriented jobs. The system programmer writes programs that help the computer do its work. The maintenance programmer is trained to upgrade and update existing programs.
4. The database analyst is primarily concerned with a company's data files, and a system analyst works with planning hardware, software, and people over the entire organization.
5. The computer consultant can plan a system for an organization, but also works with implementing the system and training people to use the system. Training personnel give specific training on using new or upgraded hardware and software.

⬤ Chapter 12

◎ EXPLORING LANGUAGES

DESCRIPTION: (2:52) This animated program explains the concept of programming. A computer program is compared to a story in which a path is followed and decisions made which lead to various courses of action.

Search Chapter 12 .... Play

Suggested Additional Resources

- <u>Understanding Computers</u>, Third Edition, by Grace Murray Hopper and Steven L. Mandell, West Educational Publishing Co.
- <u>Computers and Information Processing</u>, by Floyd Fuller and Stan Wilkinson, West Educational Publishing Co.
- Telecommunications networks and bulletin boards -- CREN, TENET, DIALOG, PRODIGY, or a local bulletin board for your city/state
- Computer magazines
- <u>The Fractal Geometry of Nature</u>, by Benoit B. Mandelbrot, W. H. Freeman and Co.

➡ PROJECTED LEARNING OUTCOMES

After studying the concepts and practicing the skills in this chapter, students should be able to:

- Distinguish between low-level and high-level languages.

- Give examples of programming languages and their purposes.

- Identify languages used with particular applications: business, science and math, robotics, general-purpose, and teaching.

- Compare and contrast programming languages (low-level, middle-level, and high-level).

- Describe the functions of an artificial intelligence language.

📖 VOCABULARY TERMS

Fractal	Interpreter
Low-level language	Pascal
Machine language	Compiler
Binary notation	Source code
Bit	Object code
Byte	Logo
Assembly language	FORTRAN
Assembler	COBOL
Mnemonic code	C
Accumulator	Middle-level language
High-level language	Case-sensitive
BASIC	Artificial Intelligence
Interactive programming	Expert systems
	LISP
Modularity	List manipulation
Run	PROLOG

Exploring
Languages

CHAPTER OVERVIEW

● Programming languages let a programmer write instructions to the computer. The only language the computer understands without translation is machine language. Machine language uses zeros and ones to communicate directly with the computer.

● Both machine and assembly languages are low-level languages. Assembly language uses abbreviations that are translated into machine language.

● High-level languages let the programmer work on problem solving rather than on the details of computer operation.

● BASIC, Pascal, and Logo were designed as teaching languages. BASIC generally uses an interpreter as its translator to machine language, while Logo and Pascal use a compiler.

● FORTRAN's main usage is in mathematical and scientific applications. COBOL's main usage is in business applications. Both were early languages.

● C is a middle-level language. It combines elements of both low- and high-level languages.

● Artificial intelligence (AI) is machine functioning that imitates human reasoning. Expert systems use AI to predict and analyze specific situations by using large databases.

● LISP and PROLOG are used primarily for AI. Both languages can be used to build expert systems, knowledge bases, and natural languages. Both languages have many future potentials.

TEACHING RESOURCES

Practicing Computer Skills 12-1. "A Taste of HyperTalk" Shows how you can talk to your computer with the HyperTalk programming language. Students view HyperTalk scripts.

Worksheet 12-1 ACTIVITY. "Programming Language Survey" Students choose a programming language to analyze. They will need to use resources, along with the text, to elaborate facts and predictions about the langage they chose.

Worksheet 12-2 RETEACHING. "Matching" Students are asked to match descriptions with terms from this chapter.

Worksheet 12-3 VOCABULARY. "Summary of Terms" Students are asked to insert the terms in the blanks provided.

Transparency Master 12A. Low-level Languages. Shows examples of Machine and Assembly languages -- Figures 12-2 and 12-5.
Transparency Master 12B. Bits and Bytes. Shows how a letter and number can be represented in a computer system -- Figure 12-3.
Transparency Master 12C. BASIC. Shows two different BASIC software programs -- Figures 12-8 and 12-9.
Transparency Master 12D Pascal and Logo. Shows programs and runs from Pascal and Logo -- Figures 12-10 and 12-11.
Transparency Master 12E. FORTRAN Program. Shows an entire FORTRAN program Figure 12-12.
Transparency Master 12F. C Program. Shows a C program and its output -- Figure 12-14.

HyperCard Lesson 12. Programming Languages. Outlines programming languages by describing and giving examples of low-level, high-level, and artificial intelligance languages. Each example provides a description, use, and advantage/disadvantage of a programming language.

TEACHING RESOURCES
(continued)

Assessment:

Test 12-A
Test 12-B

Portfolio 12 Language Exploration Students are asked to differentiate between languages.

1.   The error in Manuel's statement is that there are only two low-level languages -- machine language and assembly language.

2.   Students should be encouraged to be creative in their descriptions. Yet, they should also be encouraged to use some of the techniques for artificial intelligence that are used in this chapter.

3.   These concept maps will probably be very different. Here is one possible map:

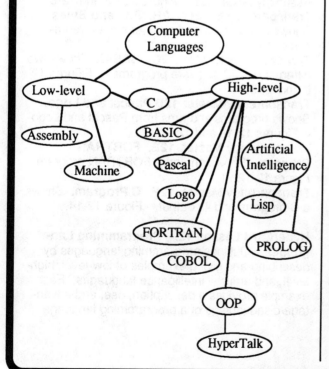

TEACHING STRATEGIES

Opening. Introduce the chapter with examples from the videodisc. Students will be able to visualize the languages and their differences more easily than reading the text first.

Teaching Tips. Encourage students to observe the differences and similarities in the languages presented in this chapter. Doing the Practicing Computer Skills, "A Taste of BASIC," will whet students appetites to wanting to learn how to problem solve through programming.

When & How.
1. Open lesson with the video clips. Discuss the stills with the class.
2. Have students read the text for each lesson.
3. Have students do the Practicing Computer Skills, "A Taste of HyperTalk," before going into the high-level languages. Do the HyperCard lesson after the Practicing Computer Skills.
4. Check for understanding orally by doing the Learning Checks together or have students print out their answers using their wordprocessor -- and then share answers with the whole class or a group.
5. Do the Chapter Review together to summarize the concepts presented.
6. Use the Portfolio to help monitor student understanding and to use for extension.
7. Use Test 12-A or 12-B to evaluate.

Classroom Management. Use groups to study the different languages. Have each group write a report on their languages and present their reports to the whole class.

Cooperative Learning. Break the class into groups to study the different languages. Each group could work cooperatively on Enrichment Activity 1 for a report. Within the group each member could do a separate language -- with more depth. The group would then combine the reports and share their information with their group and with the whole class. Make sure that students know that everyone's contribution is important.
Evaluate each group's performance. You may ask the group to evaluate their performance first on a scale of one to ten, and ask them to elaborate on why they gave themselves that rating.

TEACHING STRATEGIES

(continued)

Writing Activity. The fractal highlight in this chapter briefly discussed the Koch Snowflake. Have students write a discussion of fractals. They should include a discussion of how computers have affected fractals and how specific fractals can be created. Encourage students to include specific program coding for fractals written in different programming languages. Fractal patterns include: the Mandelbrot Set, Monkeys Tree, Minkowski Sausage, the Dragon Curve, Dragon Sweep, Twindragon, Knotted Peano Monsters, Bernoulli Clusters, Sierpinski Arrowhead, Fractal Umbrella Trees, Fractal Canopies, the Pharaoh's Breast-plate, and the Julian Set.

Reteaching. Use Worksheet 12-2, Reteaching - Matching, as reteaching instruction. Have students find the answers to the worksheet from their TutorTech lesson and their text.

Interdisciplinary Learning. Connecting with social studies . . . Have students find out the part of the world where each language was developed -- for example French scientists developed PROLOG. Have students plot the languages on a world map. Ask them to draw conclusions about their findings. Does the amount of technology a country has effect the number of languages developed? Does the wealth of a country effect that number?

Closing. Help students to understand the significance of programming a computer. Programming allows the user to control the computer. Summarize the usage of the different languages -- why some early languages are used very little, why newer languages include structured design, and why aritificial intelligence languages are important to the future of our country.

Lesson 12 - 1,2

p.236 - p.248

 PROJECTED LEARNING OUTCOMES

After studying the concepts and practicing the skills in this lesson, students will be able to:

- Distinguish between low-level and high-level languages
- Give examples of the following programming languages and their purposes: machine, assembly, BASIC, Pascal, and Logo
- Identify the above languages with their applications

 VOCABULARY TERMS

Fractal	BASIC
Low-level language	Interactive programming
Machine language	Modularity
Binary notation	Run
Bit	Interpreter
Byte	Pascal
Assembly language	Compiler
Assembler	Source code
Mnemonic code	Object code
Accumulator	Logo
High-level language	

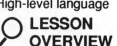 **LESSON OVERVIEW**

- Machine language is the only language that the computer understands.
- Both machine and assembly languages are low-level languages. Assembly language uses English-like abbreviations that are translated into machine language.
- High-level languages let the programmer work on problem solving rather than on the details of computer operation.
- BASIC, Pascal, and Logo were designed as teaching languages. BASIC was designed to be quickly learned. Pascal was designed to teach structured programming. Logo was designed for young children.
- BASIC generally uses an interpreter as its translator, while Pascal and Logo use a compiler.

 TEACHING RESOURCES

Practicing Computer Skills 12-1. A Taste of HyperTalk. It is not important at this time for students to worry about the HyperTalk commands used. The purpose of this exercise is for students to get a sampling of a programming language and what the computer can do in response to specific commands.

Transparency Master 12A. Low-level Languages. This readily shows the differences between the two languages. Ask students to explain what they see different in the two examples. They should observe that machine language is all zeroes and ones, which are not meaningful unless you know their code translations. They should also observe that the assembly language program is much shorter and somewhat English-like. (Figures 12-2 and 12-5)

Transparency Master 12B. Bits and Bytes. This transparency can be used to effectively show how data can be represented in binary notation in a computer system. Point out that the bytes of information translate into a single letter or number. (Figure 12-3)

Transparency Master 12C. BASIC. Have students point out the differences between the two BASIC programs -- Figures 12-8 and 12-9.

Transparency Master 12D. Pascal and Logo. Ask students to compare and contrast the two languages. Comparisons should include that both languages use English-like code and they can both program effectively with graphics. Contrasts should include that Logo looks a lot easier to program than Pascal. (Figures 12-10 and 12-11)

HyperCard Lesson 12. Programming Languages. Outlines programming languages by describing and giving examples of low-level, high-level, and artificial intelligance languages. Each example provides a description, use, and advantage/disadvantage of a programming language.

LEARNING CHECK 12-1 ANSWERS

1. machine
2. A *bit* is either the zero digit or the one digit. A *byte* is a series of bits.
3. Assembly language is easier to program. It uses English-like abbreviations, instead of zeroes and ones.
4. It is faster.
5. There is a one-to-one correspondence in coding assembly language instructions to machine language instructions.

LEARNING CHECK 12-2 ANSWERS

1. The list could include: Logo, Pascal, BASIC
2. Answers could include: BASIC, Pascal, C, HyperTalk
3. Answer could be either Assembly or Machine language
4. Answers could include Pascal, FORTRAN (even though this language hasn't been covered yet, some students may give this response), Logo, or C
5. BASIC - most versions, HyperTalk
6. High-level languages are easier to learn. They use common math terms and symbols. Fewer instructions are needed in a high-level language than a low-level language, which reduces the time needed for writing programs.
   With fewer instructions, high-level programs are shorter, easier to change, and less likely to contain input mistakes.
7. BASIC
8. BASIC
9. Logo or BASIC
10. Both Logo and Pascal are structured high-level languages. Both languages use procedures.

 PRACTICING COMPUTER SKILLS

12 - 2 Title: A Taste of HyperTalk

```
on mouseUp
     go to next card
end mouseUp
```

Discussion: Students are introduced to the HyperTalk language. The screen above shows the script for a button that takes the user to the next card (when it is clicked).

Lesson 12 - 3,4

p.249 - p.258

 ## PROJECTED LEARNING OUTCOMES

After studying the concepts and practicing the skills in this lesson, students should be able to:

- Know the purposes of the following programming languages: FORTRAN, COBOL, C, LISP, and PROLOG.
- Give examples of programming languages
- Identify languages used with particular applications.
- Compare and contrast programming languages (low-level, middle-level, and high-level).
- Describe the functions of an artificial intelligence language.

 ## VOCABULARY TERMS

FORTRAN	Artificial Intelligence
COBOL	Expert systems
C	LISP
Middle-level language	List manipulation
Case-sensitive	PROLOG

 ## LESSON OVERVIEW

- FORTRAN's main usage is in mathematical and scientific applications.
- COBOL's main usage is in business applications.
- C is a middle-level language. It combines the elements of both low-level and high-level languages. C is case-sensitive.
- Artificial intelligence (AI) is machine functioning that imitates human reasoning.
- LISP is used for list manipulation -- symbol manipulation, object oriented programming.
- PROLOG was designed for AI. The logic base in the language deals with the form and truth value of its statements.
- Both LISP and PROLOG can be used to build expert systems, knowledge bases, and natural languages. Both have future potential.

TEACHING RESOURCES
(continued)

Transparency Master 12E. FORTRAN Program. Have students study the FORTRAN program. Ask them to compare it with the Pascal and BASIC programs. They should observe that both Pascal and FORTRAN use some of the same words: *INTEGER* and *END*. All three languages use English-like words. FORTRAN has some line numbers like BASIC.

Transparency Master 12F. C Program. Ask students to look at the program and its "run" and try to determine what the printf and scanf commands do: printf: puts output on the screen; scanf: takes input from the user. Ask students which language that they have seen most closely resembles C -- the answer should be Pascal. Ask them to explain their answer.

LEARNING CHECK 12-3 ANSWERS

1. FORTRAN
2. COBOL
3. FORTRAN
4. Both use a compiler to translate its code. Both are high-level languages that use English-like code.
5. 1) Identification
   2) Environment
   3) Data
   4) Procedure
6. COBOL programs can get very wordy.
7. C came after versions A and B.
8. Programs written in C can be transferred from one computer system to another. C programs are fast and efficient. C programs can be used in a variety of machines. C can also be used to write other programming. languages.
9. It is case-sensitive.
10. It uses high-level language style, and it also uses techniques from low-level languages.

LEARNING CHECK 12-4 ANSWERS

1. Artificial intelligence (AI) is human-like reasoning performed by a computer.
2. An expert system is a software program that contains a knowledge base of specialized information about a specific problem. It uses artificial intelligence. Examples: *Belle, Taum-Meteo, Prospector.*
3. Uses of expert systems include retrieving information from large databases to make appropriate decisions and finding possible solutions to problems.
4. compilers
5. artificial intelligence, list processing
6. list manipulation
7. It's logic based.
8. Both are used to build expert systems, use customized knowledge bases, and translate human languages. PROLOG uses less code than LISP.
9. They manipulate large lists (symbols) to make computers intelligent. They use logic programming to formulate an intelligent decision.
10. These answers will vary. They should include the building of expert systems to do jobs that are now done by humans -- voice translators and script translators, opening and reading mail, etc.

Chapter 12 Summary

SUMMARY POINTS

● People use codes to accomplish many tasks. Musicians use codes to write music, so other people can play it or sing it. Mathematicians use code, or notation, to solve a problem. Other people can use a mathematician's code to interpret a solution to a problem.

● Computer programmers use code also. They use code to solve a problem using a computer. The computer can interpret the code, and other people can look at a listing of the code.

DISCUSSION QUESTIONS

1. Low-level languages use lots of code, while high-level languages use very little code for the same action. Low-level languages use code that is hard to read and understand, while high-level languages' code is similar to English statements.
2. Machine Language: used for fast execution of code
   Assembly Language: used for fast execution
   BASIC: used to learn how to program quickly
   Pascal: used to teach structured programming
   Logo: used in schools; primarily for graphics
   FORTRAN: used for math applications
   COBOL: used for business applications
   C: used as a general-purpose language; used to develop programming languages
   LISP: used for AI; makes expert systems; manipulates lists
   PROLOG: used for AI; makes expert systems, knowledge bases, and translator of human languages
3. Yes. It is easier to program.
4. They all were designed for teaching programming. BASIC uses line numbers, while Logo and Pascal don't. Logo and Pascal use procedures.
5. Many companies and employees don't want to rewrite their programs.

DISCUSSION QUESTIONS

(continued)

6. Expert systems, robots, and prediction systems
7. Logical programming could compare statistics on each team's plays, and how they respond to diferent plays. By playing a "mock" game, the program could determine the winner!
8. C is becoming a popular language because it is versatile, compatible with many machines, and very powerful.
9. Different computer systems are built differently. Each computer system has its very own identity -- the way it processes information. Since each is built differently, the commands (binary notation of its machine language) to make each process is different.

ACTIVITIES

1. Students will need to find the information for machine language, assembly language, C, and PROLOG in other sources.
2. Encourage students to use their imagination to specifically describe a system that is not currently built (at least to their knowledge). The logic processes they describe should require searching databases, making comparisons, and formulating outcomes.

Enrichment Activities.

1. Students will need to look up some of this information in reference books, magazines, or telecommunication databases -- PRODIGY contains most of the information in its encyclopedia.

1940's	machine language
1950's	assembly language
	FORTRAN
1960's	COBOL
	LISP
	BASIC
	Logo
1970's	PROLOG
	Pascal
	C
1980's	HyperTalk

Additional languages include: Ada, Forth, Modula, Modula2, and APL.

2. Encourage students to locate interesting programs -- they can search for these in telecommunications databases and in computer magazines.

CHAPTER REVIEW

Vocabulary

1. machine or assembly language
2. C
3. BASIC, Pascal, FORTRAN, C, Logo, COBOL, or HyperTalk
4. LISP or PROLOG
5. C, Pascal, or BASIC
6. Pascal, Logo, or BASIC
7. COBOL
8. FORTRAN
9. the digit zero or one
10. answers will vary, however they should contain 8 bits: example: 1111 0101

Questions

1. It is the only language that the computer understands.
2. Assembly language is much easier to program than machine language. It uses abbreviated English-like terms. It uses less code.
3. It is much easier to code. The programmer can concentrate on problem-solving rather than on the extensive use of code.
4. Logo
5. BASIC, FORTRAN -- some
6. Pascal and Logo
7. LISP and PROLOG
8. A compiler translates an entire program into machine language, and it doesn't generally execute the code. Whereas, an interpreter converts each line into machine language and executes the code on a line-by-line basis.
9. LISP was developed for list manipulation. It allows the computer to make a choice based on knowledge.
10. Several languages could be chosen:
    BASIC - easy language to use, especially with small programs and small amounts of data.
    Pascal - easy to use, easy to expand, and structured

● Chapter 13

PROBLEM SOLVING

DESCRIPTION: (3:07) A team of programmers begins to solve a problem involving a college level course by beginning the development of a course management program. The purpose of the program is to give tests, keep records, and calculate the grades of students. The concept of careful planning of the components of the program is emphasized. The development of the program is continued in subsequent video clips.

Search Chapter 13 .... Play

Suggested Additional Resources

● <u>Introduction to Computers and BASIC Programming</u>, Second Edition, by Kathleen Brenan and Steven L. Mandell, West Educational Publishing Co.

● <u>BASIC, Concepts and Structured Problem Solving</u>, by Michel Boillot, West Educational Publishing Co.

➡ PROJECTED LEARNING OUTCOMES

After studying the concepts and practicing the skills in this chapter, students should be able to:

● Contrast batch and interactive processing.

● Distinguish between dedicated and general-purpose computers.

● Explain the purpose of systems programs.

● Define structured programming and list its objectives.

● Define problem-solving techniques.

● Use problem-solving strategies to solve a problem.

📖 VOCABULARY TERMS

Dedicated computer	Algorithm
General-purpose computers	Coding
	Control structure
Interactive processing	Simple sequence
Batch processing	Selection
Boot	Loop
Operating system	Documentation
Icon	Run
Compatible	Pseudocode
Configuration	Flowchart
Structured program-ming	Syntax
	Desk checking
Top-down design	Syntax error
Stepwise Refinement	Debugging
Module	Logic error

Problem Solving with Computers

CHAPTER OVERVIEW

- Dedicated computers have their "software" built in and can do only one job. General purpose computers do many jobs.
- Software must be compatible with the computer system in order to run.
- Stages for writing a program are:
    - (1) stating the problem;
    - (2) designing the algorithm;
    - (3) coding the program; and
    - (4) debugging and testing the program.
- Structured programming methods help the programmer write a well-planned program. They include top-down design, structured coding methods, good and appropriate documentation at every stage of programming, and program testing.
- Problem solving strategies include:
    - (1) restating the problem;
    - (2) drawing a diagram;
    - (3) finding patterns;
    - (4) breaking down a problem into simpler parts;
    - (5) tracing the solution;
    - (6 checking assumptions;
    - (7) looking for similar solutions;
    - (8) using math equations;
    - (9) refining the solution;
    - (10) identifying needed information; and
    - (11) checking for reasonableness.
- Problem solving is a skill used in many subject areas and everyday life.
- Restating a problem in your own words is the first step to successful problem solving.

TEACHING RESOURCES

Practicing Computer Skills 13-1. A Little Bit More HyperTalk. This exercise can be used to get students a little bit more familiar with HyperTalk scripts.

Worksheet 13-1 ACTIVITY. Problems and Solutions. This activity helps students identify solvable problems with solutions.

Worksheet 13-2 ACTIVITY. Pseudocode. Use Worksheet 13-1, Problems and Solutions, to write an algorithm for the problem's solution.

Worksheet 13-3 RETEACHING. Related Terms. Use this activity to help students identify related concepts presented in this chapter.

Worksheet 13-4 VOCABULARY. Use this exercise to help students understand the meaning of some of the terms used in this chapter.

Transparency Master 13A. Top-Down Design. Shows a structure chart, using top-down design, of making a pizza. It shows how modules can be broken down for solving a problem -- same as Figure 13-2 in text.

Transparency Master 13B. Algorithm for Making a Pizza. Shows how to write an algorithm for solving the problem of making a pizza -- same as Figure 13-3 in text.

Transparency Master 13C. Control Structures. Same as Figure 13-4 from the text. Shows sequence, selection, and loop control structures.

Transparency Master 13D. The Programming Process. Shows how the programming process works, including emphasis on documentation -- same as Figure 13-6 in text.

Transparency Master 13E. Pseudocode and Flowchart. Shows a solution to the videocassette problem using pseudocode and a flowchart equivalent -- Figure 13-7 in text.

TEACHING RESOURCES ————
(continued)

Transparency Master 13F. Flowcharting.
Shows symbols using in flowchartting a solution to
a problem -- Figure 13-8 in text. A flowchart
example (Figure 13-9) is also shown.

**Transparency Master 13G. The Decision
Symbol.** Shows how to flowchart a decision --
Figure 13-10 in text.

**HyperCard Lesson 13. Problem
Solving.** Defines some of the vocabulary used in
this chapter. Discusses the problem solving
process. Shows a sample algorithm. Tests
flowchart symbols and explains each one's use.
Creates a simple flowchart.

Assessment:

Test 13-A
Test 13-B

Portfolio 13 Problem Solving With Computers
Students are asked to use problem solving skills
in four different activities. The second or third
activity could be used as a "skills test." These
activities give students some "hands-on" experience in solving problems that they can relate to
their everyday lives.
1.   This activity should be used in conjunction
     with the text section on "Buying Software."
     Students should come up with some
     reasonable answers.
2.   Use this activity after developing the concept
     of "Top-Down Design."
3.   Meaningful documentation can be extremely
     useful to the programmer or users of a
     program. This exercise can get students
     acquainted with documenting a problem.
4.   Use this activity with the "Problem
     Solving" section of this chapter.
These activities should help students become
involved with the problem solving process.

 **TEACHING
STRATEGIES** ————————

Opening. Computers need exact directions from
people to do a task. These directions are called
programs, which are computer software. In order to
effectively give the computer directions, programmers have learned to follow certain guidelines to
solve problems. The computer problem solving
process is essentially the same for all programming
languages. However, the more complex the
problem is, the more important it is to use good
problem solving skills.

Teaching Tips. Good problem solving skills are
the key to good solutions and programs. Emphasis
needs to be placed on these skills throughout the
remainder of this course. It is important to let
students know the value to solving a problem
systematically, using the strategies outlined in this
chapter.

When & How.
1.   Open the lesson with the videodisc clip to get
     the students' attention. Continue with the
     stills from the video lesson to introduce the
     concepts -- break the chapter down into
     two lessons, as outlined. Reinforce open-
     ended questioning during the discussion of
     the stills.
2.   Use the transparencies associated with each
     lesson to bring to focus the concepts of this
     chapter -- relate back to the video lesson.
     You could use the figures (stills) from the
     video lesson instead of this format.
3.   Have students read the text lessons and
     do the Practicing Computer Skills. Do the
     HyperCard lesson with the associated
     lesson.
5.   Do the learning checks orally with the
     students to check for understanding of
     each lesson..
6.   End of Chapter.
     .   Orally discuss the discussion questions.
     .   Assign the text activities and enrichment
         activities to students in groups.
     .   Use the Activity sheets to help students
         bring together their thoughts on the
         concepts presented.
     .   Do the Chapter Review together -- either
         orally or in groups.
7.   Assessment.
     .   Students should do their Portfolio activities
         at the places suggested.
     .   Test A and B should be given last.

Classroom Management. The two lessons in this chapter are probably best done in a "whole-class" presentation. However, the learning checks can be done in groups -- written out by the group and then compared with the other groups in the class.

Observation. These are usually very easy lessons for students to comprehend. The problem arises in trying to keep students using structured coding and structured problem-solving skills. If they can't see the reasoning behind carefully thinking, planning, and implementing a solution, they will probably tend to take the shortest solutions in the upcoming chapters.

Cooperative Learning. The activities and enrichment activities can easily be broken down into groups. Have students then share their solutions to the activities with the whole class. It can help if other students are asked to summarize or elaborate on other group presentations.

Writing Activity. Have students discuss another school class that involves problem-solving approaches -- such as math, science, social studies, or even art or music. They should include in their discussion the problem-solving strategies used. They should also be able to describe the effectiveness of the solution, and why the solution was either successful or unsuccessful -- debugging their solution in words. Students should use their word processor for this activity and turn in a hard copy of their discussion.

Reteaching. Use the Reteaching activity to help students group together common concepts, which can also help them identify and understand some of these concepts. The Chapter Review can also be used as a reteaching tool, instead of using it as a whole class activity.

 TEACHING STRATEGIES —————

(continued)

Interdisciplinary Learning. Connecting with music . . . Have students discover how a music passage is written. You may want to buy or rent the Walt Disney's CAV videodisc, <u>Fantasia</u>. The CAV version contains reasoning behind why the passages were composed as they were to form a whole. This can be related back to the top-down design problem solving process. This could help students understand modularity also, since the episodes are broken down into smaller and smaller parts. Viewing this from a problem-solving point of view gives a whole new dimension to the production.

Assessment. Use the Portfolio as a performance test to determine if further teaching is needed, and encourage students to elaborate on their answers. Test A can be used for objective testing of ideas. Test B can be used as a make-up test, or it can be used for retesting. Or, use Test A as a pre-test and test B as a post-test.

Closing. Relate the problem-solving process to the real world. Give examples of problems that were solved with systematic reasoning -- for example the designing and production of a car, airplane, school, etc.

Lessons 13 - 1,2

p.262 - p.270

 ## PROJECTED LEARNING OUTCOMES

After studying the concepts and practicing the skills in this lesson, students should be able to:

● Contrast batch and interactive processing.

● Distinguish between dedicated and general-purpose computers.

● Explain the purpose of systems programs.

● Define structured programming and list its objectives.

📖 VOCABULARY TERMS

Dedicated computer
General-purpose computers
Interactive processing
Batch processing
Boot
Operating System
Icon
Compatible
Configuration
Structured programming

Top-down design
Stepwise Refinement
Module
Algorithm
Coding
Control structure
Simple sequence
Selection
Loop
Documentation

🔍 LESSON OVERVIEW

● Dedicated computers are programmed to do a single job, whereas general-purpose computers can do many jobs and use many software programs. Systems programs run the computer, while application programs fills a user's needs.

● Writing software programs should involve structured programming: top-down design, stepwise refinement, use of modules, and structured coding with control structures, documentation, and program testing.

 ## TEACHING RESOURCES

Worksheet 13-1 ACTIVITY. Problems and Solutions. Use this activity to help students understand top-down design, stepwise refinement, and problem-solving strategies -- by having students identify the strategies they used in their solution. You may need to give students some ideas or parameters in finding a suitable problem to solve -- examples: doing laundry, making a model airplane, figuring how much their allowance would be in ten years if they get a 5% yearly increase, etc. Be sure the problems chosen are limited in scope, otherwise students will have a hard time completing this activity.

Transparency Master 13A. Top-Down Design. Shows a structure chart, using top-down design, of making a pizza. It shows how modules can be broken down for solving a problem -- same as Figure 13-2 in text. Describe the different levels of a top-down design -- Level 0 is the most broad and ambiguous while the higher the level gives the most specific details.
Transparency Master 13B. Algorithm for Making a Pizza. Shows how to write an algorithm for solving the problem of making a pizza -- same as Figure 13-3 in text. Point out to students that not every module will have refinement, except the top module which states the broad solution.
Transparency Master 13C. Control Structures. Same as Figure 13-4 from the text. Shows sequence, selection, and loop control structures. Point out that simple sequence is merely going from the first step to the last without any type of branching or repeating. Selection or decision contain simple branching. Looping contains the repetition of the same step or steps.

HyperCard Lesson 13. Problem Solving. Defines some of the vocabulary used in this chapter. Discusses the problem solving process. Shows a sample algorithm. Tests flowchart symbols and explains each one's use. Creates a simple flowchart. This lesson can be used as a transition into the next lessons. Let students view algorithms and flowcharts before discussing or reading the text of Lessons 13-3 and 13-4. This could help answer many questions that students may have.

LEARNING CHECK
ANSWERS 13-1

1. possible answers may include:
   computers to control the temperature and
   lighting in buildings, computers inside a
   microwave or in an aircraft, or computers
   that are designated as language translators
2. It can do many jobs, and it can use many
   different software programs.
3. interactive
4. systems
5. compatible
6. Answers can include:
   . What do I want to do with the software?
   . How much time do I want to spend
     learning how to use it?
   . Can I test the software at the store
     before I buy it?
   . Do I have the right equipment to run the
     software?
   . How much does the software cost?
   . Is there a hotline support number to call?
   . Is the software "compatible" with other
     programs?
   . Can I make a backup copy?
7. system program
8. Batch processing processes data all at
   once, while interactive processing involves
   processing while input is happening.
9. DOS programs direct a computer to move
   data from RAM to a data disk, they direct
   data to a peripheral device, and they
   prevent some types of data collision -- to
   name a few.
10. management of primary memory, peripheral
    devices, and data; boot the computer

LEARNING CHECK
ANSWERS 13-2

1. d -- to make the program easy to understand
   and use
2. algorithm
3. loop
4. loop
5. Documentation can help to find logic errors,
   which are hard to detect. The reason behind
   a process may be faulty, and it may be hard
   to determine without documentation.
6. Documentation should appear throughout
   the programming writing process, both within
   the program and outside of the program.
7. A good solution should:
   . be easy to read and understand
   . be dependable
   . work under all conditions
   . be easy to change
   . run as quickly as possible
8. Top-down design can help in planning a clear
   solution to a problem.
9. Structured programming can help attain a
   good solution -- see answers to question 7.
10. Bottom-up design might mean starting at
    the finest of steps and working to a more
    global solution to a big problem.

Lessons 13 - 3,4

p.271 - p.280

 PROJECTED LEARNING OUTCOMES

After studying the concepts and practicing the skills in this lesson, students should be able to:

● Define problem-solving techniques.

● Use problem-solving strategies to solve a problem.

 VOCABULARY TERMS

Run	(Hand-
Pseudocode	simulation)
Flowchart	Syntax error
Syntax	Debugging
Desk checking	Logic error

 LESSON OVERVIEW

● Problem-solving strategies are discussed:
  - (1) restating the problem
  - (2) drawing a diagram
  - (3) finding patterns
  - (4) breaking down the problem into simpler parts
  - (5) tracing the solution
  - (6) checking assumptions
  - (7) looking for similar solutions
  - (8) using math equations
  - (9) refining the solution
  - (10) identifying needed information
  - (11) checking results for reasonableness
● Problem solving is used in: math, social studies, language arts, and computer skills.
● The first step in problem solving is to restate the problem in your own words.

 TEACHING RESOURCES

Practicing Computer Skills 13-1. A Little Bit More HyperTalk. This exercise can be used to get students a little bit more familiar with HyperTalk scripts.

Worksheet 13-2 ACTIVITY. Pseudocode. Use Worksheet 13-1, Problems and Solutions, to write an algorithm for the problem's solution. You may also want to have students write a flowchart for their solution.

Worksheet 13-3 RETEACHING. Related Terms. Use this activity to help students identify related concepts presented in this chapter. Students are to circle the three terms that are related.
Answers:
1. operating system, boot, DOS
2. compatible, hardware, configuration
3. top-down design, modules, algorithm
4. simple sequence, loop, control structure
5. top-down design, stepwise refinement, structured coding
6. flowchart, design, pseudocode
7. syntax, test, debug
8. writing the program, programming language, code
9. desk checking, debugging, testing
10. code, pseudocode, algorithm

Worksheet 13-4 VOCABULARY. Use this exercise to help students understand the meaning of some of the terms used in this chapter.
Answers:
1. general-purpose, dedicated
2. boot, operating system
3. batch, interactive
4. algorithm, stepwise refinement, top-down design
5. control structures, loop, documentation, selection
6. Run
7. pseudocode, flowchart
8. debugging, logic, syntax

Transparency Master 13D. The Programming Process. Shows how the programming process works, including emphasis on documentation -- same as Figure 13-6 in text.

TEACHING RESOURCES

(continued)

Transparency Master 13E. Pseudocode and Flowchart. Shows a solution to the videocassette problem using pseudocode and a flowchart equivalent -- Figure 13-7 in text. Use this example to show students how a flowchart related to pseudocode.

Transparency Master 13F. Flowcharting. Shows symbols using in flowcharting a solution to a problem -- Figure 13-8 in text. A flowchart example (Figure 13-9) is also shown. Discuss the use of flowcharting symbols and how they can be used to show a picture of a design.

Transparency Master 13G. The Decision Symbol. Shows how to flowchart a decision -- Figure 13-10 in text. Point out to students that the decision making process in a program is important.

LEARNING CHECK 13-3 ANSWERS

1. Answers will vary. One example might be a student that needs to find out what grade he/she needs to make on a test in order to pass the class with a "B" average.
   Solutions could include figuring the other grades mathematically:
   example:
   (daily grades + Test1 + Test2)/3 = average
   To make average = 80 or above, Test2 needs to be what? Plug in values for daily grades and Test1. Set average equal to 80. To equalize the equation, what is the least value for Test2?
2. Restating the problem in your own words.
3. How a teacher or a textbook describes a problem is not necessarily how a student can understand the same problem.
4. Looking at solutions to similar problems can help determine a solution to a slightly different problem.
5. Science classes can use tables and graphs to formulate a pattern which can be used for prediction. Social studies classes can use tables and graphs to contrast different kinds of cultures, population, industry, and leaders.

LEARNING CHECK 13-4 ANSWERS

1. There are many ways to solve any given problem. The number of ways depends on the complexity of the problem.
2. State, or define, the problem.
3. algorithm or pseudocode
4. grammatical rules that must be followed when writing program instructions
5. Flowcharts are visual descriptions of needed program steps. They can show a clear picture of what is going on.
6. As solutions to programs become more complex, flowcharts can take up many pages and grow more confusing rather than being helpful.
7. Advantages: Pseudocode allows the problem solver to design a solution in terms that are understandable to him/her. It helps the programmer focus on solving the problem rather than on using the rules of a specific programming language. Disadvantage: Pseudocode can be wordy and not very visual.
8. after all syntax errors are corrected
9. Syntax errors involve the grammatical rules of a specific programming language, while logic errors involve a flaw in the design of a program.
10. at every stage of program development

PRACTICING COMPUTER SKILLS

13 - 1 Title: A Little Bit More HyperTalk.

```
on mouseDown
  -- go to the next card
  -- if the shift key is down go to the next marked card
  visual effect wipe right very fast
  if the shiftKey is down then go next marked card
  else if the commandKey is down then go last card of
this bkgnd
  else go next card of this bkgnd
  play "boing"
end mouseDown
on mouseStillDown
  -- Requires handler: mouseDown
  mouseDown
end mouseStillDown
```

Discussion: Students alter the script of a button from the Address stack. They insert the statement *play "boing"* into an existing HyperTalk script.

● Chapter 13 Summary

SUMMARY POINTS

● Computers need software to do jobs. Some computers are dedicated to specific jobs, while others can do many jobs with many different software programs.

● Software is designed for users. It must be compatible with the hardware in order to operate.

● Writing programs involves first designing a solution to a problem, using problem solving strategies. Problem-solving is a part of many subjects and the real world.

DISCUSSION QUESTIONS

1. Answers will vary. Have students identify different types of software they used: games, programming languages, application programs, etc. You could divide students into groups for this and have them identify why they felt their software was easy or difficult to use.
2. Answers will vary. One example may be to break a word problem into parts. Find the solution to each part, and then determine how the parts fit together to determine a solution to the whole problem.
3. Design or planning. Because without a good design, solutions could have bad logic or they may not be efficient.
4.

Pseudocode		Flowchart	
Advantage	Disadv.	Advantage	Disadv.
helps put in own words sequential outline	too wordy too long	visual shows flow	too long too confusing

5. Answers will vary. They could help a student plan out how to redesign his/her room.
6. They could help in many ways. With jobs becoming more skilled, problem-solving skills are essential.

ACTIVITIES

1. Pseudocode
   1) Enter test grades
   2) Calculate: Add the three tests and divide the sum by 3
   3) Print the results

Flowchart

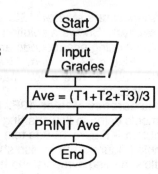

2. errors:
20 LET C + 500 = D
30 PRNT C
END

3.

4. ABC   BAC   CAB
    ACB   BCA   CBA

→ 1) Find first position of set
   2) Keep first the same and arrange the other two positions.
└ 3) Repeat for each object.
    Note: Permutation N!

Problem-solving strategies used:
. draw a diagram   . find patterns
. trace solution   . check assumptions
. check result for reasonableness

ACTIVITIES

(continued)

5. Pseudocode for Activity 4
   1) Read objects
   2) Make Sets
      1. Place first object in position one.
         Place second object in position two.
         Place third object in position three.
      2. switch second and third objects
         for set two.
   3) Repeat step 2 -- changing the objects

Enrichment Activities.

1. Answers will vary. Encourage students to write with well-developed sentence structure and paragraph form.
2. Answers will vary. Have students write a report, using their word processor that describes the program.
3.

Strategies	Steps
1) Restate the problem 2) Draw a diagram 3) Check assumptions 4) Use math equations 5) Refine solution 6) Identify needed information 7) Check results for Reasonableness	1) Measure room (yds) 2) Find standard carpet width (yd) that would best fit room 3) Multiply standard width by length of your room (yds) 4) Multiply solution in step 3 by $10.00. 5) Check answer by hand simulation 6) Check for reasonableness -- ask salesman or someone who knows about carpeting

4. Answers will vary. They include:
water supply, navigation to work (employment -- roads, subway, bus, etc.), climate, available jobs, and available housing. Graphs will vary. Some steps used might include:
. draw diagrams   . find patterns
. check assumptions   . check for reasonableness

CHAPTER REVIEW

Vocabulary

1. user enters input
2. Macintosh, Apple II, or IBM computer
3. Microsoft Works, PageMaker, Super Paint
4. ⬤ ⬭ ☝ are some examples
5. Simple sequence or loop
6. Answers will vary. They should include a design.
7. transference may be one answer
8. Answers will vary. Some might include: DOS program.
9. Answers will vary. Some might include breaking steps into finer details -- example, breaking down steps in making a pizza.
10. syntax error or logic error

Questions

1. Answers might include managing
   1) primary memory;
   2) printer;
   3) monitor;
   4) keyboard;
   5) data in secondary storage.
2. d -- pseudocode
3. a -- algorithm
4.
   1) State the problem;
   2) Design the solution;
   3) Write the program; and
   4) Debug and test the program.
5. Syntax errors involve the grammatical rules of the programming language, while logic errors involve the algorithm or design of a program.
Syntax error -- misspelling a command.
Logic error -- wrong or incorrect formula.
6. It is useful to both the programmer and the program user. It can help a programmer debug his/her solution. It can help a program to be more "user friendly."
7. A loop is a control structure that causes a set of instructions to be run over and over again.
8. Control structures can be in the form of a simple sequence. They can be in the form of a loop. Control structures help you solve problems in an orderly fashion.
9. Program testing involves trying out a program with sample data. It should be used throughout a program -- from beginning to end.
10. Estimating the results can help you check for the reasonableness of an answer.

Chapter 14

 Creating with HyperCard

DESCRIPTION: (2:58)) A tour of Apple Hyper-Card is provided. The index card metaphor is employed to explain the operation of HyperCard. Various applications of HyperCard are displayed. HyperCard terminology, including cards, backgrounds, fields, buttons, and graphics are shown.

Search Chapter 19 .... Play

Suggested Additional Resources

● Computer Magazines.

● Telecommunications networks and bulletin boards

● The Complete HyperCard 2.0 Handbook, by Danny Goodman, Bantam Computer Books

● Berkeley Macintosh User Group

● The Boston Computer Society

 PROJECTED LEARNING OUTCOMES

After studying the concepts and practicing the skills in this chapter, students should be able to:

● Understand some uses of HyperCard stacks.

● Give examples of HyperCard stacks.

● Navigate in HyperCard.

● Describe HyperCard and how it is organized.

● Use HyperCard commands.

● Change text on a card.

● Add a card to a stack.

● Copy graphics from the Scrapbook, and use them on a card.

 **VOCABULARY TERMS**

HyperCard	String
Script	Command
Home Stack	Field
Card	Paint
Stack	Background
Home Card	Foreground (Card Layer)
Browse	Recent
Button	Preferences Card
Link	Pixel
Hidden Button	

Getting Started with HyperCard

CHAPTER OVERVIEW

● HyperCard is used to look for and store information.

● HyperTalk is the programming language for HyperCard.

● HyperCard can be used to create databases, presentations, and CAI.

● HyperCard works by using cards that contains fields, buttons, and graphics. Fields contain text, buttons make things happen, and graphics are used to make the card attractive.

● The background of a card is shared by other cards in the stack. The foreground layer (also called the card layer) is specific to each card.

● Searching for information, like a specific name in a database, can be done using the Find command.

● User levels are set to customize cards using the Preferences card.

TEACHING RESOURCES

Practicing Computer Skills 14-1. Looking at the Address Stack. Students browse through the cards in the Address stack. They also look at some of the traits (aspects) of a card.

Practicing Computer Skills 14-2. Looking at the Appointments Stack. Students go from the Appointments stack to the Address stack. They search text by using the Find command.

Practicing Computer Skills 14-3. Using the Message Box. Students use the message box to find the current time and date. They also use the message box to find text.

Practicing Computer Skills 14-4. Changing the Background and Foreground. Students change the background and foreground of cards in the Address stack. They use the Recent command to view the cards they have visited. They customize their cards with paint.

Practicing Computer Skills 14-5. Copying a Picture. Students copy a picture from the scrapbook onto a card and change the appearance of the graphic.

Worksheet 14-1 ACTIVITY. HyperCard Basics. Helps students identify HyperCard basics.

Worksheet 14-2 ACTIVITY. Parts of a Card. Students label the parts of a card (field, button, or paint).

Worksheet 14-3 VOCABULARY. Use this to help students identify and review vocabulary used in this chapter.

Transparency Master 14A. HyperTalk Example. Shows an example of a HyperTalk script. Point out the HyperTalk commands (put, repeat, if, and go) -- same as Figure 14-1.

Transparency Master 14B. Sample HyperCard Card. Shows one of the cards from the Address stack -- see Figure 14-2.

Transparency Master 14C. Home Card Icons. Shows the Home Card from the HyperCard Development Kit -- Figure 14-3.

TEACHING RESOURCES
(continued)

Transparency Master 14D. HyperCard Tools. Shows the Tools menu -- Figure 14-4.

Transparency Master 14E. Button Icons. Shows some of the readymade icons available with the HyperCard Development Kit -- Figure 14-8.

Transparency Master 14F. File Menu. Shows the File menu options and describes their functions -- Figure 14-12.

Transparency Master 14G. Elements of a Card. Shows the diffewrent parts of a card (paint, text, and buttons) -- Figure 14-13.

Transparency Master 14H. Foregound. Points out the specific information used in the foreground layer -- Figure 14-15.

Transparency Master 14I. Go Menu. Shows the G0 menu options and their functions-- Figure 14-17.

Transparency Master 14J. Preferences Card. Displays the Preferences Card, with level 5 active-- Figure 14-19.

Transparency Master 14K. Art Bits Card. Shows the Art Bits Card, Beasts, from the HyperCard Development Kit-- Figure 14-25.

HyperCard Lesson 14. Getting Started. This stack outlines the basic concept of HyperCard, describes the various elements involved, and gives examples of their use.

HyperCard Worksheet 14.

Assessment:

Test 14-A
Test 14-B

Portfolio 14 Getting Started This portfolio asks students to respond to a question about foreground, background, and painting tools. Students design posters using vocabulary from HyperCard, and illustrate how to copy a picture from another card using top-down design.

Skills Test 14. Making an Electronic Address Book. Students customize the Address stack. They enter the names, addresses, and telephone numbers of five of their friends. They use paint to make their cards more attractive.

TEACHING STRATEGIES

Opening. HyperCard was considered to be the first easy-to-access software erector set and information organizer. HyperCard allows users to quickly and easily build application software, like making an address stack.

Teaching Tips. It is extremely beneficial to have the HyperCard Development Kit. With the Kit comes many readymade templates -- buttons, fields, art, etc. Also included in the Kit is invaluable reference books. Another big help is the Educator HomeCard (EHC) from Apple Computer. A comprehensive manual can be purchased from Intellimation. The Educator HomeCard contains the following stacks: Education Home, Seating Chart, Gradebook, Student Info, Planner, Lesson Plans, Classroom Ideas, Teacher Resources, Classroom Clip Art, Presenter, and Education Help.

You will need sufficient memory to run these programs. If you only have 1 Megabyte of RAM, you won't be able to create extensive stacks. However, turning off the RAM Cache from the Control Panel can help. You can also trash some of your RAM eating programs to help some -- virus checking programs, screen savers, the notepad, etc.

When & How.

1. Open the lesson with the video clip. Discuss the stills with the class -- you may want to use the stills of the figures from the chapter instead of using the transparencies when introducing each lesson.
2. Have students do the Practicing Computer Skills associated with each lesson.
3. Have students read each lesson.
4. Use the transparencies associated with each lesson to help clarify ideas and concepts presented in the text portion of the lesson.
5. Use the HyperCard lessons associated with each lesson. Use the HyperCard worksheet as an evaluative tool.
6. Do the learning checks, with each lesson, orally.
7. Do the written activity sheets associated with each lesson.

When & How. (continued)
8. Have students do the Activities and Enrichment Activities, at the end of the chapter, in groups. You can use this also for performance evaluation. Have each group present their activites to the whole class for discussion.
9. Do the Chapter Review together orally. This could also be done in groups. It can help students review the concepts presented, before they are tested with the Chapter Test or the Skills test.
10. Use the Portfolio to help monitor student understanding. This can also be used for students to take home to show their progress.
11. Use Test 14A or 14B to evaluate understanding. Use Skills Test 14 to evaluate progress and understanding of the concepts.

Observation. Students will probably breeze through the concepts presented in this chapter. It may be difficult, though, for some students to visualize the background layer apart from the foreground layer.

Computer Demonstration. Show students how to navigate in HyperCard. Use the Address stack to show the different card components. Show the information about the objects on a card in the Address stack. View some of the scripts associated with objects on one of the cards.
Show how to tear off the Tools menu.

Interdisciplinary Learning. Connecting to science and math . . . Have students research HyperCard stacks created for science and mathematics. Students should cooperatively make a list of available software and their purposes.

Classroom Management. Use groups to do the activities and enrichment activities. Do the written activities individually, to check for understanding.

Cooperative Learning. When working with groups on the activities and enrichment activities, break the class into several small, manageable groups -- three to four students in a group.

Writing Activity. Have students compare and contrast HyperTalk to other high-level programming languages. Some criteria might be:
. compiler/interpreter
. graphics capabilities
. ease of use
. object-oriented
. syntax of the language
. application programs developed with the language
. expandability
. speed

Trouble shooting. Since HyperCard saves so frequently, you will need to have students save their stack templates (like the Address stack) before they experiment with it. Otherwise, the original template will be gone.

Reteaching. If available, use the HyperCard Tour stack for reteaching. This is a very visual stack that can be used for self-paced instruction.

Closing. One of the most important features of HyperCard is its ease of use. Even the "non-programmer" can operate HyperCard. Hyper-Card allows the user to easily navigate from one idea to the next, even if it is not in sequential order!

Lesson 14 - 1

p.284 - p.294

 PROJECTED LEARNING OUTCOMES

After studying the concepts and practicing the skills in this lesson, students should be able to:

● Understand some uses of HyperCard stacks.

● Give examples of HyperCard stacks.

● Navigate in HyperCard.

 **VOCABULARY TERMS**

HyperCard	Browse
Script	Button
Home Stack	Link
Card	Hidden Button
Stack	String
Home Card	Command

LESSON OVERVIEW

● HyperCard is used to look for and store information.

● HyperTalk is the programming language for HyperCard.

● HyperCard can be used to create databases, presentations, and CAI.

● A card is similar to an index card in a library. A stack is one or more cards, stacked together.

● HyperCard is considered to be circular in nature.

● Many HyperCard commands are similar to Microsoft Works commands.

 TEACHING RESOURCES

Practicing Computer Skills 14-1. Looking at the Address Stack. Students browse through the cards in the Address stack. They also look at some of the traits (aspects) of a card.
Practicing Computer Skills 14-2. Looking at the Appointments Stack. Students go from the Appointments stack to the Address stack. They search text by using the Find command.
Practicing Computer Skills 14-3. Using the Message Box. Students use the message box to find the current time and date. They also use the message box to find text.

Worksheet 14-1 ACTIVITY. HyperCard Basics. Helps students identify HyperCard basics.
Answers:
1. HyperTalk
2. presentations
3. first card of the Home stack
4. stack
5. active buttons
6. browse
7. I-Beam, Browse, Arrow
8. Option plus the Command key
9. Command [M]
10. print selected areas of a card

Transparency Master 14A. HyperTalk Example. Shows an example of a HyperTalk script. Point out the HyperTalk commands (put, repeat, if, and go) -- same as Figure 14-1.
Transparency Master 14B. Sample HyperCard Card. Shows one of the cards from the Address stack -- see Figure 14-2.
Transparency Master 14C. Home Card Icons. Shows the Home Card from the HyperCard Development Kit -- Figure 14-3.
Transparency Master 14D. HyperCard Tools. Shows the Tools menu -- Figure 14-4.
Transparency Master 14E. Button Icons. Shows some of the readymade icons available with the HyperCard Development Kit -- Figure 14-8.
Transparency Master 14F. File Menu. Shows the File menu options and describes their functions -- Figure 14-12.

HyperCard Lesson 14. Getting Started. This stack outlines the basic concept of HyperCard, describes the various elements involved, and gives examples of their use.

1. Possible answers:
   . build application software
   . create databases
   . create presentations
   . CAI
   . navigate through a videodisc
2. HyperTalk is HyperCard's programming (authoring) language.
3. A card is similar to a library index card. A card can contain graphics, text, and animation. It is circular in format -- rather than linear, and it allows branching.
4. (1) clicking the icon
   (2) use the Open Stack command from the File menu
   (3) double-clicking the stack icon from the desktop level
5. It allows more than just words and pictures. It can contain graphics, pictures, and animation.
6. the Browse tool
7. Buttons are used to move around stacks and cards, to link cards, and to perform tasks -- like dialing a phone number.
8. I-beam, browse, arrow
9. The Find command allows the user to search text fields for information.
10. Answers will vary. Encourage students to be creative in their uses.

PRACTICING COMPUTER SKILLS

14 - 1 Title: Looking at the Address Stack.

His birthday is April 26.

He used to work at Acme Dot Company.

FAX: 555-1111

Discussion: When the Show Notes button is activated, the above text would be displayed.

 PRACTICING COMPUTER SKILLS

(continued)

14 - 2 Title: Looking at the Appointments Stack.

Discussion: The Appointments stack contains a calendar with the current month, year, and date displayed. Students look at the traits of the different objects on the card.

14 - 3 Title: Using the Message Box.

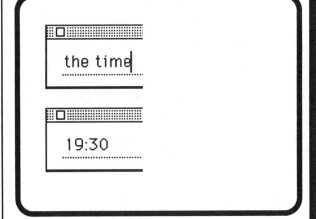

Discussion: Students use the Message box to find the current time. After pressing the return key the current time is displayed, in a 24-hour clock mode. The above time would be 7:30 PM.

Lesson 14 - 2

p.295 - p.308

 ## PROJECTED LEARNING OUTCOMES

After studying the concepts and practicing the skills in this lesson, students should be able to:

● Describe HyperCard and how it is organized.

● Use HyperCard commands.

● Change text on a card.

● Add a card to a stack.

● Copy graphics from the Scrapbook, and use them on a card.

 ## VOCABULARY TERMS

Field
Paint
Background
Foreground (Card Layer)
Recent
Preferences Card
Pixel

LESSON OVERVIEW

● HyperCard works by using cards that contains fields, buttons, and graphics. Fields contain text, buttons make things happen, and graphics are used to make the card attractive.

● The background of a card is shared by other cards in the stack. The foreground layer (also called the card layer) is specific to each card.

● Searching for information, like a specific name in a database, can be done using the Find command.

● User levels are set to customize cards using the Preferences card.

 ## TEACHING RESOURCES

Practicing Computer Skills 14-4. Changing the Background and Foreground. Students change the background and foreground of cards in the Address stack. They use the Recent command to view the cards they have visited. They customize their cards with paint.

Practicing Computer Skills 14-5. Copying a Picture. Students copy a picture from the scrapbook onto a card and change the appearance of the graphic.

Worksheet 14-2 ACTIVITY. Parts of a Card. Students label the parts of a card (field, button, or paint).

Answers:
1. field
2. field
3. button
4. field
5. button
6. paint
7. button
8. button
9. paint
10. field

Worksheet 14-3 VOCABULARY. Use this to help students identify and review vocabulary used in this chapter.

Answers:
1. field
2. background
3. foreground
4. button
5. link
6. string
7. command
8. script
9. Recent
10. paint

TEACHING RESOURCES ————

(continued)

Transparency Master 14G. Elements of a Card. Shows the diffewrent parts of a card (paint, text, and buttons) -- Figure 14-13.

Transparency Master 14H. Foregound. Points out the specific information used in the foreground layer -- Figure 14-15.

Transparency Master 14I. Go Menu. Shows the G0 menu options and their functions-- Figure 14-17.

Transparency Master 14J. Preferences Card. Displays the Preferences Card, with level 5 active-- Figure 14-19.

Transparency Master 14K. Art Bits Card. Shows the Art Bits Card, Beasts, from the HyperCard Development Kit-- Figure 14-25.

LEARNING CHECK 14-2 ANSWERS ————

1. fields, buttons, paint
2. Field text can be searched using the Find command, whereas Paint text cannot. Paint text is created using the A paint tool. Field text is created using the I-beam tool over a text field.
3. The **background** layer is the lowest layer of a card. It is used as a template for all cards in a stack. The **foreground** (card layer) contains the text, graphics, and buttons that are specific to a particular card.
4. The foreground layer contains the specifics for each card. While the background layer contains what is shared by every card.
5. when the stack is first created
6. The new card is added immediately after the card that is on the screen.
7. HyperCard places cards in a stack in circular order, starting with the first card created and continuing with the last card.
8. Recent shows the cards that you have seen.
9. **Browsing (level 1)** -- allows the user to explore stacks but not make changes.
   Typing (level 2) -- allows the user to enter and edit text in fields.
   Painting (level 3) -- allows the user the paint tools to change the appearance of cards and backgrounds.
   Authoring (level 4) -- allows the user to create buttons and fields, link buttons to cards and stacks.
   Scripting (level 5) -- allows the user to edit scripts of buttons, fields, cards, backgrounds, and stacks.
   Each higher level also contains the features of all the levels below it.
10. Answers will vary. Frequent automatic saving helps the user save time from continually having to manually save.

PRACTICING COMPUTER SKILLS

14- 4 Title: Changing the Background and Foreground.

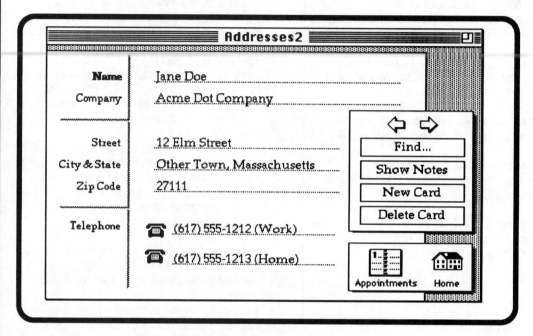

Discussion: The button icons have been changed in the background of the above card. The foreground telephone fields have been changed from the original card.

14- 5 Title: Copying a Picture.

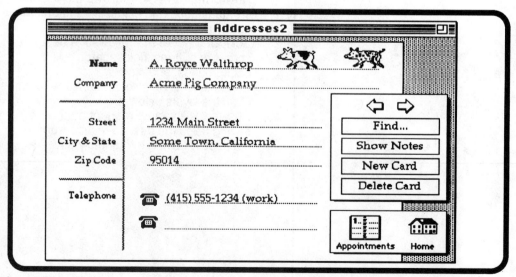

Discussion: The above card has a picture copied from the Art Bits stack. The picture is copied again, and altered using the pencil tool (with Fat bits active).

Skills Test 14. Making an Electronic Address Book. Students customize the Address stack. They enter the names, addresses, and telephone numbers of five of their friends. They use paint to make their cards more attractive.

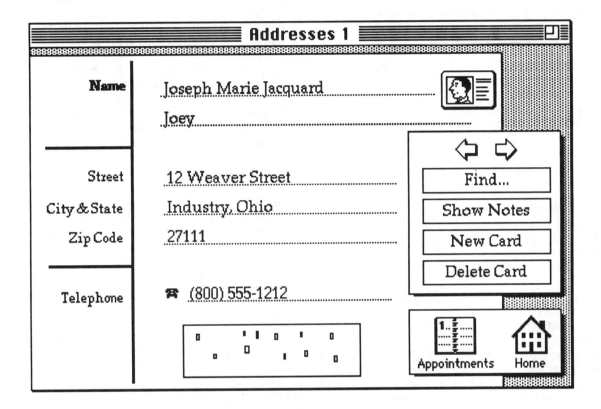

Discussion: The above card has a picture copied from the Art Ideas stack. You can also select a picture from a MacPaint file and copy it onto the clipboard. Or, you could also scan a picture and copy it onto the clipboard.

Paint was used to draw an example of a punched card. The background was altered -- some fields were deleted, some fields were changed, and paint was added.

● Chapter 14
Summary

SUMMARY POINTS

● HyperCard works by using cards that contain objects -- buttons, fields, text, and graphics.
● The Find commands is used to search for information.
● Fields contain text.
● Buttons make things happen.
● Graphics are used to make the card attractive.

DISCUSSION QUESTIONS

1. because of its graphics capabilities
2. to quickly build application software
3. Answers will vary. They could include person alizing home uses.
4. They both contain specific information about a particular topic.
5. They allow the creator to make one template -- saves time.
6. to protect cards in a stack -- a security measure
7. When you're experimenting with a stack, you might not want all of your changes saved. Use the Save a Copy command to make a copy of your file when your're experimenting.

ACTIVITIES

1. use the New Card command from the Edit menu
2. use the Delete Card command from the Edit menu
3. use the Find command from the Go menu
4. use the Print Card command from the File menu
5. use the Print Field command from the File menu, while at the first card
6. use the Print Stack command from the File menu
7. If you don't have access to the Art Bits stack, use graphics from MacPaint or other graphics programs.
8. Go to the button info, select icon, and select a different icon.
9. Select the Show Notes button, while in the background. Delete the button.
10. Use the same editing techniques used in Microsoft Works.

Enrichment Activities.

1. Students will need to be in the background layer -- stripes in the menu bar.
2. Students will need to separate the database fields with tabs. They should get a screen similar to the one below:

Field 1	Jane Doe
Field 2	Acme Dot Company
Field 3	12 Elm Street
Field 4	Other Town, Massachusetts
Field 5	27111
Field 6	(617) 555-1234
Field 7	
Field 8	
Field 9	
Field 10	Her birthday is September 24. H
Field 11	

CHAPTER REVIEW

Vocabulary

1. A <u>card</u> is a screen that can contain buttons, fields, and graphics.
2. A <u>stack</u> contains one or more cards.
3. A <u>button</u> is a "hot spot" on a card that makes things happen.
4. An <u>icon</u> is a picture or symbol. It can be used as a pointer device.
5. A <u>field</u> is a rectangular area of a card that can contain text.
6. <u>Paint</u> is graphics created using the paint tools.
7. The <u>background</u> is the lowest level of a card. It is a template shared by other cards.
8. The <u>foreground</u> layer of a card contains the text, graphics, and buttons specific to a particular card.
9. A <u>link</u> is a connection between information.
10. A <u>script</u> is a collection of instructions, thngs to do.

Questions

1. New Card, Edit
2. Go
3. (1) clicking the icon
    (2) using the Open Stack command from the File menu
    (3) double-clicking the stack's icon from the desktop level
4. browse
5. circular
6. Buttons
7. Option, Command
8. Recent
9. Home
10. Bill Atkinson
11. HyperCard automatically saves all inser tions and changes as they are made.
12. The **Print Field...** command allows you to print selected fields of a card.
    The **Print Card** command allows you to print selected fields of a card.

CHAPTER REVIEW

(continued)

The **Print Stack...** command allows you to print the whole stack, with options for printing half-size cards.
The **Print Report...** command allows you to print selected areas in a stack.

13. Parts of a card:
    fields -- rectangular reas of a card that can contain text
    paint -- graphic created using painting tools
    buttons -- "hot spots" on a card
    Card examples will vary.
14. Position the I-beam pointer over the text to be changed and click to mark an insertion point. Use the same editing tools used in Microsoft Works.
15. **Browsing (level 1)** -- allows the user to explore stacks but not make changes.
    Typing (level 2) -- allows the user to enter and edit text in fields.
    Painting (level 3) -- allows the user the paint tools to change the appearance of cards and backgrounds.
    Authoring (level 4) -- allows the user to create buttons and fields, link buttons to cards and stacks.
    Scripting (level 5) -- allows the user to edit scripts of buttons, fields, cards, backgrounds, and stacks.
    Each higher level also contains the features of all the levels below it.
16. To tear off a menu, drag through the menu and pass the bottom (or sides), then place it where you want it on the screen.
17. (1) Use the Find command. (2) Activate the Message box from the Go menu, and use type find and the text in quotes.
18. HyperCard can be used to create databases, presentations, CAI, and navigate through videodiscs.
19. Use the Browse tool on buttons. Use the Go menu's commands. Use "hot keys."
20. dial telephone numbers, personalize stacks, create databases, make presentations, etc.

Chapter 15

UNDERSTANDING GRAPHICS

DESCRIPTION: (2:40) Various computer graphics, including fractals produced by the CRAY super computer, are included in this program. The NASA computer graphics laboratory is shown. Commercial art applications, simulations, modeling, and computer-aided design applications are shown.

Search Chapter 15 .... Play

Suggested Additional Resources

● The Complete HyperCard 2.0 Handbook, by Danny Goodman, Bantam Computer Books
● HyperCard Authoring Tool , by Dennis Myers and Annette Lamb, Career Publishing Inc.
● Computer Magazines: MacWorld, MacUser, BYTE
● Telecommunications networks and bulletin boards.
● Berkeley Macintosh User Group
● The Boston Computer Society

PROJECTED LEARNING OUTCOMES

After studying the concepts and practicing the skills in this chapter, students should be able to:

● Examine the characteristics of a button, field, card, and stack.

● Use Readymade backgrounds.

● Create a background.

● Use Readymade fields.

● Create a field and set its traits.

● Use Readymade buttons.

● Create a button and set its traits.

● Create a HyperCard stack.

VOCABULARY TERMS

Authoring
Transparent
Opaque
Rectangle
Shadow
Scrolling Field
Trait

Authoring with HyperCard

CHAPTER OVERVIEW

● Authoring is the process of changing existing stacks and creating new stacks. Authoring stacks requires planning. The planning process should include:
. planning the background and foreground
. designing the fields
. designing the buttons
. determining the card's traits

● To find out information about a button or field, double-click the object (button or field) while the object's tool is selected from the Tools menu.

● To find out information about a card or stack, choose Card Info (or Stack Info) from the Objects menu.

● To create a new stack:
. choose New Stack... from the File menu
. choose a name for the new stack
. choose a card size

● To create a background, you must be in the background layer (stripes in the menu bar).

● Backgrounds can contain text, graphics, and buttons. Background graphics can be copied from other stacks or created using the graphic tools from the Tools menu.

● Fields can be copied from readymade stacks or created with selected styles and text.

● Buttons can be copied from readymade stacks or created as transparent, with text, or with icons.

● Making cards involves the same processes as making backgrounds.

TEACHING RESOURCES

Practicing Computer Skills 15-1. Examining the Address Card. Students look at the buttons and fields of cards in the Address stack.
Practicing Computer Skills 15-2. Changing the Notes. Students are asked to change the notes on each card in the address stack.
Practicing Computer Skills 15-3. Changing a Field's Style. Students are asked to change the style of the fields in the Address stack.
Practicing Computer Skills 15-4. Creating a Background. Students are asked to create a background for a stack that contains the names of state capitols, a description of the State, and navigation buttons.
Practicing Computer Skills 15-5. Entering Information. Students are asked to enter text into the fields created in Creating a Background Practicing Computer Skills.
Practicing Computer Skills 15-6. Adding Buttons. Students are asked to add additional buttons to the Practicing Computer Skills, Entering Information.

Worksheet 15-1 ACTIVITY. Planning a Stack. Students are asked to write a plan for a stack that contains the names of their teachers, subject he/she teaches, and period of the day. The stack should also include navigation buttons.

Worksheet 15-2 RETEACHING. Matching the Concepts. Students are asked to match descriptions with concepts covered in this chapter.

Transparency Master 15A. Button Information. Shows the Button information dialog box -- Figure 15-4.
Transparency Master 15B. Field Information. Shows the Field information dialog box -- Figure 15-6.
Transparency Master 15C. Card Information. Shows the Card information dialog box -- Figure 15-7.
Transparency Master 15D. Creating a New Stack. Shows the necessary steps to create a new stack.

Transparency Master 15E. New Stack Dialog Box. Shows the New Card dialog box -- Figure 15-8.
Transparency Master 15F. Creating Buttons. Shows the necessary steps to create a button.

HyperCard Lesson 15. Creating and Using HyperCard Objects. This stack describes the process involved in creating and using Hyper-Card objects as well as creating a new stack.
HyperCard Worksheet 15.

Assessment:

Test 15-A
Test 15-B

Portfolio 15. Cards. This portfolio asks students to respond to questions about buttons, Virtus Vision, creating a new stack, and creating a concept map on how to examine an existing card. Looking at an existing card involves examining the card information, field information, button information and graphics. The following concept map details the major concepts, and refines the button information.

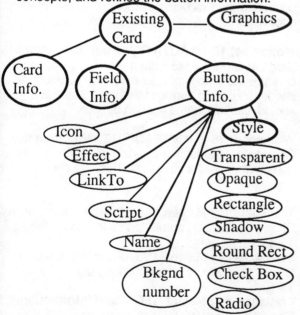

Note: Students would need to also detail card information, field information, and the card's graphics.

Skills Test 15. Creating a New Stack. Students are to plan a new stack that contains their classes. Each card will contain:
. class name
. description of class
. grades for each six-week period
. buttons to navigate through the stack
. graphic description of the subject
Students are then to create the stack they planned.

 TEACHING STRATEGIES ————

Opening. Authoring is the process of changing old stacks and creating new stacks. It can also be called tinkering. This chapter shows how to make your own stacks from scratch.

Teaching Tips. This is usually a fun chapter for students. They really like working with making their own stacks -- especially creating their own graphics. Take advantage of their interest and include other programming techniques that you would like to see them continually use -- like good planning.

When & How.
1. Open the lesson with the videodisc clip to get the students' attention. Continue with the stills from the video lesson to introduce the concepts -- break the chapter down into two lessons, as outlined.
2. Have students do the HyperCard activity and worksheet.
3. Do the Practicing Computer Skills associated with each lesson.
4. Have students read the text, associated with each lesson.
5. Do the Worksheets associated with each lesson.
6. Do the learning checks orally with the students to check for understanding of each lesson.

TEACHING STRATEGIES ———————
(continued)

When & How. (continued)

7. End of Chapter.
   . Orally discuss the discussion questions.
   . Assign the text activities and enrichment activities to students in groups.
   . Do the Chapter Review together -- either orally or in groups.
8. Assessment.
   . Students should do their portfolio before starting the text activities.
   . The SkillsTest should be done after the portfolio.
   . Test A and B should be given last.

Observation. If you start by having students plan carefully their stacks, they will probably continue to do so. It is important to carefully plan the background. Use as many readymade buttons as possible, as it saves time in creating scripts (which may have some bugs).

Computer Demonstration. Show students how to examine an existing card. Look at the different traits of a card. Show what happens when you change the traits of a button -- change its style. Show how to change the traits of a field.

Cooperative Learning. Do the activities and enrichment activities in heterogeneous groups of four to five students. Monitor the activities by making your presence known, but don't be too anxious to jump in with help. Let students try to figure out their problems first. Assist them with some suggestions in designing their stacks. Help students in each group to get actively involved with the group -- team spirit. Encourage creativity and extension to the activities, and reward groups for their efforts -- display their activity in a special place for all students to see, give additional points, or even verbally praise them individually or as a whole group.

Writing Activity. Have students discuss the different uses of HyperCard in our world today. Discussions should include using HyperCard in multimedia, electronic mail, and 3-D representations.

TEACHING STRATEGIES ———————
(continued)

Trouble shooting. Students frequently work at the card level when they want to be at the background level. Remind students that the stripes must be in the menu bar when they are working in the background.

Interdisciplinary Learning. Connecting to Reading . . . Have students relate to the "Create Your Own Adventure" books how conditions can change the output of an event. Have students bring in samples of "creating your own adventure stories" and try to flowchart these stories to determine the possible outcomes. Have students plan a stack that would contain cards for each of the paths in the adventure. Ask students to think about how they would link the cards from one path to another.

Closing. Bring these lessons to a close by emphasizing the importance of good planning. Planning a stack can save valuable time, and it can help with the appearance of a stack along with the navigation.

# Lesson 15 - 1

p.312 - p.319

➡️ PROJECTED LEARNING OUTCOMES

After studying the concepts and practicing the skills in this lesson, students should be able to:

● Examine the characteristics of a button, field, card, and stack.

● Plan a stack.

📖 VOCABULARY TERMS

Authoring   Rectangle
Transparent   Shadow
Opaque   Scrolling Field

🔍 LESSON OVERVIEW

● Authoring is the process of changing existing stacks and creating new stacks. Authoring stacks requires planning. The planning process should include:
    . planning the background and foreground
    . designing the fields
    . designing the buttons
    . determining the card's traits

● To find out information about a button or field, double-click the object (button or field) while the object's tool is selected from the Tools menu.

● To find out information about a card or stack, choose Card Info (or Stack Info) from the Objects menu.

TEACHING RESOURCES

Practicing Computer Skills 15-1. Examining the Address Card. Students look at the buttons and fields of cards in the Address stack.

Practicing Computer Skills 15-2. Changing the Notes. Students are asked to change the notes on each card in the address stack. They first make a copy of the Address stack, so that the original stack is not altered.

Practicing Computer Skills 15-3. Changing a Field's Style. Students are asked to change the style of the fields in the Address stack.

Worksheet 15-1 ACTIVITY. Planning a Stack. Students are asked to write a plan for a stack that contains the names of their teachers, subject he/she teaches, and period of the day. The stack should also include navigation buttons.
Answers will vary. They should include planning for the foreground and background, design of the fields, design of the buttons, and the card size.

Transparency Master 15A. Button Information. Shows the Button information dialog box -- Figure 15-4.

Transparency Master 15B. Field Information. Shows the Field information dialog box -- Figure 15-6.

Transparency Master 15C. Card Information. Shows the Card information dialog box -- Figure 15-7.

HyperCard Lesson 15. Authoring. This lesson introduces the terms used in medium-resolution graphics.

HyperCard Worksheet 15 Authoring

LEARNING CHECK 15-1 ANSWERS

1. Authoring is the process of changing old stacks and creating new stacks.
2. (1) Who will use the stack.
   (2) What's the purpose.
   (3) Experience level of the user
   (4) Simplicity
   (5) Easy to read and search
3. Planning:
   . background and foreground
   . designing the fields
   . designing the buttons
   . determing the card size
4. Select the Button tool from the Tools menu. Choose *Button Info* from the Objects menu to see information about a selected button or double-click the button (if you're at the Authoring or Scripting level).
5. Choose the Field tool from the Tools menu. Select a field (click on the field). Choose *Field Info* from the Objects menu or double-clicking the field.
6. Graphic text
7. Transparent is a see-through object with no visible borders, while opaque is a white object with visible borders.
8. Repeatedly use the Tab key in selected fields.
9. Select *Don't Search Card* from the Card Info dialog box.
10. Answers will vary. They should include, though, the fact that naming cards, fields, and buttons can be useful in linking.

 ## PRACTICING COMPUTER SKILLS

15 - 1 Title: Examining the Address Card.

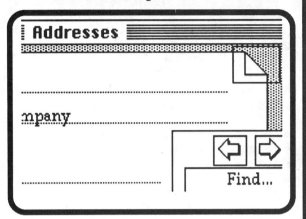

Discussion: When the button tool is selected, the hidden button is outlined. The button toggles the "dog-ear" of the card.

15 - 2 Title: Changing the Notes.

Her birthday is September 24.
Her FAX number is 555-1111.
Her favorite food is pizza.

Discussion: The changed notes field of Jane's card is shown above.

15 - 3 Title: Changing a Field's Style.

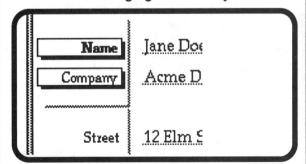

Discussion: The style of the Name and Company fields are changed from transparent to Shadow.

Lesson 15 - 2

p.319 - p.336

PROJECTED LEARNING OUTCOMES

After studying the concepts and practicing the skills in this lesson, students should be able to:

- Use Readymade backgrounds.
- Create a background.
- Use Readymade fields.
- Create a field and set its traits.
- Use Readymade buttons.
- Create a button and set its traits.
- Create a HyperCard stack.

VOCABULARY TERMS

Trait

LESSON OVERVIEW

- To create a new stack:
  . choose New Stack... from the File menu
  . choose a name for the new stack
  . choose a card size
- To create a background, you must be in the background layer (stripes in the menu bar).
- Backgrounds can contain text, graphics, and buttons. Background graphics can be copied from other stacks or created using the graphic tools from the Tools menu.
- Fields can be copied from readymade stacks or created with selected styles and text.
- Buttons can be copied from readymade stacks or created as transparent, with text, or with icons.
- Making cards involves the same processes as making backgrounds.

TEACHING RESOURCES

Practicing Computer Skills 15-4. Creating a Background. Students are asked to create a background for a stack that contains the names of state capitols, a description of the State, and navigation buttons.

Practicing Computer Skills 15-5. Entering Information. Students are asked to enter text into the fields created in Creating a Background Practicing Computer Skills.

Practicing Computer Skills 15-6. Adding Buttons. Students are asked to add additional buttons to the Practicing Computer Skills, Entering Information. Students add buttons with icons and transparent buttons.

Worksheet 15-2 RETEACHING. Matching the Concepts. Students are asked to match descriptions with concepts covered in this chapter.
Answers:
1. Authoring or Scripting level
2. Objects menu
3. Scrolling field
4. Transparent button
5. Stripes in the menu bar
6. background layer
7. field tool
8. trait
9. Shared text
10. buttons with text

Transparency Master 15D. Creating a New Stack. Shows the necessary steps to create a new stack.

Transparency Master 15E. New Stack Dialog Box. Shows the New Card dialog box -- Figure 15-8.

Transparency Master 15F. Creating Buttons. Shows the necessary steps to create a button.

LEARNING CHECK 15-2 ANSWERS

1. Authoring, Scripting
2. text, graphics, buttons
3. the same order that you created the fields
4. in the background
5. It is used to modify existing fields.
6. The only limit to the number of fields that you can have on a card or background is the number that will fit.
7. The Scrolling option is chosen when you have more text to insert than you have available space in the visual field box.
8. button
9. You can edit your selected icon with the *Edit...* command. The Icon Editor tells you how many icons are in your current task.
10. Creating buttons and fields are similar in that they both must have their traits set: name, id, style, script, and other characteristics.

PRACTICING COMPUTER SKILLS

15- 4 Title: Creating a Background.

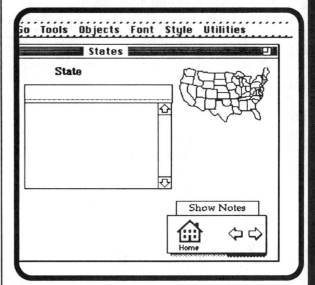

Discussion: Background buttons, fields, and graphics are created for this card. The background buttons include: Next button, Previous button, Home button, and Show Notes button. The buttons were copied from the Address stack. The background fields include: a State title field (with Shared Text selected), a state field (with text to be entered at the card level), and a description field (with text to be entered at the card level).

Notice the stripes in the menu bar.

15- 5 Title: Entering Information.

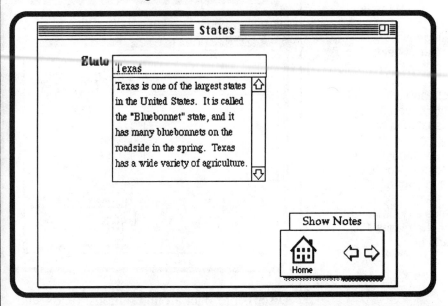

Discussion: Information is entered into the two text fields. The first text field on this card is the "state" field. The second text field is a scrolling field that contains a description of the state. Information is entered into these fields at the card layer (foreground).

15 - 6 Title: Adding Buttons.

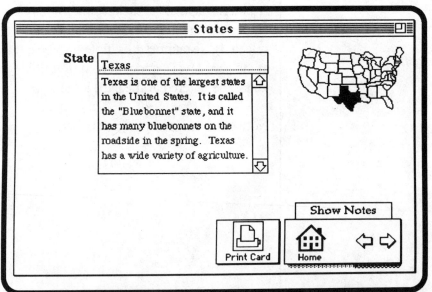

Discussion: One transparent button is added -- the button that outlines the state of Texas. This button would show additional notes about the state. The button was created by copying the script from the Show Notes button from the Address stack.

SKILLS TEST

Skills Test 15. Creating a New Stack. Students are to plan a new stack that contains their classes. Each card will contain:

- . class name
- . description of class
- . grades for each six-week period
- . buttons to navigate through the stack
- . graphic description of the subject

Students are then to create the stack they planned.

Assessment should be based on:

(1) the design
(2) completion of the stack
(3) navigation
(4) printout
(5) extensions -- colors added,
     animation, graphics

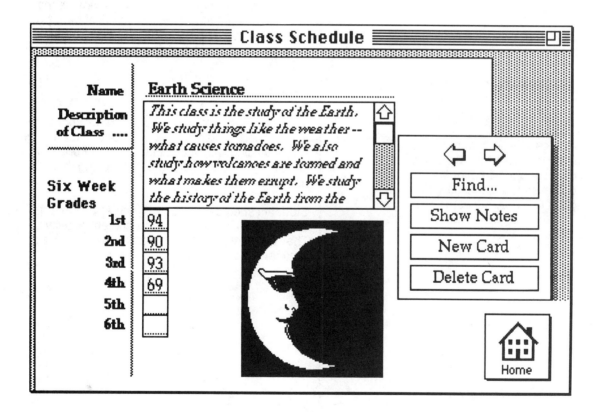

Note: The card above shows the requirements of this assignment. It has buttons to go Home, to the next and previous cards, notes, new cards, and deleting a card. The graphic used came from the Art Bits stack of the HyperCard Development Kit (Claris).

● Chapter 15 Summary

SUMMARY POINTS

● Authoring can be a lot of fun. It involves changing old stacks and creating new stacks.

● To find out information about an object, select the appropriate tool from the Tools menu and double-click on the desired object.

● The planning process should be emphasized. Without adequate planning, stacks can be difficult to create and maintain for future changes.

DISCUSSION QUESTIONS

1 In both cases, you copy the object and then paste.
2. Fields can be searched using the Tab key by the order they were created.
3. It can make the creation of the stack much easier. It can also look at future factors that may affect the design.
4. Some text you don't want to search -- for example titles.
5. They can save lots of time.

ACTIVITIES

(continued)

1-4. Students will need to plan their stacks with the ideas suggested in this chapter. Each student's stack should be different. Students should start with a readymade stack -- like the Address stack. They can then delete unwanted buttons and fields. The navigation buttons will already be there, though. Have students print out each of these stacks before continuing with the next Activity -- that way you will be able to break these Activities into several different grades. You could also have them print the cards in half size.

Note: Sorting can be done linearly as the cards are created (in alphabetical order). Or, it can be done using the Sort button. Cards should be sorted by the name field.

Enrichment Activities.

1 and 2. Programs will vary. Students should be encouraged to plan out their designs. Students will like practicing with visual effects for buttons. They should try out the visual effects by using them to navigate through their cards.

Students should start out with the Appointments stack as their template for Enrichment Activity 2. They can then modify this stack to meet the requirem this activity.

CHAPTER REVIEW

Vocabulary

1. changing the icon of a button
2. no visible borders on the field
3. white field
4. has a vertical scroll bar in the field
5. characteristic of an object - scrolling, Shared Text, Show Lines, etc.

Questions

1. c. planning
2. Button dialog box
3. lines
4. Home
5. Home, Stack Kit
6. stripes
7. Shared Text
8. browse
9. button
10. Opaque
11. The planning process should include:
    . planning the background and foreground
    . designing the fields
    . determining a card size, and what folder to save the card in
12. a. while the button tool is active, double-click the desired button
    b. while the field tool is active, double-click the desired field
    c. choose *Card Info...* from the Objects menu
    d. choose *Stack Info...* from the Objects menu
13. The Tab key will go in the same order that you created the fields. It can be used for easy navigation.
14. . Go to the background layer. Press the Command key and [B] key.
    . Choose New Field from the Objects menu.
    . Move and resize the field. Use the arrow pointer to move and resize.
    . Press Command key and [B] key to get back to the card layer -- to enter text in each individual card

CHAPTER REVIEW

(continued)

15. **Transparent** -- no visible border
    Opaque -- field is white with no border
    Rectangle -- white field with thin black border
    Shadow -- white field with a shadow along the right side and bottom
    Scrolling -- white field with a border and scrolling bar on the right side
16. Buttons make things happen in HyperCard.
17. A transparent button can allow hidden information. They can also allow further information about a specific subject or graphic.
18. . Choose *Background* from the Edit menu
    . Select a general tool from the Tools menu
    . Choose *New button* from the Objects menu
    . Double-click the button
    . Type the text that you want displayed in the Button Name box
    . Check *Show Name*
    . Click *OK* to accept the changes
19. **Transparent** -- button is transparent, no visible border -- used for further information
    Opaque -- white button, with no border -- used to cover a background image
    Rectangle -- white button with a thin black border -- same uses as Opaque
    Shadow -- white button with a shadow on the right side and bottom -- same uses as Opaque, but may need to be used on larger buttons
    Round Rect -- rounded rectangular button -- used in many dialog boxes, also used to show names
    Check Box -- opaque square button -- used for dialog boxes
    Radio Button -- small round opaque button -- are usually grouped with other radio buttons; only one of the group will be able to have a black dot (like an old car radio button)
20. Choose *New Stack...* from the File menu
    Choose a name for the new stack
    Choose a card size
    Click the *New button*

Chapter 16

 ENTERING DATA

DESCRIPTION: (2:35) Various means of entering data including keyboarding, bar code scanners, optical character recognition, and source-data automation are shown in this program.

Search Chapter 16........Play

Suggested Additional Resources

● Programming bulletin boards on local user group networks.
● CREN - telecommunications network for computer scientists.
● The Complete HyperCard 2.0 Handbook, by Danny Goodman, Bantam Computer Books
● HyperCard Authoring Tool , by Dennis Myers and Annette Lamb, Career Publishing Inc.
● Computer Magazines: MacWorld, MacUser, BYTE
● Berkeley Macintosh User Group
● The Boston Computer Society

PROJECTED LEARNING OUTCOMES

After studying the concepts and practicing the skills in this chapter, students should be able to:

● Use message handlers to execute statements.
● Use system messages.
● Create handlers that include command messages.
● Use command messages with buttons.
● Create a button and write its script.
● Use containers for text and numbers.
● Create and use variables.
● Use operators in a script.
● Use built-in functions in a script.
● Use function handlers to return a value.
● Create a stack with graphics, fields, and buttons to solve a given problem.

 VOCABULARY TERMS

HyperTalk	Command
Object	Go
Message	Hide
Idle	Show
System Message	Put
MouseUp	Container
MouseDown	Variable
MouseStillDown	It
Comment Statement	Global variable
Keywords	Local variable
Send	String value
Do	Numeric value
On	Logical value
End	Logical Operator
Handler	Function Handler
Message Handler	

Scripting with HyperTalk

CHAPTER OVERVIEW

● Scripts use English-like words that contain messages sent to objects. Some kind of message is always active in HyperCard. A message is sent when something happens. (When nothing is being done, an *"idle"* system message is sent.) A system message is a message sent to an object -- like *mouseUp* .

● Names in HyperTalk must follow certain rules.

● Scripts contain a collection of statements. Comments help document scripts. Keywords are used to control statements.

● A handler tells HyperCard how to deal with a message. A command message tells HyperCard what to do.

● A variable is a container (a location in the computer's memory). A container can be the Message box, a field, or a variable. Global variables can be accessed throughout HyperCard, while local variables can only be accessed in the handler where they were created.

● All values in HyperTalk are initially strings. However, HyperTalk can convert strings to numeric or logical values. Logical and arithmetic operators are available.

● Many predefined functions are available. A function handler returns a value. A function call contains the function's name and parameter list.

TEACHING RESOURCES

Practicing Computer Skills 16-1. Adding Visual Effects. Students make a new stack called Geometric Figures. They add visual effects to the navigation buttons.
Practicing Computer Skills 16-.2 Adding a New Card Button. Students make a button and write a script to make a new card.
Practicing Computer Skills 16-3. Adding Sound. Students make a button that plays sound. They add the button to the Geometric Figures stack.
Practicing Computer Skills 16-4. Putting Values Into Containers. Students practice putting values into containers -- the message box.
Practicing Computer Skills 16-5. Creating Labels. Students create Label fields by writing a script for their stack. They use these labels to put values into fields.
Practicing Computer Skills 16-6. Working with Variables. Students work with local and global variables in this exercise.

Worksheet 16-1   ACTIVITY. Scripting Practice. Students practice writing scripts for handlers.
Worksheet 16-2   ACTIVITY. System Message Practice. Students are to identify the system message that belongs tothe explanation.
Worksheet 16-3   ACTIVITY. COMMANDS. Students are asked to identify the commands that match their actions.
Worksheet 16-4   ACTIVITY. Operators. Students are asked to insert the operators in the blanks provided.
Worksheet 16-5   Enrichment. Repeating. Students use the repeat structure to write scripts that contain commands that are used one or more times.

Transparency Master 16A. Names in HyperCard. Give the rules for naming in HyperTalk -- Figure 16-2 in text.
Transparency Master 16B. System Messages. Shows a chart of HyperTalk system messages with their explanations -- Figure 16-3 in text.

TEACHING RESOURCES

(continued)

Transparency Master 16C. Statements. Shows a sample HyperTalk script, including comment statements -- Figure 16-5.

Transparency Master 16D. Keywords. Shows a list of the HyperTalk keywords -- Figure 16-6.

Transparency Master 16E. Message Handler. Shows a script with one message handler -- Figure 16-7.

Transparency Master 16F. Commands. Shows a list of HyperTalk commands, their actions, and examples -- Figure 16-8.

Transparency Master 16G. Message Handler. Shows a script with one message handler -- Figure 16-7.

Transparency Master 16H. Variable Rules. Shows HyperTalk restrictions in the use of variables.

Transparency Master 16I. Logical Operators. Shows a chart with HyperTalk's logical operators (also called relational operators) -- Figure 16-10.

Transparency Master 16J. Arithmetic Operators. Shows a list of HyperTalk operators, their jobs, examples, and results -- Figure 16-11.

Transparency Master 16K. Order of Precedence. Shows how calculations are made in order of hierarchy -- Figure 16-12.

Transparency Master 16L. Built-in Functions. Shows a list of HyperTalk functions, their actions, and examplesr -- Figure 16-13.

HyperCard Lesson 16. Scripting. This stack introduces the use of the HyperTalk language by providing examples of scripts which carry out a variety of tasks.

HyperCard Worksheet 16.

Assessment:

Test 16-A
Test 16-B

Portfolio 16 Scripting. Students are asked to respond to questions about scripting, to write a script for a button, and to draw a concept map about HyperTalk system messages. The concept map helps students visualize what system messages do.

TEACHING RESOURCES

(continued)

Skills Test 16 Make a Stack. Students are asked to build from the Geometric Figures stack. They are to write message handlers for buttons that:
- . show the current time
- . play music
- . navigate through cards
- . add and delete cards from the stack
- . print the current card
- . display a name in the message box
- . sort cards
- . display the area of a triangle

Each card contains field with information about a specific geometric figure, a diagram of the figure, and graphics that use patterns.

TEACHING STRATEGIES

Opening. Scripting involves using the HyperTalk language that is built into HyperCard. Scripts use English-like words that contain messages sent to objects -- buttons, fields, cards, etc. The purpose of a script is to give a list of things for HyperCard to do.

Teaching Tips. It doesn't matter to HyperTalk how words are capatilized or not capitalized. However, for easy reading, it helps to use some capitals in a lower-case word -- for example, mouseUp is easier to read and understand its function than MOUSEUP. Using a combination of upper and lower case letters can make scripts more readable and understandable!

If statements are longer than a line, you need to break the statement into the next line. Press the Option key and Return key at the end of the line. This puts a soft return character (¬) in the script, which ties together the entire statement.

Encourage students to use card (cd) or background (bkgnd or bg) in scripts when referring to buttons and fields. If card (or cd) is leftout of a script, HyperCard assumes that you mean the background field. If background (or bg) is left out of a script for a button, HyperCard assumes that you mean you mean the card button. It is good programming practice, especially for beginning programmers, to specify the object. This type of error would be a logic error, and could be difficult to find.

When & How.

1. Open the lesson with the videodisc clip to get the students' attention. Continue with the stills from the video lesson to introduce the concepts. Break the chapter down into two lessons, as outlined.
2. Have students do the HyperCard activity and worksheet.
3. Do the Practicing Computer Skills associated with each lesson. There are a lot of them in this chapter! Use these before introducing the concepts with the text. Students seem to understand what they do better if they see them in use before they're discussed orally.
4. Have students read the text, associated with each lesson.
5. Do the Worksheets associated with each lesson.
6. Do the learning checks orally with the students to check for understanding of each lesson.
7. End of Chapter.
    - Orally discuss the discussion questions.
    - Assign the text activities and enrichment activities to students in groups.
    - Do the Chapter Review together, either orally or in groups.
8. Assessment.
    - Students should do their portfolio before starting the text activities.
    - The Skills test should be done after the portfolio.
    - Test A and B should be given last.

Computer Demonstration. Show several script examples to students. Let them see what happens when you make a syntax and logic error, and how you correct those errors. Using variables (both global and local) will probably be a difficult concept for students to grasp. Do several demonstrations using these types of variables. Students need to see how variables work in a HyperTalk program. They also need to see how to debug their errors in using variables.

Cooperative Learning. Divide the class into groups of three to four students. Ask each group to write a stack that asks five to ten questions about material in this section or about material covered in previous chapters. The questions should be placed on individual cards, with the answers referenced with transparent buttons on each card. Keep the questions short (ten words or less, if possible) and make the answers one or two words only. Save the stacks. Print out the cards in each stack.

Writing Activity. Have students describe a specific logic error they have encountered. They should give details about why they made the error, how they corrected the error, and how they can prevent such errors from happening in the future.

Modeling. Use students as human models to show what occurs when a "wrong type" of data is put into a designated container. The container could be the Boys' or Girls' shower room. Students can immediately visualize that in specified circumstances it is extremely important for data to match the specification! This exercise can also help clarify why HyperCard converts string values to numeric values in some instances.

Reteaching. Use the worksheet **Summing Up** to help students with concepts that were not mastered with the original presentation of the material.

Interdisciplinary Learning. Connecting to Social Studies. . . Break the class into small groups. Have each group find the longitude and latitude of a city in each of the continents. They should then design a card that will display the information on a chart with titles: Continent, City, Longitude, Latitude. Have each class share their design with the other groups. Combine each group's design to make a stack of cards with their information.

Closing. When HyperCard was first designed, the authors thought that very few people would be interested in actually writing scripts. They were certainly wrong. HyperTalk has become a viable and much used programming language.

Lesson 16 - 1

p.342 - p.350

 ## PROJECTED LEARNING OUTCOMES

After studying the concepts and practicing the skills in this lesson, students should be able to:

- Use message handlers to execute statements.
- Use system messages.
- Create handlers that include command messages.
- Use command messages with buttons.
- Create a button and write its script.

VOCABULARY TERMS

HyperTalk	Keywords
Object	Send
Message	Do
Idle	On
System Message	End
MouseUp	Handler
MouseDown	Message Handler
MouseStillDown	Command
Comment Statement	

 ## LESSON OVERVIEW

- Scripts use English-like words that contain messages sent to objects. Some kind of message is always active in HyperCard. A message is sent when something happens. (When nothing is being done, an *"idle"* system message is sent.) A system message is a message sent to an object -- like *mouseUp* .

- Names in HyperTalk must follow certain rules.

- Scripts contain a collection of statements. Comments help document scripts. Keywords are used to control statements.

- A handler tells HyperCard how to deal with a message. A command message tells HyperCard what to do.

 ## TEACHING RESOURCES

Practicing Computer Skills 16-1. Adding Visual Effects. Students make a new stack called Geometric Figures. They add visual effects to the navigation buttons.

Practicing Computer Skills 16-.2 Adding a New Card Button. Students make a button and write a script to make a new card.

Practicing Computer Skills 16-3. Adding Sound. Students make a button that plays sound. They add the button to the Geometric Figures stack.

Worksheet 16-1 ACTIVITY. Scripting Practice. Students practice writing scripts for handlers. Answers:
1. on moouseUp
     go to previous card
   end mouseUp
2. on mouseUp
     go to next card
   end mouseUp
3. on mouseUp
     visual effect scrool left very fast
     go to next card
   end mouseUp
4. on mouseUp
     visual effect dissolve slowly black
     go to previous card
   end mouseUp
5. on mouseUp
     play "harpsichord" tempo 150
   end mouseUp

Transparency Master 16A. Names in HyperCard. Give the rules for naming in HyperTalk -- Figure 16-2 in text.
Transparency Master 16B. System Messages. Shows a chart of HyperTalk system messages with their explanations -- Figure 16-3 in text.
Transparency Master 16C. Statements. Shows a sample HyperTalk script, including comment statements -- Figure 16-5.
Transparency Master 16D. Keywords. Shows a list of the HyperTalk keywords -- Figure 16-6.
Transparency Master 16E. Message Handler. Shows a script with one message handler -- Figure 16-7.

TEACHING RESOURCES

(continued)

Worksheet 16-2   ACTIVITY. System Message Practice. Students are to identify the system message that belongs to the explanation.
Answers:
1.   idle
2.   closeCard
3.   returnKey
4.   doMenu
5.   mouseDown
6.   mouseUp
7.   mouseStilldown
8.   openCard
9.   mouseEnter
10.   mouseWithin

HyperCard Lesson 16. Scripting. This stack introduces the use of the HyperTalk language by providing examples of scripts which carry out a variety of tasks.
HyperCard Worksheet 16.

LEARNING CHECK 16-1 ANSWERS

1.   HyperCard creates easy to program multimedia presentations.
2.   examples: buttons, fields, backgrounds, cards, stacks
3.   always
4.   examples: mouseUp, mouseDown
5.   Each line in a HyperTalk script is a statement, for example
     put the time into the message box
6.   on mouseUp
     end mouseUp
7.   They are used to control statements in a script.
8.   HyperTalk script
9.   A message handler tells HyperCard how to deal with a message.
10. Comments help document scripts so that the programmer can tell what action is supposed to occur in a statement.

PRACTICING COMPUTER SKILLS

16 - 1 Title: Adding Visual Effects.

```
on mouseDown
  -- go to the next card
  visual effect dissolve slowly to white
  go to next card
end mouseDown
```

Discussion: The above screen shows the script of the background button Next.

16 - 2 Title: Adding a New Card Button.

```
▣□▤▤▤▤▤▤▤▤     Script of bkgnd
on mouseUp
  doMenu "New Card"
end mouseUp
```

Discussion: Being able to add a new card, with a click of a button, to a stack is very convenient.

16 - 3 Title: Adding Sound

```
on mouseUp
  play "boing"
end mouseUp
```

Discussion: Students experiment with making sounds. They use the *play* command. The general form of the *play* command:
 play sound [tempo] [notes]
Examples: play "boing"
            play "harpsichord" tempo 100
where 100 is a medium tempo, numbers higher have a faster tempo (numbers lower, have a slower tempo).

● Lesson 16 - 2

p.350 - p.360

 PROJECTED LEARNING OUTCOMES

After studying the concepts and practicing the skills in this lesson, students should be able to:

● Use containers for text and numbers.
● Create and use variables.
● Use operators in a script.
● Use built-in functions in a script.
● Use function handlers to return a value.
● Create a stack with graphics, fields, and buttons to solve a given problem.

 VOCABULARY TERMS

Hide	Local Variable
Show	String Value
Put	Numeric Value
Container	Logical Value
Variable	Precedence
It	Logical Operator
Global Variable	Function Handler

○ LESSON OVERVIEW

● A variable is a container (a location in the computer's memory). A container can be the Message box, a field, or a variable. Global variables can be accessed throughout Hyper-Card, while local variables can only be accessed in the handler where they were created.

● All values in HyperTalk are initially strings. However, HyperTalk can convert strings to numeric or logical values. Logical and arithmetic operators are available.

● Many predefined functions are available. A function handler returns a value. A function call contains the function's name and parameter list.

 TEACHING RESOURCES

Practicing Computer Skills 16-4. Putting Values into Containers. Students practice putting values into containers -- the message box.

Practicing Computer Skills 16-5. Creating Labels. Students create Label fields by writing a script for their stack. They use these labels to put values into fields.

Practicing Computer Skills 16-6. Working with Variables. Students work with local and global variables in this exercise.

Worksheet 16-3   ACTIVITY. COMMANDS.
Students are asked to identify the commands that match their actions.
Answers:
1. hide
2. show
3. put
4. sort
5. ask
6. answer
7. go
8. play
9. visual effect
10. find

Worksheet 16-4   ACTIVITY. Operators.
Students are asked to insert the operators in the blanks provided.
Answers:
1. not equal to
2. modular divide
3. present within
4. divide
5. raise to a power
6. equal to
7. integer divide
8. multiply
9. greater than or equal to
10. present witin

TEACHING RESOURCES

(continued)

Worksheet 16-5   Enrichment. Repeating.
Students use the repeat structure to write scripts that contain commands that are used one or more times.
Possible Answers:

1. repeat 4 times
       wait 2 second
    end repeat
2. repeat
       put the time into message box
    end repeat
3. put 0 into message box
    repeat until message box contains 50
       add 5 to message box
    end repeat
4. on mouseUp
       hide menuBar
       repeat 10 times
          play "harpsichord" tempo 120
       end repeat
       show menuBar
5. on mouseUp
       repeat 10 times
          visual effect dissolve slowly
          go to next card
       end repeat
    end mouseUp

Transparency Master 16F. Commands. Shows a list of HyperTalk commands, their actions, and examples -- Figure 16-8.
Transparency Master 16G. Message Handler. Shows a script with one message handler -- Figure 16-7.
Transparency Master 16H. Variable Rules. Shows HyperTalk restrictions in the use of variables.
Transparency Master 16I. Logical Operators. Shows a chart with HyperTalk's logical operators (also called relational operators) -- Figure 16-10.
Transparency Master 16J. Arithmetic Operators. Shows a list of HyperTalk operators, their jobs, examples, and results -- Figure 16-11.
Transparency Master 16K. Order of Precedence. Shows how calculations are made in order of hierarchy -- Figure 16-12.
Transparency Master 16L. Built-in Functions. Shows a list of HyperTalk functions, their actions, and examplesr -- Figure 16-13.

LEARNING CHECK 16-2 ANSWERS

1.   A command tells HyperCard what to do.
2.   The *put* command takes a value and puts it somewhere.
3.   A container is a location in the computer's memory.
4.   some examples of variables:
     MyName
     Address
     Total
     test1
5.   local and global
6.   The *&* symbol joins text together without spaces. The *&&* symbol joins text together with a space.
7.   string, numeric, and logical
8.   logical and arithmetic
9.   A function returns a single evaluated value.
10. A function handler returns a value. It begins with the keyword *function*. A message handler begins with the keyword *on*, and it executes statements. Message handlers <u>sometimes</u> have additional parameters, while function handlers <u>usually</u> have parameters.

16 - 4 Title: Putting Values into Containers.

```
on mouseUp
    put the time into message box
end mouseUp
```

Discussion: The above script for a button would display the current time in the message box, when the button was clicked. This script could generate the following message:

```
18:11
```

The time is in a 24-hour clock. The time shown would be 6:11 PM.

16-5 Title: Creating Labels.

```
on openCard
  put "Card" && the number of this card into
  ¬ background field "Card Label"
end openCard
```

```
Card 2
```

Discussion: Notice that the script contains a soft return character, since the statement is too long for a line in the window. If the background name field was not exactly as written in the quotes, a syntax error would occur (if there was a space before Card -- " Card Label" instead of "Card Label"). The button shown above would be displayed for card 2 of this stack.

16-6 Title: Working with Variables.

```
on mouseUp
  create_Global_Name
  global Name
  put Name into the message box
end mouseUp

on create_Global_Name
  global Name -- Name will be a global variable
  ask "What's your name?"
  put it into Name
end create_Global_Name
```

Discussion: The script above has two handlers. The first handler calls the second handler with the statement:

create_Global_Name

It then uses the global variable's value. This value will be available throughout HyperCard after this script has been executed.

Handlers are called in HyperTalk by executing a statement that contains the handler's name (create_Global_Name). These handlers work like subroutines in BASIC or procedures in Pascal.

When the above script is activated the ask statement would display the following:

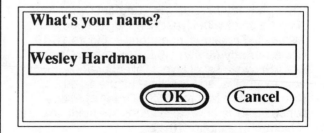

The user would enter a name and select OK. Since the name is global it would be available for the message box.

Make a Stack. Students are asked to build from the Geometric Figures stack. They are to write message handlers for buttons that:
. show the current time
. play music
. add and delete cards from the stack
. display the area of triangles in the message box

. navigate through cards
. print the current card
. sort cards
. display a name in the message box

Each card contains fields with information about a specific geometric figure, a diagram of the figure, and graphics that use patterns. The following is an example of a possible card from this stack.

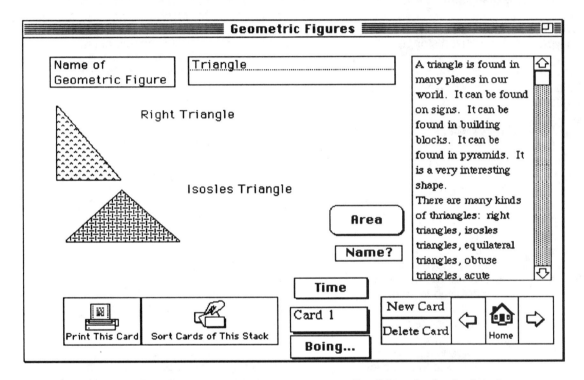

Note: There are several field types: scrolling fields, fields with text for each card, and fields with titles. Students should be encouraged to be creative and use as many of the concepts presented in these chapters as possible. Variables would be used to send calculations to the message box as a calculation of the area for the base and height of different triangles.

The following message box would be shown for a base of 8 and height of 8:

8 is the area of your triangle...

Possible script for the Area button:

```
on mouseUp
  global base
  ask "What's the base?"
  put it into base
  global height
  ask "What's the height?"
  put it into height
  put area_Triangle (base,height) into Message box
  put " is the area of your triangle ..." after Message box
end mouseUp

function area_Triangle base, height
  return (.5 * base * height)
end area_Triangle
```

● Chapter 16
Summary

SUMMARY POINTS

● Scripting in the HyperTalk languag is easy to do. Many of the statements are English-like, and they don't seem as foreign as other programming language statements.
● Some kind of message is always active in HyperCard.
● All values in HyperTalk are initially strings. However, HyperTalk can convert strings to numeric or logical values.
● Handlers are the basic structures of the HyperTalk language. They tell HyperCard how to deal with messages.

DISCUSSION QUESTIONS

1. It is easy to program multimedia presentations. Its inventor had multimedia in mind. HyperCard authors can add sound, text, graphics, and video easily.
2. Messages are continually sent on what is happening in the system.
3. They use English-like words. They must follow a prescribed format (syntax).
4. They can help the programmer remember the thought process involved in an old script.
5. They lose their meaning and their values.
6. Command messages tell HyperCard what to do. A system message is a message sent to an object, a response to an action. They both take action.
7. They both return a single value after calculations have been made.

ACTIVITIES

1-3. Encourage students to be creative with these activities. These activities can also be used as a review for the vocabulary used in this chapter. Students can copy buttons from other exercises, or they can make their buttons from scratch. Sorting can be done linearly by the name field, by creating the cards in alphabetical order, or students can create a sort button (or copy one from another stack and revise it to fit this stack).
4-5. This stack can also be used as a review or for reteaching the concepts about functions. This activity also allows students the opportunity to work with the Message Box as a container for values. A transparent button might be the best solution for doing Activity 5.

Enrichment Activities.

1. This will take some practice. Students may not be able to do this the first time. The fields will need to be designed with field numbers or names. A sample state ment that might be used:

   put abs(-9) into field 4

   or
   put abs(-9) into first word of field "Absolute"

2. Encourage students to be creative. This stack will need to be graded on a perfor mance basis. The appearance and navigation of this stack will be important. Using the Find command in a button will extend lessons presented in this text. Students will need to discover how to do this. They may need to examine a card that uses the Find command first.

Vocabulary

1. button, field, graphics, card, stack
2. mouseUp, mouseDown
3. show all cards
4. on, end, send, do, if, else, exit, function, global
5. on mouseUp
   go to previous card
   end mouseUp
6. on mouseUp
   go to next card
   end mouseUp
7. answer, ask, find, go, hide, play, put, show, sort, visual effect
8. memory location -- It
9. MyName
10. It -- predefined local variable
11. "Teddy Toenail"
12. 155
13. 10 > 5
14. abs()
15. convert (112, F)

Questions

1. script
2. Idle
3. statement
4. Handlers
5. handler
6. command message
7. variable
8. local
9. strings
10. single
11. function
12. return
13. message

114. A script is used to send messages to objects. Every object has a script associated with it that is capable of sending and receiving messages.
15. HyperCard names:
   . must begin with a letter
   . can contain additional letters, digits, or the underscore character
   . should be meaningful to the programmer
   . should not have negatives
   . are not limited in length

(continued)

16. A system message is a message sent to an object in response to an action.
17. on mouseUp
    end mouseUp
18. *on* and *end*
19. All values in HyperTalk are intially strings (a set of characters), for example, "State of Arizona" is a string value. **String values** are sets of ASCII characters, a list of characters. **Numeric values** are sets of characters that represent numbers. The characters include the digits and the period, for example 100 is a numeric value. **Logical values** are the values of "true" and "false." They are used as the result of comparisons, for example 5 > 10 has a logical value of "false."
20. A script contains one or more message handlers. So, a handler is part of a script. All of the messages in a script are sent to objects. Whereas, a handler would be a segment of messages within a script.
21. **Put** is a HyperTalk command that takes a value and puts it someplace. It takes a value (either text or numeric) and puts it in a designated container.
22. **Global variables** can be used throughout Hypercard for any session until you quit. **Local variables** can be used only in the handler where they are created.
23. A logical operator compares two values and produces a "true" or "false" result (>, <, <>, is in, is not in). An arithmetic operator is used in an arithmetic expression (+, -, ^).
24. They can be used as a calculated value.
25. A function call occurs when a function is executed. Examples:
    put time() into the message box
    put date() into the message box
    Both of these examples would call pre-defined functions to find their current values.

Appendix A

West Computer Literacy System
Videodisc Index and User's Guide

Production Coordinator:
Robert V. Price, Ph.D.

This videodisc was produced in cooperation with
Texas Tech University

West's Computer Literacy System Videodisc

The laser videodisc is an organized collection of motion segments and still visuals provided as part of the WEST COMPUTER LITERACY SYSTEM. The videodisc can be used as a teaching aid when presenting lessons, or it can be used directly by students in a cooperative learning setting, for special individual assignments, or for reteaching. Use of the videodisc can help clarify important concepts and motivate students.

The videodisc is organized to work with other components of the system. The table of contents is the same as that of the LEARNING SYSTEM and the text, COMPUTERS: TOOLS FOR TODAY. The videodisc contains motion clips to introduce each chapter, and over 1,400 still visuals. Each vocabulary term contained in the text is illustrated as part of the Visual Glossary on the videodisc. All of the figures from the text are also contained on the videodisc. Additionally, there are many supplementary visuals provided which help to illustrate the material presented in the text or which you can use to design your own presentations.

The first part of the videodisc contains the video programs. The second part contains the visual glossary and figures for each chapter. The third part contains supplementary visuals. Chapters 1-9 are contained on side 1 of the videodisc. The rest are contained on side 2.

Using the Bar Code Reader

The bar codes provided are a convenient way to control your videodisc player if you have a bar wand remote control. You will find the bar codes for the motion segments both in the SYSTEM INTEGRATOR at the opening of each chapter, as well as in the following pages of this index. To use the bar code reader:

1. Hold the bar code reader like a pencil. It should be at a perpendicular angle. Scan the bar code which corresponds to the motion segment or the term you wish to display. Press and hold down the READ button on the bar code reader. The reader will beep when the code has been successfully read. If a beep is not heard, scan the bar code again until a beep is heard.

2. If you are not directly wired into the player, you need to also do the following: Point the bar code reader at the videodisc player and press the SEND button on the bar wand. You should hear another beep. The motion segment or still image that you have selected will be displayed.

   Note: Start scanning far enough to the left of the bar code and continue holding down the READ button bar enough to the right.

Using the Remote Control

You can also access the motion segments and the still visuals on the videodisc by using your videodisc player's standard remote control unit. Frame numbers are provided for all motion segments, the Visual Glossary, the chapter figures, and supplemental visuals. To use a standard videodisc remote control, follow these steps:

1. Point the remote control toward the videodisc player and press CHAPTER/FRAME once or twice until the word FRAME appears on the screen.

2. Enter the frame number corresponding to the visual you wish to see using the remote control unit keypad. The frame numbers will appear on the screen as you enter them.

3. Press the CHAPTER/FRAME SEARCH. The visual you have selected will appear on the screen. For terms which are represented by a motion segment, press PLAY to play the segment. Press PAUSE when the segment pertaining to the term is finished.

4. Repeat the procedure to see another visual.

You can also play a video program by using the following sequence:

1. Press CHAPTER.

2. Enter the number of the chapter desired (1-19).

3. Press SEARCH. The chapter title will appear.

4. Press PLAY.

The video program will play. It will stop automatically when the program is over.

A convenient way to use the videodisc is to start the lesson with a video program in the manner described above and then use the bar code reader or remote control to jump to the visual glossary for the same chapter. Use the STEP command to display each visual in the Visual Glossary as you move through the lesson.

For more information on using the videodisc player and hand controller, see the instructions that accompany your videodisc player.

Using the Videodisc Index

The Videodisc Index includes both the bar codes and the frame numbers for the motion segments, the Visual Glossary and the figures for every chapter. For the supplementary visuals only the frame numbers are provided. The index is organized as follows:

1. For each chapter you will find a set of bar codes with frame numbers for the Visual Glossary. Where a range of frame numbers is shown (such as 50110—51235), a brief motion segment is used to illustrate the term.

2. Next, a set of bar codes with frame numbers for the figures is given. Using these bar codes or frame numbers, you can access the beginning figure for each chapter. Then you can STEP through the sequence of figures.

3. Next you will find a complete frame number index for the Visual Glossary terms and the figures for each chapter.

4. The last item in the Videodisc Index is a complete listing of the frame numbers for all of the supplementary still visuals.

MAC Still Visuals - Chapter1	Keyboard	Read
frame 51730	frame 51734	frame 51738
Visual Glossary - Chapter 1	Monitor	Microcomputer
frame 51731	frame 51735	frame 51739
Computer	Disk	Primary Memory
frame 51732	frame 51736	frame 51740
Program	Disk Drive	Secondary Storage
frame 51733	frame 51737	frame 51741
Data Processing	Output	Information
frame 51742	frame 3250 to 2883	frame 51745
Input	Soft Copy	Hardware
frame 2255 to 2350	frame 4709	frame 51746
Processing	Hard Copy	Peripheral Device
frame 51743	frame 51744	frame 43091 to 43379
Calculate	Data	Software
frame 3882	frame 3420 to 3536	frame 51747

Videodisc Index

System Software	Printer	Command
frame 51748	frame 51751	frame 2668

Application Software	Kilobyte	Floppy Disk
frame 51749	frame 51752	frame 51754

Programming Language	Character	Access
frame 51750	frame 51753	frame 51755

Compatible	Cursor	Load
frame 43420 to 43848	frame 24814 to 24902	frame 51756

Simulation
frame 51757

Menu
frame 51758

Visual Glossary - Chapter 2

frame 52025

Program Disk

frame 52026

Data Disk

frame 52028

Word Processing Program

frame 51779

Write Protected

frame 52027

File

frame 52029

Database Manager Program

frame 19040

Save

frame 8930 to 9346

Backup Copy

frame 51789

Electronic Spreadsheet

frame 51780

Format

frame 10394

Prompt

frame 52030

Videodisc Index

Visual Glossary - Chapter 3

frame 51792

Buffer

frame 52279

Typefaces

frame 52282

Format

frame 10394

Text

frame 10024

Point Size

frame 52283

Default

frame 18304

Graphics

frame 52280

Justify

frame 11817

Clip Art

frame 52281

Visual Glossary - Chapter 4

frame 51812

File

frame 16015

Entry

frame 16741

Database Manager Program

frame 51813

Record

frame 16161

Single Record Layout

frame 16265

Database

frame 15487 to 16015

Field

frame 16451

Multiple Record Layout

frame 19001

Retrieve

frame 51814

Category

frame 16451

Open

frame 51815

Update

frame 20230

Comparison Information

frame 20065 to 20656

Videodisc Index

Visual Glossary - Chapter 5

frame 52314

Communication Channel

frame 52316

Protocol

frame 52319

Comparison Criteria

frame 19783 to 20906

Modem

frame 22599

Baud Rate

frame 52320

Format

frame 22851 to 23154

Digital Signals

frame 52317

Bits Per Second

frame 52321

Telecommunications

frame 52315

Analog Signals

frame 52318

Packet

frame 52322

Noise

frame 52326

Parity

frame 52327

Odd Parity

frame 52328

Even Parity

frame 52329

Start Bits

frame 52323

Stop Bits

frame 52324

Data Bits

frame 52325

Electronic Bulletin Board

frame 51837

Password

frame 24815 to 25010

Electronic Mail (E-Mail)

frame 24142

Commercial Database

frame 25010

Information Network

frame 22447

Videodisc Index

Visual Glossary - Chapter 6

frame 52346

Value

frame 29777

Forecast

frame 52347

Cell

frame 28124 to 28440

Entry

frame 58154

Coordinate

frame 28440

Formula

frame 29100 to 29833

Label

frame 28729

Function

frame 28833 to 30135

Visual Glossary - Chapter 7
frame 52359

Calculator
frame 52360

Punchcard a
frame 52361

Punchcard b
frame 52362

Silicon
frame 51876

Real Time
frame 52369

Integrated Circuitry
frame 52370

Silicon Chip
frame 52371

Punchcard c
frame 52363

Vacuum Tubes
frame 52364

Binary Notation
frame 52364

Electronic Digital Computer
frame 42050

Minicomputer
frame 52372

Large Scale Integration
frame 39039 to 39578

Microprocessor
frame 52371

Personal Computer
frame 52373

Stored Program Concept
frame 32435 to 33100

Generation
frame 52366

Language Translator Program
frame 52367

Transistor
frame 52368

Very Large Scale Integration
frame 52374

Videodisc Index

Visual Glossary - Chapter 8	Bit	Arithmetic/Logic Unit
frame 52395	frame 52399	frame 3871
Analog Computer	Byte	Primary Memory
frame 52396	frame 52400	frame 3340
Digital Computer	Central Processing Unit	Processor
frame 52397	frame 52371	frame 3750 to 4016
Binary Number System	Control Unit	Read-Only Memory
frame 52398	frame 4036 to 4274	frame 3348
Read	Gigabyte	Magnetic Tape
frame 52401	frame 52405	frame 52408
Write	Mainframe	Tape Drive
frame 52402	frame 52406	frame 52409
Random Access Memory	Supercomputer	Read/Write Head
frame 52403	frame 39027 to 39844	frame 52410
Megabyte	Secondary Storage Media	Back Up
frame 52404	frame 52407	frame 52411

Sequential Access Storage

frame 52412

Optical Disk

frame 52414

Track Ball

frame 52417

Format

frame 52403

Video Display Terminal

frame 4823

Graphics Tablet

frame 52418

Direct Access Storage

frame 52413

Joystick

frame 52415

Light Pen

frame 52419

Hard Disk

frame 42230

Mouse

frame 52416

Scanner

frame 52420

Touch Screen

frame 52421

Flat Panel Display

frame 52425

Letter Quality Printer

frame 52429

Voice Recognition Unit

frame 52422

Impact Printer

frame 52426

Non-Impact Printer

frame 52430

Monochrome Monitor

frame 52423

Dot Mtrix Printer

frame 52427

Plotter

frame 52431

Resolution

frame 52424

Daisy Wheel Printer

frame 52428

Voice Response Unit

frame 52432

Videodisc Index

Voice Synthesizer

frame 52433

Visual Glossary - Chapter 9

frame 52459

Download

frame 52463

Natural Language

frame 52467

Ethics

frame 52460

Privacy

frame 52464

Figures - Chapter 9

frame 52468

Computer Ethics

frame 52461

Piracy

frame 52465

Computer Crime

frame 52462

Artificial Intellegence

frame 52466

Videodisc Index

Macintosh Still Visuals frame 50377	**Electronic Funds Transfer** frame 50381	**Electronic Mail (E-Mail)** frame 944
Visual Glossary - Chapter 10 frame 50378	**Point of Scale Terminal** frame 50382	**Data Imaging Processing** frame 50385
Automation frame 50379	**Optical Recognition Device** frame 50383	**Information Retrieval** frame 50386
Source Data Automation frame 50380	**Bar Code** frame 50384	**Teleconferencing** frame 50387
Materials Planning Requirement frame 50388	**ComputerAxial Tomography** frame 50392	
Computer Aided Design (CAD) frame 50389		
Computer Aided Manufacturing frame 50390		
Computer Aided Manufacturing frame 50391		

Visual Glossary - Chapter 11

frame 50408

Application Programmer

frame 50412

Computer Engineer

frame 50414

Data Processing Librarian

frame 50409

Maintenance Programmer

frame 4685

Computer Consultant

frame 4861

Data Entry Operator

frame 50410

System Analyst

frame 49986

Tenchinal Writer

frame 50415

Computer Operator

frame 50411

Database Analyst

frame 50413

Computer Technician

frame 50416

Security Specialist

frame 50417

Videodisc Index

Visual Glossary - Chapter 12

frame 50426

Binary Notation

frame 50429

Assembler

frame 50433

Fractal

frame 26977 to 27481

Bit

frame 50430

Mnemonic Code

frame 50434

Low Level Language

frame 50427

Byte

frame 50431

High Level Language

frame 50435

Machine Language

frame 50428

Assembly Language

frame 50432

BASIC

frame 50436

Accumulator

frame 50437

Interpreter

frame 50438

Object Code

frame 50442

Interactive Programming

frame 6894 to 7168

PASCAL

frame 50439

LOGO

frame 50443

Modularity

frame 14847

Compiler

frame 50440

FORTRAN

frame 50444

RUN

frame 12545 to 13249

Source Code

frame 50441

CoBol

frame 50445

C Language

frame 50446

List Processing (LISP)

frame 50450

Middle Level Language

frame 50447

List Manipulation

frame 50451

Artificial Language

frame 50448

Prolog

frame 50452

Expert Systems

frame 50449

Videodisc Index

Visual Glossary - Chapter 13

frame 50474

Boot

frame 50479

Structured Programming

frame 23398

Dedicated Computer

frame 50475

Icon

frame 49568

Stepwise Refinement

frame 50482

Interactive Computer

frame 50477

Compatible

frame 21236

Module

frame 37399

Batch Processing

frame 50478

Configuration

frame 50481

Algorithm

frame 24187 to 24712

Logic Error

frame 39380 to 40285

Visual Glossary – Chapter 14
frame 50498

Card
frame 50501

Button
frame 50507

HyperCard
frame 50499

Stack
frame 50504

Link
frame 47939 to 48378

Script
frame 50500

Home Card
frame 50505

Hidden Button
frame 50508

Home Stack
frame 49937

Browse
frame 50506

Command
frame 50509

Field
frame 49002

Recent
frame 50513

Paint
frame 50510

Preferences
frame 50514

Background
frame 50511

Figures – Chapter 14
frame 50515

Foreground (card layer)
frame 50512

Videodisc Index

Visual Glossary – Chapter 15	Rectangle	Figures – Chapter 15
frame 50545	frame 50547	frame 50551
Authoring	Shadow	
frame 49456	frame 50548	
Transparent	Scrolling Field	
frame 45317	frame 50549	
Opaque	Trait	
frame 50546	frame 50550	

Visual Glossary – Chapter 16

frame 50570

HyperTalk

frame 50571

Object

frame 50572

Idle

frame 50573

Do

frame 50582

On

frame 50583

End

frame 50584

Handler

frame 50585

Message

frame 50574

System Message

frame 50575

Mouse Down

frame 50576

Mouse Up

frame 50577

Message Handler

frame 50586

Command

frame 50587

Go

frame 50588

Hide

frame 50589

Command Statement

frame 50578

Mouse Stilldown

frame 50579

Keywords

frame 50580

Send

frame 50581

Show

frame 50590

Put

frame 50591

Container

frame 50592

Variable

frame 50593

Videodisc Index

It	Numeric Variable	Figures – Chapter 16
frame 50594	frame 50598	frame 50602
Global Variable	**Logical Operator**	
frame 50595	frame 50599	
Local Variable	**Precedence**	
frame 50596	frame 50600	
String Variable	**Function Handler**	
frame 50597	frame 50601	

Figure - Chapter 1
frame 52247

Figure - Chapter 2
frame 52272

Figure - Chapter 3
frame 52284

Figure - Chapter 4
frame 52303

Figure - Chapter 10
frame 50393

Figure - Chapter 11
frame 50418

Figure - Chapter 12
frame 50453

Figure - Chapter 13
frame 50487

Figure - Chapter 5
frame 52330

Figure - Chapter 6
frame 52348

Figure - Chapter 7
frame 52375

Figure - Chapter 8
frame 52434

Figure - Chapter 14
frame 50515

Figure - Chapter 15
frame 50551

Figure - Chapter 16
frame 50602

Figure - Chapter 9
frame 52468

◀ ❚❚ STILL/STEP ❚❚ ▶

West Computer Literacy System Videodisc
Index for Users of Macintosh Computers

Side 1

Frame Number	Visual Title
1-11	Introduction & Credits
12	Table of Contents 1
13	Table of Contents 2

Video Programs - Chapters 1-9

14	Chapter 1: Exploring Your Computer
5362	Chapter 2: Introduction to Word Processing
10375	Chapter 3: Desktop Publishing
14500	Chapter 4: Database Management
21397	Chapter 5: Desktop Publishing
27021	Chapter 6: Electronic Spreadsheets
31982	Chapter 7: Looking Back
39847	Chapter 8: Examining Hardware
47385	Chapter 9: Using Computers Responsibly

52218	**Macintosh Still Visuals**
52219	**Visual Glossary - Chapter 1**
52220	Computer
52221	Program
52222	Keyboard
52223	Monitor
52224	Disk
52225	Disk Drive
52226	Read
52227	Microcomputer
51989	Primary Memory
52228	Secondary Memory
52229	Data Processing
2255-2355	Input
52230	Processing
3882	Calculate
2350-2883	Output
52231	Soft Copy
52232	Hard Copy
3420-3536	Data
52233	Information
52234	Hardware
43091-43379*	Peripheral Device
52235	Software

52236	System Software
52237	Application Software
52238	Programming Language
43420-43848*	Compatible
52239	Printer
52240	Kilobyte
52241	Character
24814-24902	Cursor
2668	Command
52242	Floppy Disk
52243	Access
52244	Load
52245	Simulation
52246	Menu

52247 Figures - Chapter 1

52248	1-1 A Typical Home Computer
52249	1-2a Storage
52250	1-2b Storage
52251	1-3 The Data Processing Flow
52252	1-4 A Software Packages
52253	1-5 Macintosh Computers
52254	1-6 A Macintosh Classic
52255	1-7 Inside The Computer
52256	1-8 Back View Of A Macintosh Computer Showing Parts
52257	1-9 The Cursor
52258	1-10 The Macintosh Keyboards
52259	1-11 Dot Matrix Printer Print head
52260	1-12 A Floppy Disk
52261	1-13 WestSoft Main Menu

52262 Visual Glossary - Chapter 2

51779	Word Processing Program
19040	Database Manager Program
51780	Electronic Spreadsheet Program
52263	Program Disk
52264	Write Protected
8930-9346	Save
10394	Format
52265	Data Disk
52266	File
52267	Backup Copy
52268	Filename
52269	Prompt
52270	Dialog Box
52271	Document
10393-10597	Scroll
7312-7956	Delete
9600-10150*	Insert
8399-8713*	Word Wrap

Visual Glossary - Chapter 8 (continued)

52416	Mouse
52417	Track Ball
52418	Graphics Tablet
52419	Light Pen
52420	Scanner
52421	Touch Screen
52422	Voice Recognition Unit
52423	Monochrome Monitor
52424	Resolution
52425	Flat Panel Display
52426	Impact Printer
52427	Dot Matrix Printer
52428	Daisy Wheel Printer
52429	Letter Quality Printer
52430	Non-Impact Printer
52431	Plotter
52432	Voice Response Unit
52433	Voice Synthesizer

52434 Figures - Chapter 8

52435	8-1 The ASCII Code
52436	8-2 The Central Processing Unit
52437	8-3 Central Processing Unit Of A Microprocesor
52438	8-4 Primary Memory
52439	8-5 Mainframe Computer
52440	8-6 Minicomputer
52441	8-7 A Small Computer a
52442	8-7 A Small Computer b
52443	8-8 Supercomputer
52444	8-9 Magnetic Tapes
52445	8-10 Recording On Magnetic Tape
52446	8-11 Top View Of A Disk Surface
52447	8-12 Removable Disk Packs
52448	8-13 Optical Disk
52449	8-14 Video Display Terminal
52450	8-15 Membrane Keyboard
52451	8-16 Input Devices
52452	8-17 Scanner
52423	8-18 Touch Screen
52454	8-19 Voice Recognition System
52455	8-20 RGB Color Monitor
52456	8-21 Flat Panel Display
52457	8-22 Daisy Wheel Printer
52458	8-23 Flat-bed Plotter

52459 Visual Glossary - Chapter 9

52460	Ethics
52461	Computer Ethics
52462	Computer Crime
52463	Download

Visual Glossary - Chapter 9 (continued)

52464   Privacy
52465   Piracy
52466   Artificial Intelligence
52467   Natural Language

52468   ## Figures - Chapter 9

52469   9-1 Access To Computer
52214   9-2 Financial Crime
52215   9-3 Storage of Data
52216   9-4 Federal Privacy Legislation
52217   9-5 Copyright Notice

Videodisc Side 2

Frame
Number   **Visual Title**

1	Title
2-3	Table of Contents

Video Programs - Chapters 10 - 19

Note: The video programs for Chapters 14 - 18 are not specifically covered in the Macintosh version of <u>Computers: Tools for Today</u>. They are included on the videodisc as supplementary information.

4	Chapter 10: Computers in the World Around Us
5236	Chapter 11: Careers in Computing
11240	Chapter 12: Computer Languages
15467	Chapter 13: Problem Solving with Computers
21062	Chapter 14: Beginning Programming
26955	Chapter 15: Understanding Graphics
31725	Chapter 16: Entering Data
36339	Chapter 17: Using Control Structures
40287	Chapter 18: Looping & Structured Programming
44584	Chapter 19: Creating with HyperCard

50377	## Macintosh Still Visuals

50378	**Visual Glossary - Chapter 10**

50379	Automation
50380	Source-Data Automation
50381	Electronic Funds Transfer
50382	Point of Scale Terminal
50383	Optical Recognition Device
50384	Bar Code
00944	Electronic Mail (E-Mail)
50385	Data Imaging Processing (DIP)
50386	Information Retrieval
50387	Teleconferencing
50388	Materials Planning Requirement (MRP)
50389	Computer Aided Design (CAD)
50390	Computer Aided Manufacturing a (CAM)
50391	Computer Aided Manufacturing b (CAM)
50392	Computerized Axial Tomography (CAT Scan)

50393	**Figures - Chapter 10**

50394	10-1 Automatic Teller
50395	10-2 Wand Scanner
50396	10-3 Counter Mounted Scanner
50397	10-4 Video Teleconferencing
50398	10-5 Computer Aided Design Software Package
50399	10-6 Computer Aided Manufacturing

50439	Pascal
50440	Compiler
50441	Source Code
50442	Object Code
50443	LOGO
50444	FORTRAN
50445	COBOL
50446	Middle Level Language A
50447	Middle Level Language B
50448	Artificial Intelligence
50449	Expert Systems
50450	List Processing (LISP)
50451	List Manipulation
50452	Prolog

50453	**Figures - Chapter 12**

50454	12-1 Koch Snowflake Fractal
50455	12-2 Machine Language
50456	12-3 Bits and Bytes
50457	12-4 Assembly Language
50458	12-5 Assembly Language Code Example
50459	12-6 Sample HyperCard Card
50460	12-7 BASICA Program
50461	12-8 AppleSoft BASIC
50462	12-9 Microsoft BASIC
50463	12-10 Pascal Program
50464	12-11 LOGO
50465	12-12 FORTRAN Program
50466	12-13 Segments of COBOL Program
50467	12-14 C Program
50468	12-15 C Programming Language
50469	12-16 AI Program
50470	12-17 Software Program Using LISP
50471	12-18 Game Program
50472	12-19a Turbo Prolog
50473	12-19b Turbo Prolog

50474	**Visual Glossary - Chapter 13**

50475	Dedicated Computer
50476	General Purpose Computer
50477	Interactive Processing
50478	Batch Processing
50479	Boot
50480	Operating System
49568	Icon
21236	Compatible
50481	Configuration
23398	Structured Programming
50053	Top-Down Design
50482	Stepwise Refinement
37399	Module

24187-24712	Algorithm
37699	Coding
43327	Control Structure
40866	Simple Sequence
50483	Selection
50484	Loop
50485	Documentation
24712	RUN
14291	Pseudocode
14738	Flowchart
43179	Syntax
38259-39126*	Debugging
50486	Desk Checking
39074	Syntax Error
39380-40285*	Logic Error

50487   **Figures - Chapter 13**

50488	13-1a Video Keying 1
50489	13-1b Video Keying 2
50490	13-2 Top-Down Design
50491	13-3 Algorithm
50492	13-4 Control Structure
50493	13-5 Big Dipper Program
50494	13-6 The Programming Process
50495	13-7 PseudoCode and Flowchart
50496	13-8 Flowchart Symbols
14738	13-9 Flowchart Example
50497	13-10 The Decision Symbol

50498   **Visual Glossary - Chapter 14**

50499	HyperCard
50500	Script
49937	Home Stack
50501	Card 1
50502	Card 2
50503	Card 3
50504	Stack
50505	Home Card
50506	Stack
50507	Button
47939-48378	Link
50508	Hidden Button
50084	String
50509	Command
49002	Field
50510	Paint
50511	Background
50512	Foreground (Card Layer)
50513	Recent
50514	Preferences Card
50094	Pixel

Figures - Chapter 16 (continued)

Supplementary Visuals - Side One

Components of Computer Systems (continued)

52517	Apple II Disk Drive
52518	Disk II - Disk Drive
52519	Back View Of Apple II Computer 1
52520	Back View Of Apple II Computer 2
52521	Mac IIfx Computer
52522	Thermal Printer
52523	Mac SE/30 Computer
52524	Mac SE Computer
52525	Macintosh Computer
52526	Mouse
52527	Mac With Microphone
52528	Mac II Central Processing Unit
52529	Mac Plus
52530	Mac Plus Computer 1
52531	Mac Plus Computer 2
52532	Mac Plus With Laser Printer And Software
52533	Macintosh Portable
52534	Personal System/2 Model 30
52535	4869 5.25" External Diskette Drive
52536	IBM Porable
52537	IBM PC Convertible
52538	PC Convertible Model 3
52539	IBM PC Convertible
52540	IBM Computers Display
52541	IBM PS/2 Model 25
52542	IBM PC/AT
52543	IBM Personal Typing System
52544	IBM 3270 PC
52545	IBM 3351 Industrial Computer
52546	IBM PS/2 With Toys
52547	IBM PS/2 With Books
52548	IBM PS/2 Models 30,50,60,80
52549	IBM PC XT
52550	IBM PC
52551	Computer With Copy Holder
52552	Printer With Collator

Productivity Software and Applications

52553	Word Processing Station
52554	Word Processor 1
52555	Word Processor 2
52556	Word Processor 3
52557	Report Cover
52558	Desk Top Publishing Graphic
52559	Dinosaur Graphic
52560	Graphics And Publishing Examples
52561	Desk Top Publishing Display
52562	Hand Held Page Scanner
52563	Page Scanner
52564	Apple Desk Top Publishing Advantages Graphic

52565	Apple Desk Top Publishing Organizational Chart
52566	Apple Desk Top Publishing Display
52567	Desk Top Publishing User
52568	Desk Top Publishing User Montage
52569	Graph of Desktop Publishing Software
52570	Desk Top Publishing Printer 1
52571	Printer With Collator
52572	Apple Laser Writer II
52573	Laser Computer
52574	Data Products Printer
52575	ThunderScan Software Disks
52576	Click Art Software Disks
52577	Desk Top Publishing Magazine Covers
52578	Ready, Set, Go Software
52579	Desk Top Publishing Product Display
52580	Mac SE With Radius Full Page Display
52581	Mac II With Apple Monitor
52582	Abaton Flat Bed Scanner
52583	Desk Top Publishing Monitor
52584	IBM Personal Publishing System
52585	IBM Personal Publishing System With Printer
52586	Mac Desk Top Publishing System
52587	Apple Desk Top Publishing System
52588	Desk Top Publishing Example - Newsletter
52589	Laser Print Sample 1
52590	Laser Print Sample 2
52591	Freehand Software Graphic Example
52592	Ready, Set, Go Software Example
52593	Quark Express Example
52594	Image Studio Graphic
52595	Adobe Illustrator Graphic
52596	Superior User Environment
52597	Desk Top Publishing - School Newspaper 1
52598	Desk Top Publishing - School Newspaper 2
52599	Desk Top Publishing - Title Page
52600	Desk Top Publishing - Crossword Puzzles
52601	Desk Top Publishing - Transparencies
52602	Ragtime Software
52603	Cricket Draw Graphic
52604	Mac Draw Graphic
52605	Super Paint Graphic
52606	Graphic Works Graphic
52607	Layout Of A School Newspaper
52608	Desk Items Clip Art
52609	Fullwrite Professional Software
52610	Desk Top Publishing - Poem Project
52611	Producing A School Newspaper
52612	Desk Top Publishing - Letterheads
52613	Desk Top Publishing - Computer Use And Applications Graphic
52614	Desk Top Publishing - Student/Parent Handbook
52615	Graphic Of Teacher

Productivity Software and Applications (continued)

52616	Desk Top Publishing - Weekly Bulletin
52617	Desk Top Publishing - Office Stationery
52618	Desk Top Publishing - Banquet Program
52619	Desk Top Publishing - Play Program
52620	Desk Top Publishing - Screen
52621	MicroSoft Works Screens
52622	Fonts Example Screen
52623	Everex Modem
52624	Telecommunications Graphic
52625	Satellite Antenna On Skyscrapers

Historical Development of Computers

52626	Commodore 64 Modem
52627	Acustic Modem
52628	Herman Hollerith Photo
52629	ENIAC Computer
52630	Memory Core
52631	Leibnitz Calculator - Model
52632	Hollerith Punch Card Machine
52633	Abacus
52634	Charles X. Thomas - Photo
52635	Thomas Arithometer
52636	Pascaline
52637	Ada Lovelace Photo
52638	Difference Engine
52639	Machine Language Program
52640	Hollerith Tabulator
52641	Hollerith Tabulator - Drawing
52642	Punch Card Close Up
52643	Plugboard
52644	Early Computer Use Site
52645	Vacuum Tubes
52646	Transistors
52647	Magnetic Core Storage
52648	Disc from Disc Pac
52649	Magnetic Tape Photo
52650	Magnetic Tape
52651	JP Eckert And ENIAC Computer
52652	JP Eckert And ENIAC Computer Control
52653	Operator Console For Univac 1
52654	Early IAS Computer/Princeton 1940's
52655	Vacuum Tubes And Wiring In Early Computers
52656	Circuit Board With Transistors
52657	Core Memory From 1960's Computer
52658	Core Memory Module Made From Ferite "donuts"
52659	Magnified Memory Core With 8080 Chip
52660	4K Memory Chip And 4K Core Plane
52661	Magnified View Of Power Transistor
52662	Monoscope - A Pencil Type Vacuum Tube Of 1960's
52663	Read Only Memory Board From 1960's

Historical Development of Computers

52664	Read Only Memory Memory Plane With Eye of Needle
52665	Control Panel From Univac 1110 Computer
52666	Back Panel Wiring For Univac 1110
52667	Close Up Showing Wires In Univac
52668	Sperry 1110/80 Computer
52669	Water Cooled Sperry 1110/90 Computer
52670	Back Panel Of Sperry 1110/90 Computer
52671	The ABC Computer
52672	Stretch Computer Information
52673	Magnetic Tape
52674	Transistor Board
52675	Osborne Computer
52676	TRS 80-1 Computer
52677	TRS 80-1 Computer
52678	TI/99-4 User
52679	Early Modem
52680	TRS 80 II Computer
52681	Heath Computer
52682	TI 99 Computer
52683	

Computer Hardware

52684	IBM Magnetic Tape Unit
52685	IBM 3480 Magnetic Tape Subsystem 1
52686	IBM 3430 Magnetic Tape Subsystem 2
52687	Magnetic Tapes And Tape Drives
52688	Magnetic Tape And Storage
52689	Mainframe Computer
52690	IBM 3480/3420 Comparison
52691	Gallium Arsenide Chip
52692	Electron Beam LithoGraphic System
52693	Magnified Electron Beam
52694	Optical Scanner
52695	Scanner Forms
52696	IBM Scanner
52697	Scantron Machine 1
52698	Scantron Machine 2
52799	Scantron Machine 3
52800	IBM Scanner 1
52701	IBM Scanner 2
52702	Magnification Of Circuitry
52703	Red Light And Plotter
52704	Laser Tec Technology
52705	Microphoto Of Atoms
52706	Gas Panel Display Screen
52707	Gas Panel Display Screen
52708	Thin Film Recording Heads
52709	Thin Film Head Teachnology
52710	Videodisc System

Computer Hardware (continued)

52711	Videodisc Draw System
52712	High Speed Bipolar Logic Chip
52713	4 Million Bit Chip
52714	Magnification Of 4 Million Bit Chip
52715	4 Million Bit Chip
52716	Bipolar Logic Chip Magnified
52717	1 Million Bit Chip Magnified
52718	Experimental Computer Chips
52719	1 Million Bit Memory Chips on Wafer
52720	1 Meg Memory Chip
52721	Superconductivity 1
52722	Superconductivity 2
52723	Superconductivity Squids
52724	Wheel Printer
52725	Quietwriter Printer
52726	IBM Printer 1
52727	IBM Printer 2
52728	Xerox 4020 Printer
52729	IBM Pageprinter 1
52730	IBM Pageprinter 2
52731	Line Printer
52732	IBM 4710 Printer
52733	IBM 4248 Printer
52734	LaserPrinter II
52735	TP1 Printer
52736	WheelWriter
52737	IMB Proprinter
52738	Proprinter XL24
52739	Proprinter XL
52740	Quietwriter III
52741	Epson LG 500
52742	Proprinter II
52743	"Dot Band" Computer Printing Technology
52744	"Resistive Ribbon" Printing Technology
52745	Magnetic Disk Pack
52746	IBM 6157 Streaming Tape Drive
52747	Desk with Recessed Monitor
52748	Macintosh With Videodisc Player
52749	Amdek CD Player
52750	Interactive Video Display
52751	Videodisc User
52752	IBM Computer System With CDRom Player
52753	Macintosh With Interactive Video
52754	Apple Printer
52755	Printer Cable
52756	Apple Network Cable
52757	3151/3162 Cartridge
52758	IBM 7372 Color Plotter
52759	6186 Color Plotter
52760	Monitor And Plotter
52761	Video Projector Used In Classroom 1

Computer Hardware (continued)

52762   Video Projector Used In Classroom 2
52763   Video Projector Used In Classroom 3
52764   Electronic Tablet With Han21 Characters
52765   Paddles For Video Games
52766   Amiga Keyboard
52767   Light Pen
52768   CBM Drives
52769   3163 ASCII Display Station 1
52770   3151 ASCII Display Station 2
52771   3151 ASCII Display Station 3
52772   Redwood Products
52773   IBM Computer With Laserdisc Player
52774   Second Generation Computer Center
52775   Unisys Ergonomic Keyboard
52776   Laser Computer
52777   Control Data Computer
52778   NEC Computer With Printer
52779   Tandy Computer
52780   IBM 4700 Family
52781   IBM Computer Comparison
52782   IBM PS/2 Models 30,50,60,80
52783   IBM 9370 Model 90
52784   Computer Display
52785   IBM 9370 Computer
52786   Laptop Computer
52787   Epson Laptop
52788   Graphics Tablet and User
52789   IBM Mass Storage System
52790   Terminal Multiplexer
52791   IBM Small Cluster
52792   Communication Controller
52793   Terminal Unit Interface
52794   IBM 3624 Con Tran Facility
52795   IBM 3603 II Terminal Attachment
52796   Fiber Optic Channel Extender Link
52797   Power Unit
52798   IBM 3088 Communication Unit
52799   Coolant Distribution Unit
52800   IBM Personal Banking Machine
52801   IBM Administrative System
52802   IBM 4702 Model 1
52803   IBM 5090
52804   IBM 5360
52805   IBM 5362 System Unit
52806   IBM Storage Control
52807   IBM System/88
52808   IBM 8150 Processor
52809   IBM 3174 Large Cluster
52810   IBM 5360 System Unit With Optional Expansion Unit
52811   IBM 7552 Panel Mounted
52812   IBM 7552 Floor Mounted

52813	IBM ROLM CBX
52814	RISC Architecture
52815	Satellite Graphic
52816	Systems Application Architecture
52817	IBM S/36 And S/38 Connectivity
52818	IBM Token-ring Network
52819	Information Management System
52920	Local Area Networking
52821	IBM 3090 Model 600E
52822	Holographic Optical Disc
52823	Thermal Conduction Module
52824	IBM 3687 Holographic Disk
52825	Electron Erosion Printing
22826	Circuit Board 1
52827	Circuit Board 2
52828	Work Station
52829	IBM Panel Display
52830	IBM Model C Color Display
52831	IBM Information Panel
52832	Model C Color Display
52833	Tandy Computer 1
52834	Tandy Computer 2
52835	Tandy Computer 3
52836	Tandy Computer 4
52837	Tandy Laptop
52838	Compaq Computer 1
52839	Compaq Computer 2
52840	Control Data Computer 1
52841	Control Data Computer 2
52842	Label Printer
52843	Macintosh Computer With Interactive Media
52844	Control Data Computer 3
52845	Zenith Laptop
52846	Marketing/Point Of Purchase Terminal
52847	Video Editing System
52848	Media Link And PC/ID
52849	Multimedia/authoring System
52850	Interactive Media
52851	Interactive Video
52852	Digital Audio System
52853	CDTV
52854	Robotic Plugboard Control Box
52855	Cordless Mouse
52856	Unisys Computer
52857	Unisys Computer With Laserdisc
52858	Mac With Synthesizer
52859	Mac With Jukebox 5 Disk Changer
52860	Atari Portfolio Laptop
52861	Atari Computer
52862	Mac With Compact Disc Player
52863	

Computer Hardware (continued)

52864   Magnified View Of Data On A Diskette
52865   Magnified View Of 3.5" Macintosh Diskette
52866   Magnified View Of Tape Disk
52867   Read Only Memory Generated Characters
52868   Videodisc Production

Supplementary Visuals - Side Two

Educational Software and Applications

50615	Computer Security Devices
50616	Surveillance Mirror
50617	Virex Title
50618	Virex Introduction
50619	Virex Menu
50620	Virex Volume Scan
50621	Virex Volume Scan
50622	Student Using IBM
50623	Student In IIe Lab
50624	IIe User
50625	Students In IIc Lab
50626	Girls Using PC
50627	PC User
50628	Girl Using PC
50629	Students With IBM PS/2 Model 25
50630	Students In Library With PC Convertible
50631	Girl And Father With PC Convertible
50632	Student On Steps With PC Convertible
50633	Student In IBM Lab
50634	IBM Computer Lab 1
50635	IBM Computer Lab 2
50636	Computer Lab User
50637	Students In Macintosh Lab 1
50638	Students In Macintosh Lab 2
50639	User In IIe Lab
50640	Students In Apple IIc Lab
50641	Child Using IIe
50642	Student Using IIc With Keyboard Diagram 1
50643	Student Using IIc With Keyboard Diagram 2
50644	Student Using IIc With Keyboard Diagram 3
50645	Students With IIe
50646	Teacher And Student Using IIe
50647	Students And Teacher With Television Monitor 1
50648	Students And Teacher With Television Monitor 2
50649	Student With TI 99/4a
50650	Students Using Computers
50651	Students In IBM PS/2 Lab
50652	Students Using Computer In Science Experiment
50653	Student With Apple II
50654	Girl Using Computer With Screen Viewer
50655	Student Using Apple IIgs
50656	Students Using Apple IIe 1
50657	Students Using Apple IIe 2
50658	Students Using Apple IIe 3
50659	Student Using A TI99/4 Computer
50660	Students In Write To Read Program
50661	Students In Write To Read Program
50662	Elementary Computer Center
50663	Students Using Computer With Headphones

50664	Elementary Computer Lab 1
50665	Elementary Computer Lab 2
50666	Word Processed Story
50667	Hand Written Story
50668	Write To Read Teacher
50669	TI 99/4a Computer And Printer
50670	Acorn Computer Lab
50671	School Hall
50672	"For School" Graphic
50673	Body Transparent Software
50674	European Nations And Locations Software
50675	Artificial Intelligence - An Experiment In Artificial Intelligence Software 1
50676	Artificial Intelligence - An Experiment In Artificial Intelligence Software 2
50677	Artificial Intelligence - An Experiment In Artificial Intelligence Software 3
50678	Weather Fronts Software 1
50679	Weather Fronts Software 2
50680	Logic Builders Software 1
50681	Logic Builders Software 2
50682	Logic Builders Software 3
50683	Logic Builders Software 4
50684	Logic Builders Software 5
50685	Scholastic Slide Shop - Title
50686	Scholastic Slide Shop - Introduction
50687	Scholastic Slide Shop - Directions
50688	Greek Mythology Program
50689	Spellicopter Program
50690	Software Package - Higher Ed.
50691	Chemistry Program
50692	Math Maze Program
50693	Conduit Catalog Of Software
50694	Desk Mate 1 Program
50695	Desk Mate 2 Program
50696	Key Lingo Software
50697	Designasaurus Software
50698	Dinosaur Days Software
50699	States And Traits Software
50700	Crypto Cube Software
50701	W.O.R.K. Software
50702	Math Shop Software 1
50703	Math Shop Software 2
50704	The Factory Software 1
50705	The Factory Software 2
50706	Kids At Work Software
50707	Learning Programs For The Apple Software
50708	Starburst Design Software
50709	Multiplication Bingo Software
50710	Vocabulary Builder Software
50711	History Trivia Software
50712	States And Capitals Software
50713	Techno Trivia Software
50714	Techno Trivia Software 2

Educational Software and Applications (continued)

50715	Typing Tutorial Program
50716	Popper's Penguins Software 1
50717	Popper's Penguins Software 2
50718	Strategy In Problem Solving
50719	Strategy In Problem Solving Software
50720	Ant Farm Software
50721	Incredible Laboratory
50722	Computer Aided Instruction 1
50723	Computer Aided Instruction 2
50724	Computer Aided Instruction 3
50725	Computer Aided Instruction 4
50726	Voyage To The Planets Program
50727	Computer Aided Instruction 5
50728	Computer Aided Instruction 6
50729	Computer Aided Instruction 7
50730	Computer Aided Instruction 8
50731	Botanical Gardens Program 1
50732	Botanical Gardens Program 2
50733	Botanical Gardens Program 3
50734	Botanical Gardens Program 4
50735	Botanical Gardens Program 5
50736	The Friendly Computer Program
50737	Paint With Words Program
50738	LOGO Shapes
50739	Teacher's Manual
50740	Quickspell Program
50741	AppleWorks Spreadsheet
50742	AppleWorks Word Processing
50743	AppleWorks Planning Calendar
50744	AppleWorks Time Out Menu
50745	AppleWorks Files Menu
50746	AppleWorks Main Menu
50747	Graphic: Computer Aided Instruction
50748	Dilemma: Which Ending Will You Choose?
50749	Wheels For The Mind
50750	Educational Resources Display
50751	Consumers And The Law
50752	MECC Display
50753	Scholastic Display 1
50754	Scholastic Display 2
50755	Computer In A Military Environment
50756	Computer In A Military Office
50757	Magnetic Stripe Banking Card
50758	Computers In The Bank
50759	Computers In The Bank
50760	Drive Up Automatic Teller Machine
50761	Drive Up Automatic Teller Machine
50762	Drive Up Automatic TellerMachine

Recreational Software and Applications

50763	Sub Battle Software - Title
50764	Sub Battle - Game Example
50765	Sub Battle - Game Example
50767	The Ancient Art Of War At Sea - Titles
50768	The Ancient Art Of War At Sea - Game Example 1
50769	The Ancient Art Of War At Sea - Game Example 2
50770	The Ancient Art Of War At Sea - Game Example 3
50771	Video Games In Arcade
50772	Mac And Synthesizer
50773	Computerized Musical Keyboard
50774	IBM PS/2 With Synthesizer
50775	Musician Using Computerized Synthesizer
50776	Music Software 1
50777	Music Software 2
50778	Deluxe Music Construction Software
50779	IBM With Synthesizer
50780	Racing Game 1
50781	Racing Game 2
50782	Racing Game 3
50783	California Game 1
50784	California Game 2
50785	California Game - Skateboarding 1
50786	California Game - Skateboarding 2
50787	California Game - Skateboarding 3
50788	California Game - Kawasaki 1
50789	California Game - Kawasaki 2
50790	Choplifter 1
50791	Choplifter 2
50792	Choplifter 3
50793	Prince Of Persia Game 1
50794	Prince Of Persia Game 2
50795	Prince Of Persia Game 3
50796	Prince Of Persia Game 4
50797	GBA Basketball Game 1
50798	GBA Basketball Game 2
50799	GBA Basketball Game 3
50800	Risk Computer Game
50801	Golf Computer Game
50802	Space Invaders
50803	Marble Madness
50804	Wagon Train 1848
50805	Quick Solve 1
50806	Murphy's Minerals
50807	Word Munchers

Robotics

50808	Human Like Robot With Arms Raised
50809	Human Like Robot At Podium
50810	Robot Dinosaur Among Buildings
50811	Robot Dinosaur In Natural Habitat 1

Robotics (continued)

50812 Robot Dinosaur In Natural Habitat 2
50813 Arm Controlling Joystick
50814 Robot Dinosaur In Natural Habitat 3
50815 Robot Dinosaur "Skeleton"
50816 Computer With Controls For Robot Dinosaur
50817 Robot Dinosaur In Natural Habitat 4
50818 Robot Dinosaur Control Panel
50819 Person Controlling Robot Arm 1
50820 Person Controlling Robot Arm 2
50821 Robot Arm
50822 Piano Playing Robot
50823 Chem Lab Robot
50824 Robot Bio Lab
50825 Viking Mars Lander
50826 Viking 1 Sampler Scoop And Robot Arm
50827 Viking Lander 1
50828 Viking Lander 2
50829 Robot Dinosaur Cut Away

Computers In The World Around Us

50830 Computer In Doctor's Office
50831 Computer In Doctor's Lab
50832 Computer In Pharmacy
50833 Computer In Dentist's Office 1
50834 Computer In Dentist's Office 2
50835 Computer In Dentist's Office 3
50836 Sales Report On Computer
50837 IBM 468 Store System
50838 Computer Designed Constructions
50839 IBM Engineering Design System Information
50840 Computer Assisted Manufacturing Site
50841 Engineering Verification Engine
50842 Computer Assisted Manufacturing Site 1
50843 Computer Controlled Laser Cutting Steel
50844 IBM PS/2 Monochrome Display With Computer Aided Drafting Drawing
50845 Man Using PC Convertible
50846 Computer In Office Setting
50847 System/38 PC In Office
50848 System/38 Architecture
50849 Xerox Computer In Office
50850 Man And Woman At Xerox Computer
50851 Woman Using Computer In Office
50852 Computers In Office 1
50853 Computers In Office 2
50854 Handshake In Front Of Computer
50855 Man At Computer In Office
50856 Woman Using Computer Controlled Copier
50857 Computers In Office Setting 1
50858 Computers In Office Setting 2
50859 Man Using Phone

Computers In The World Around Us

50860	Word Processor System
50861	Man And Woman In Office At Computer
50862	Office Management Program
50863	Office Software Display 1
50864	Office Software Display 2
50865	Office Software Display 3
50866	Storyboard Screen
50867	Personal Typing System
50868	Relational Database Method
50869	Get Organized Software
50870	Topview Software
50871	Computer Support Center 1
50872	Computer Support Center 2
50873	Computers In Financial Office
50874	IBM PS/2 In Office
50875	Computer In A Stock Room
50876	Computer Center
50877	Computer Terminal Group
50878	Computer Center
50879	Computers In Office
50880	Automated Telephone
50881	Office Montage
50882	Computer With Printout
50883	Computers In Carrels In Office
50884	Office Desktop Publishing System
50885	Desktop Publishing System
50886	Computer In A Science Lab
50887	Woman Using Mac At Desk
50888	IBM RT RC in Office
50889	Bar Graph on Monitor
50890	Woman Using Macintosh Computer
50891	Spreadsheet On A Computer Screen
50892	PC Convertible At Construction Site
50893	Software Usability Lab
50894	PC Convertible In Office
50895	Computers At NASA
50896	LCD Projection Panel On Overhead Projector
50897	Word Processing Work Station
50898	IBM PS/2 Model 50 In Office
50899	IBM PS/2 Model 30 In Office
50900	IBM PS/2 Model 30 In Office
50901	IBM PS/2 Model 30 In Office
50902	IBM PS/2 With Quietwriter III
50903	Service Management System

Programs and Programming

50904	Hand Drawn Flowchart
50905	Peanut Butter And Jelly Sandwich Flowchart
50906	Flowchart Examples
50907	Intel 8088 Assembly Language Example

Programs and Programming (continued)

50908	User Programming In BASIC
50909	LEGO LOGO Title Screen
50910	"No Limits" LEGO LOGO Poster
50911	Display Of LEGO LOGO Models 1
50912	Display Of LEGO LOGO Models 2
50913	Display Of LEGO LOGO Models 3
50914	Display Of LEGO LOGO Models 4
50915	Display Of LEGO LOGO Models 5
50916	Display Of LEGO LOGO Models 6
50917	Display Of LEGO LOGO Models 7
50918	Display Of LEGO LOGO Models 8
50919	Display Of LEGO LOGO Models 9
50920	Blaise Pascal Information
50921	Leibniz Information
50922	Leibniz - Photo
50923	Pascal Program Example
50924	Basic Arithmetic Operators
50925	Problem Solving With Computers Information
50926	Coding A BASIC Program

Computer Graphics

50927	Screen Layout Form
50928	Graphic Design 1
50929	Graphic Design 2
50930	Graphic Design 3
50931	Graphic Design 4
50932	Fractal Geometry
50933	Graphic Design 5
50934	Graphic Design 6
50935	Cray Graphics
50936	Abstract Face Graphic
50937	Eye Graphic
50938	House Graphic
50939	IBM PS/2 Graphics
50940	Pie Chart
50941	Bar Graph
50942	Cray Graphics - Head
50943	Puffins Graphic 1
50944	Puffins Graphic 2
50945	Woman Graphic
50946	Computer Graphic
50947	Graphics Print-out
50948	Computer With Graphic On Screen
50949	MAC Graphic
50950	Church Graphic
50951	Fund Raiser Graphic
50952	Dancers Graphic 1
50953	Dancers Graphic 2
50954	Dancers Graphic 3
50955	Space Plane Graphic

Computer Graphics (continued)

50956   Abstract Graphic
50957   Mummy Graphic
50958   Puffins Graphic 3
50959   Puffins Graphic 4
50960   Car Graphic
50961   Pie Chart
50962   IBM PS/2 Color Display
50963   Earth Structure Graphic
50964   Mac Paint : Tools
50965   Mac Paint : Patterns
50966   Mac Paint : F-16 Picture
50967   Mac Paint : F-16 Edit 1
50968   Mac Paint : F-16 Edit 2
50969   Mac Paint : Clip Art 1
50970   Mac Paint : F-16 Edit 3
50971   Mac Paint : Clip Art 2
50972   Mac Paint : Steven Jobs
50973   Mac II Astronaut Graphic
50974   TNET Screen
50975   Shapes On A Monitor
50976   Graphics Tablet
50977   Shooting Stars Graphic
50978   Line Configuration - Cray Graphics

HyperCard

50979   Your Tour Of HyperCard - Title
50980   HyperCard - Like Using Index Cards
50981   HyperCard - Buttons
50982   HyperCard - Clicking On Buttons
50983   HyperCard - Buttons Cont.
50984   HyperCard - Buttons Are Hot Spots
50985   HyperCard - GO Menu
50986   HyperCard - Home Cards
50987   HyperCard - Review Of Points
50988   HyperCard - Shared Backgrounds
50989   HyperCard - Foreground Information
50990   HyperCard - Review Card
50991   HyperCard - Elements of Cards
50992   HyperCard - Entering Text
50993   HyperCard - Scanned Images
50994   HyperCard - Field Size
50995   HyperCard - Organizes Information

Computers In Space

50996   NASA Supplementary Visuals Title
50997   Milky Way
50998   Horsehead Nebula
50999   Saturn V Rocket

Computers In Space (continued)

51000	IMAX Theater Screen
51001	Space Shuttle
51002	American Nebula
51003	Great Nebula
51004	Space Telescope
51005	Whirlpool Galaxy
51006	Space Plane
51007	Rocket Garden
51008	Spaceman at Spaceport USA
51009	Launch Pad
51010	Simulated Lunar Landing Site
51011	Access Arm
51012	Columbia's Launch
51013	Rocket Garden
51014	Saturn V And VAB
51015	Columbia Landing
51016	Mars
51017	Phobos
51018	Martian Sunset
51019	China Tibet Plateau
51020	Mars Eclipse with Corona
51021	Sun's Corona
51022	Solar Eruptions
51023	Solar Eruptions
51024	Skylab 3 View Of Sun
51025	Launch Pad
51026	Apollo Soyuz
51027	Shuttle Conceptual Drawing
51028	Shuttle Liftoff
51029	Gemini Space Craft
51030	Lunar Rover
51031	Space Exploration Mural
51032	Below Launch Pad
51033	Rocket Booster Recovery
51034	Rocket Booster Separating From Shuttle
51035	Solar Eruption

Appendix B

Answers to
Chapter Tests

The chapter tests which are provided as copyables are designed as one of the assessment tools available in the System Integrator. The chapter tests can be used as a written check-for-understanding of concepts presented in each chapter. There are two versions for each chapter (Test A and Test B). Having two tests gives the teacher the option of using one test for make-up or for retesting. However, these tests should be used in relation to the whole assessment process.

A Word About Assessment

The System Integrator helps provide the teacher with a wealth of assessment tools and strategies. Daily assessment in more informal settings can help provide a realistic view of students' abilities. The portfolios can help establish a reflection of student understanding of concepts presented, and they can be very useful in showing parents samples of student work and progress. The skills tests are available to help evaluate students' progress on a performance basis. Self-evaluation can also be used to help promote self-directed learning, with students taking ownership in the learning process.

With the wide variety of assessment tools available in this system, teachers have the opportunity to capture more of what students can do.

● Chapter 1
Exploring Your Computer

MULTIPLE CHOICE		MATCHING	FILL IN THE BLANK	TRUE/FALSE
1. D	6. B	11. C	16. Input	21. TRUE
2. C	7. C	12. D	17. Output	22. TRUE
3. B	8. A	13. A	18. Processing	23. FALSE
4. A	9. C	14. E	19. Storage	24. FALSE
5. C	10. D	15. B	20. Information	25. TRUE

26. Describe what you can do to make computer equipment last as long as possible.

Keep all equipment away from dust and moisture. Store disks in protective dust proof box. Do not leave disks in direct sunlight. Make sure the room is at a comfortable temperature. Always touch a piece of metal before you touch your computer.

27. How did people feel about computers in the 1940s and how have those feelings changed?

Most people did not even know what a computer was. The scientists who made them thought they needed only a few more computers to handle all the world's computer needs. Today, computers in businesses are necessities and home computers are common. Even some cars have microcomputers in them. People have come to accept computers as useful tools for everyday activities.

Chapter 1
Exploring Your Computer

MULTIPLE CHOICE		MATCHING	FILL IN THE BLANK	TRUE/FALSE
1. C	6. D	11. D	16. Disk drive	21. FALSE
2. A	7. B	12. C	17. Printer	22. FALSE
3. C	8. D	13. A	18. Keyboard	23. TRUE
4. C	9. C	14. E	19. Monitor	24. TRUE
5. A	10. A	15. B	20. Disk	25. FALSE

26. Why would a computer not be a good baby sitter?

The computer has no emotions and could not give any loving care. There are too many different situations for the computer to handle. The computer has no common sense. It would take everything the children would say literally, as it does not understand different figures of speech.

27. We call computers, printers, and disk drives "hardware". We call printouts "hardcopies". Yet we call programs either "software" or "soft copies". Why is that?

Something is "hard" if it can be seen or touched. All computer equipment, disks, paper, etc. are physical objects. However, the programs cannot be seen or touched. They are intangible. Hence, they are not "hard". If they are not "hard," they are "soft".

Chapter 2 <u>Test A</u>
Getting Started with Microsoft Works and the Word Processor

MULTIPLE CHOICE		MATCHING	FILL IN THE BLANK	TRUE/FALSE
1. B	6. A	11. B	16. DELETE	21: TRUE
2. D	7. D	12. E	17. INSERT	22. TRUE
3. D	8. A	13. A	18. Document	23. FALSE
4. A	9. D	14. D	19. File	24. TRUE
5. C	10. B	15. C	20. Backup Copy	25. TRUE

26. What is the difference between loading a file and saving a file?

When you load a file, the computer finds a file on your disk and puts a copy of it in the computer's memory. When you save a file, the computer copies what is in its memory to a file on a disk or hard drive.

27. Why does a computer keyboard have more keys than a typewriter?

Computers can do so much more than typewriters, that some special keys are needed just for these features. For example: The <command> key typed with <S> is for "save". The <command> key types with <P> is for "print".

Chapter 2

<u>**Test B**</u>

Getting Started with Microsoft Works and the Word Processor

MULTIPLE CHOICE		MATCHING	FILL IN THE BLANK	TRUE/FALSE
1. C	6. D	11. D	16. Insert	21. TRUE
2. B	7. D	12. B	17. Delete	22. FALSE
3. D	8. B	13. E	18. Word Processing	23. TRUE
4. A	9. B	14. A	19. Database	24. TRUE
5. D	10. A	15. C	20. Spreadsheet	25. TRUE

26. How does the Microsoft Works "Desktop" help you save time?

If you are working with more than one file, you can load all of them (up to 14) at the same time. You do not have to constantly reload a file every time you switch from one to another.

27. Why will a Macintosh disk not work on an IBM computer?

A Macintosh disk has been formatted for the Macintosh and will only work on the Macintosh and maybe some Apple computers. Apple and IBM do not have compatible formats. Only disks that are formatted for the IBM or its clones will work on the IBM computers.

Chapter 3
Learning More About Word Processing and Desktop Publishing

<u>Test A</u>

MULTIPLE CHOICE		MATCHING	FILL IN THE BLANK	TRUE/FALSE
1. A	6. B	11. C	16. Justify	21. TRUE
2. C	7. A	12. D	17. Buffer	22. FALSE
3. D	8. C	13. A	18. Typeface	23. TRUE
4. B	9. D	14. B	19. Clip art	24. TRUE
5. A	10. D	15. E	20. Point size	25. FALSE

26. Explain why a safety message appears every time you try to delete a file from your disk.

The message is checking if you really want to delete that file. It is possible you chose the wrong file. It is also possible you pushed the wrong key and really did not want to delete any file.

27. Why is a word processor better than a typewriter?

Word processors allow you to correct your mistakes; move, copy, center, and justify text; and some can check your spelling. Most typewriters cannot do any of that. To fix your mistakes on a typewriter, you must retype the whole thing.

Chapter 3
Learning More About Word Processing and Desktop Publishing

MULTIPLE CHOICE		MATCHING	FILL IN THE BLANK	TRUE/FALSE
1. C	6. C	11. D	16. Line spacing	21. FALSE
2. B	7. D	12. C	17. Margins	22. TRUE
3. C	8. B	13. E	18. Underline	23. TRUE
4. B	9. C	14. A	19. Bold	24. FALSE
5. C	10. A	15. B	20. Subscript or Superscript	25. TRUE

26. There are two ways to back up a file. You can save it on a second disk, or you can save it on the same disk with a different name. Which one is safer?

It is safer to save it on a second disk. If you have 2 copies of the same file on the same disk, and the whole disk goes bad, you will lose both files.

27. What type of information appears in a dialog box?

Information relating to whatever you are doing at the time. It may have a list of choices. It may have a message for you.

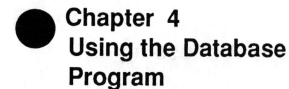

Chapter 4
Using the Database
Program

<u>**Test A**</u>

MULTIPLE CHOICE		MATCHING	FILL IN THE BLANK	TRUE/FALSE
1. D	6. D	11. C	16. Open	21. TRUE
2. A	7. D	12. E	17. Retrieve	22. TRUE
3. B	8. B	13. B	18. Form window	23. FALSE
4. C	9. B	14. A	19. Sort	24. TRUE
5. A	10. A	15. D	20. Comparison Information	25. FALSE

26. Explain the difference between a word processing program and a database manager program.

A word processing program is used to write letters, memos, and reports. A database manager program is used to store information in an organized way.

27. If a library does not have a computer, and they use the old "card catalog" system, why must they have three different card catalogs?

Some people need to find a book written by a certain author. Some need a book with a certain title. Some need a book on a certain subject. Unless you have three different catalogs sorted by these three different categories, you will constantly be sorting and resorting your one file.

Chapter 4
Using the Database
Program

MULTIPLE CHOICE		MATCHING	FILL IN THE BLANK	TRUE/FALSE
1. D	6. C	11. E	16. Database	21. TRUE
2. D	7. C	12. B	17. Record	22. FALSE
3. A	8. B	13. A	18. Field	23. TRUE
4. B	9. A	14. C	19. Entry	24. TRUE
5. D	10. C	15. D	20. File	25. TRUE

26. What is the difference between a form window and a list window?

A form window shows only one record at a time. A list window shows many records.

27. Why is it important to update a file?

If a file is not updated, the information will not be accurate. You will have old, outdated information in your file.

Chapter 5   <u>Test A</u>
Learning More about the Database Program
and Telecommunications

MULTIPLE CHOICE		MATCHING	FILL IN THE BLANK	TRUE/FALSE
1. D	6. C	11. C	16. Parity	21. FALSE
2. B	7. B	12. D	17. Integrated	22. TRUE
3. A	8. D	13. A	18. Commercial	23. TRUE
4. D	9. C	14. B	19. Bulletin Board	24. TRUE
5. A	10. D	15. E	20. Information Network	25. FALSE

26. What can go wrong when data is transmitted over a phone line?

When data is transmitted over a phone line it is changed into sound signals. If there is noise in the background, and the noise it sent on the phone line as well, it will interfere with the transmission of the data message.

27. What is the advantage of doing a print review?

It lets you see exactly how your file will look when you print it. If you have made any mistakes, you can change them before you print. This will save time and paper.

Chapter 5 **Test B**
Learning More about the Database Program and Telecommunications

MULTIPLE CHOICE		MATCHING	FILL IN THE BLANK	TRUE/FALSE
1. C	6. B	11. A	16. Noise	21. TRUE
2. A	7. D	12. D	17. Modem	22. FALSE
3. D	8. A	13. E	18. Packet	23. TRUE
4. C	9. D	14. C	19. Format	24. FALSE
5. B	10. C	15. B	20. Baud rate	25. FALSE

26. Why does Microsoft Works allow you to have up to eight reports for a data base file?

At any given time you may need to print different information about the same file. All the reports are saved. You can call up the information on any report and print it at any time.

27. How does telecommunication technology allow more people to work at home?

People can work at home on their computers. Computers can link with others by modems. Any paper work they need to send in can be sent electronically to their editors, publishers, bosses, etc.

Chapter 6
Using the Spreadsheet

MULTIPLE CHOICE		MATCHING	FILL IN THE BLANK	TRUE/FALSE
1. D	6. B	11. A	16. Entry	21. TRUE
2. A	7. A	12. E	17. Forecast	22. FALSE
3. B	8. A	13. B	18. Formula	23. FALSE
4. C	9. B	14. C	19. Function	24. TRUE
5. C	10. B	15. D	20. Spreadsheet	25. FALSE

26. Microsoft Works calculates its formulas from left to right. It does not use order of operations. What do you have to do to the formula 7 + 2 * 4 - 9 / 3 to get the correct answer of 12?

You need to put parentheses around the 2*4 and the 9/3, and type 7 + (2 * 4) - (9 / 3).

27. How can the copy and paste routine help you save time when entering formulas?

Without this routine, you need to type in every formula separately. In some situations, the formulas that are being used are almost identical to other formulas. If you use copy and paste, you can type one formula, copy it and paste it to new locations.

Chapter 6
Using the Spreadsheet

MULTIPLE CHOICE		MATCHING	FILL IN THE BLANK	TRUE/FALSE
1. A	6. B	11. E	16. Cell	21. TRUE
2. A	7. C	12. A	17. Row	22. TRUE
3. D	8. C	13. D	18. Column	23. TRUE
4. C	9. C	14. C	19. Label	24. TRUE
5. B	10. D	15. B	20. Value	25. FALSE

26. Explain why entering the formula A1+A2+A3 will be interpreted by the computer as a label. How do you fix it?

The first symbol you type determines if the cell is a value or a label. Since the "A" in "A1" was the first thing typed, the computer assumes this will be a label. To fix this, put a = sign in front and type = A1 + A2 + A3.

27. Why do some of the formulas change when you add or delete rows or columns?

When you add or delete rows or columns, part of the spreadsheet is shifted over. This causes coordinate of the numbers to change. To keep the formulas accurate, Microsoft Works automatically changes the formulas to make them match.

 **Chapter 7**   <u>Test A</u>
Looking Back

MULTIPLE CHOICE		MATCHING	FILL IN THE BLANK	TRUE/FALSE
1. C	6. B	11. A	16. Binary	21. FALSE
2. D	7. B	12. C	17. Minicomputer	22. FALSE
3. C	8. A	13. D	18. Vacuum tube	23. TRUE
4. D	9. D	14. B	19. Microprocessor	24. FALSE
5. A	10. C	15. E	20. Transistor	25. TRUE

26. Describe some of the problems with the early electronic computers like the ENIAC.

The early electronic computers used vacuum tubes. This made the computers very large. The vacuum tubes would heat up and burn out frequently. The computers required constant repair. Also, the heat from the vacuum tubes made the computer rooms very hot.

27. How did people write programs ifor the early electronic computers?

Programs were written by rewiring the entire computer system. Every time you wanted to change the program, you had to re-wire the computer.

Chapter 7
Looking Back

MULTIPLE CHOICE		MATCHING	FILL IN THE BLANK	TRUE/FALSE
1. A	6. D	11. B	16. Calculator	21. FALSE
2. C	7. A	12. D	17. Silicon	22. TRUE
3. C	8. C	13. A	18. Real time	23. FALSE
4. B	9. A	14. C	19. Generation	24. FALSE
5. A	10. B	15. E	20. Personal Computer	25. TRUE

26. Describe some of the changes that occurred with every new generation of computers.

In every new generation, computers became smaller, faster, more powerful, less expensive, and easier to use.

27. Why were people concerned after they finished the 1880 census? How was this problem resolved?

The 1880 census was not completed until late 1887. With the growing population, it was feared that the 1890 census would not be finished before they had to take the 1900 census. Herman Hollerith developed a machine called the Punchcard tabulator which made the process of accumulating the data much faster.

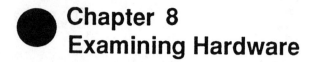

Chapter 8
Examining Hardware

MULTIPLE CHOICE		MATCHING	FILL IN THE BLANK	TRUE/FALSE
1. C	6. B	11. B	16. Analog	21. FALSE
2. D	7. A	12. C	17. Bit	22. TRUE
3. B	8. D	13. D	18. Mainframe	23. FALSE
4. C	9. A	14. A	19. Megabyte	24. TRUE
5. D	10. A	15. E	20. Hard disk	25. TRUE

26. Describe the similarities and difference of RAM and ROM.

Both RAM and ROM have information in them that can be read. However, the user is able to change the information stored in RAM. The information stored in ROM is unchangeable. Also, RAM is erased when the computer is turned off, while ROM is permanent.

27. Why do we call the CPU the brain of the computer?

It is the part of the computer that determines what is going to be done, how it will be done, and in what order it will be done.

Chapter 8
Examining Hardware

MULTIPLE CHOICE		MATCHING	FILL IN THE BLANK	TRUE/FALSE
1. C	6. D	11. D	16. Digital	21. FALSE
2. B	7. D	12. B	17. Byte	22. TRUE
3. D	8. B	13. E	18. Super computer	23. FALSE
4. A	9. B	14. A	19. Gigabyte	24. FALSE
5. D	10. A	15. C	20. Tape drive	25. FALSE

26. Describe some of the uses we have today for supercomputers.

Supercomputers can solve very complicated math problem (the type that would take regular computers weeks to do) in a matter of minutes. They are being used by movie makers for computer animation, and. they are being used by government and businesses for complicated simulations, such as pilot training simulations.

27. Why would an artist want to use a mouse instead of a keyboard?

A computer keyboard is great for typing text, but for drawing pictures it can be slow. A mouse allows the computer to copy the motion of your hand. An artist can draw images on the screen by moving his hand in the same way he or she would draw on paper.

Chapter 9
Using Computers Responsibly

Test A

MULTIPLE CHOICE		MATCHING	FILL IN THE BLANK	TRUE/FALSE
1. B	6. B	11. B	16. Privacy	21. TRUE
2. A	7. D	12. D	17. Computer Crime	22. FALSE
3. C	8. D	13. E	18. Ethics	23. TRUE
4. A	9. A	14. A	19. Copyright	24. FALSE
5. C	10. B	15. C	20. Artificial Intelligence	25. FALSE

26. Why do many people think that computer crime is not important?

Since the people who commit computer crimes are often committing them at home behind their computers, they never see the people or business that are being hurt by it. And often, small amounts are stolen from any one account, only adding up to big thefts over time.

27. Describe some of the things we can do to prevent computer crimes.

Use access codes on our systems. Make software disk copy-protected. Set standards so more honest people are hired into computer companies. Scramble messages in transmissions.

Chapter 9
Using Computers Responsibly

MULTIPLE CHOICE		MATCHING	FILL IN THE BLANK	TRUE/FALSE
1. A	6. D	11. A	16. Piracy	21. FALSE
2. D	7. A	12. B	17. Computer ethics	22. TRUE
3. B	8. C	13. C	18. Download	23. TRUE
4. B	9. D	14. E	19. Access	24. FALSE
5. B	10. C	15. D	20. Natural language	25. TRUE

26. List some types of computer crime.

Common types of computer crime include software piracy, sabotage of equipment, theft of services or property, and illegal transference of funds.

27. Describe "ethics".

Ethics are the morals upon which we base our behavior. They are the standards by which we tell the difference between right and wrong and act accordingly.

Chapter 10
Finding Computers in the World
Around You

<u>Test A</u>

MULTIPLE CHOICE		MATCHING	FILL IN THE BLANK	TRUE/FALSE
1. D	6. B	11. E	16. Automation	21. TRUE
2. A	7. D	12. D	17. Bar code	22. TRUE
3. A	8. C	13. A	18. Point of sale	23. FALSE
4. B	9. B	14. B	19. Dip	24. TRUE
5. C	10. B	15. C	20. Computer aided design	25. FALSE

26. Describe how computers help the health care profession.

Computers are used to store patient records, plan schedules, keep a list of specialists, order supplies, and perform CAT scans.

27. Describe how computers are used to improve the condition of athletes.

Computer programs have been written that test the strength of muscles, check endurance, and find weaknesses in the athlete that need improving. They can also compare the athlete's form with the "ideal" form for different activities and events.

Chapter 10
Finding Computers in the World
Around You

MULTIPLE CHOICE		MATCHING	FILL IN THE BLANK	TRUE/FALSE
1. B	6. B	11. C	16. Source-data	21. FALSE
2. A	7. A	12. D	17. Teleconference	22. FALSE
3. A	8. C	13. B	18. Electronic funds	23. TRUE
4. D	9. D	14. A	19. Electronic Mail	24. TRUE
5. C	10. B	15. E	20. Optical recognition	25. FALSE

26. Describe source-data automation and why it is useful.

Source-data automation is any method that captures data in computer-readable form when and where an event takes place. It is useful because it improves speed and accuracy.

27. How does the UPC code save store employees time when prices change?

The UPC code is printed on all products. Each product has a different code. The prices for these code are stored in the computer that scans them at checkout. When a price changes, you do not need to change prices on the products; you just need to change the price for that UPC code once in the computer.

Chapter 11
Investigating Careers

MULTIPLE CHOICE		MATCHING	FILL IN THE BLANK	TRUE/FALSE
1. A	6. A	11. D	16. Computer operator	21. FALSE
2. B	7. B	12. A	17. System programmer	22. TRUE
3. D	8. C	13. E	18. Database analyst	23. TRUE
4. C	9. D	14. B	19. Computer technician	24. FALSE
5. C	10. D	15. C	20. Computer engineer	25. FALSE

26. Describe some of the responsibilities of a security specialist.

A security specialist is responsible for the safety of all equipment and information. He or she must see to it that hardware is stored in such a way that it can not easily be stolen easily damaged by the elements. He or she would install security codes and scrambling devices to safeguard the software.

27. Describe some of the things a computer consultant does.

A computer consultant works independently. He or she goes to various companies and finds out what type of software they need. If they require special customized software, he or she can write it for them.

Chapter 11
Investigating Careers

MULTIPLE CHOICE		MATCHING	FILL IN THE BLANK	TRUE/FALSE
1. B	6. A	11. A	16. Data-entry operator	21. TRUE
2. D	7. A	12. B	17. Application programmer	22. FALSE
3. D	8. D	13. E	18. Computer consultant	23. TRUE
4. B	9. C	14. C	19. System analyst	24. TRUE
5. C	10. B	15. D	20. Technical writer	25. FALSE

26. Describe what a data processing librarian does.

A data processing librarian sees to it that computer files and disks are properly stored, cleaned, and maintained. When necessary, the information can be transferred electronically to anyone who requests it.

27. Describe what a maintenance programmer does.

When companies expand or make other changes, their software usually needs to be adapted to the new situations. A maintenance programmer sees to it that the program is kept up to date, and that it can handle all of the <u>current</u> business needs.

Chapter 12
Exploring Languages

<u>**Test A**</u>

MULTIPLE CHOICE		MATCHING	FILL IN THE BLANK	TRUE/FALSE
1. A	6. C	11. B	16. BASIC	21. FALSE
2. C	7. D	12. C	17. Lisp	22. FALSE
3. D	8. A	13. D	18. C	23. FALSE
4. B	9. A	14. E	19. LOGO	24. TRUE
5. A	10. C	15. A	20. Interpreter	25. FALSE

26. When Nicholas Wirth invented the language Pascal, he put in some features of FORTRAN and some features of COBOL. There was another language called PL/1 that had all the features of both languages. Why do think Pascal was more popular?

Since PL/1 had ALL the features of both languages, it had hundreds of commands and was very difficult to learn. Wirth's "leaner" Pascal was more popular because it was able to do a little of what both FORTRAN and COBOL could do, but still be understood.

27. Why is a LISP program able to generate another LISP program? How is this useful for artificial intelligence development?

The syntax of a LISP program and its data are both series of lists. The data lists a LISP program generates can be another program because they are the same form. This helps AI because one of the things a human can do that a computer cannot is come up with new ideas on his or her own. A program that could write other programs would be the first step in the development of self thought.

Chapter 12
Exploring Languages

MULTIPLE CHOICE		MATCHING	FILL IN THE BLANK	TRUE/FALSE
1. B	6. B	11. A	16. FORTRAN	21. FALSE
2. A	7. A	12. E	17. COBOL	22. TRUE
3. C	8. C	13. D	18. Pascal	23. TRUE
4. D	9. D	14. C	19. Compiler	24. TRUE
5. A	10. C	15. B	20. Machine	25. FALSE

26. Why do the vast majority of people who write programs write them in a language other than machine language?

Machine language is nothing but 1's and 0's. It is very complicated. It takes a long time to write a program in machine language, and debugging a machine language program is incredibly difficult.

27. Why is C considered to be a middle-level language?

Like a high-level language, C is much easier to understand than machine language, but it is not as understandable as the rest of the high-level languages. Like a low-level language, C is very powerful, but not as powerful as machine language.

Chapter 13
Problem Solving with Computers

MULTIPLE CHOICE		MATCHING	FILL IN THE BLANK	TRUE/FALSE
1. A	6. B	11. B	16. Module	21. TRUE
2. C	7. D	12. D	17. Loop	22. FALSE
3. B	8. C	13. C	18. Pseudocode	23. TRUE
4. A	9. B	14. E	19. Syntax	24. FALSE
5. D	10. D	15. A	20. Coding	25. FALSE

26. How does "structured programming" and "top-down" design help you debug a program? What happens if you did not use them?

If you use structured programming and top-down design, you are writing your program in small modules. Each module is checked before you go on to the next one. If there is a problem in your program, it must be with the most recent module. If you do not use this method, your error could be anywhere in the program.

27. What are the four steps to writing a program?

a. Understand the problem. (Put it in your own words.)
b. Develop an algorithm. (Design a solution.)
c. Code the algorithm. (Write the program.)
d. Test and debug the program. (Check it!)

Chapter 13
Problem Solving with Computers

MULTIPLE CHOICE		MATCHING	FILL IN THE BLANK	TRUE/FALSE
1. A	6. A	11. C	16. Algorithm	21. FALSE
2. C	7. C	12. B	17. Flowchart	22. FALSE
3. D	8. C	13. A	18. Boot	23. FALSE
4. D	9. B	14. D	19. Configuration	24. TRUE
5. B	10. D	15. E	20. Stepwise refinement	25. TRUE

26. What is the difference between "simple sequence" and "selection"?

In simple sequence, every command is executed one after the other in turn. In selection, different commands may be performed. The computer makes the decision based on certain circumstances.

27. What is the difference between a "dedicated" and a "general-purpose" computer?

A dedicated computer is designed to do only one task, like the computer in a digital clock or microwave. A general purpose computer is design to accept different programs. A computer can do any task as long as it has the program for it.

Chapter 14
Getting Started with HyperCard

MULTIPLE CHOICE		MATCHING	FILL IN THE BLANK	TRUE/FALSE
1. A	6. A	11. A	16. Script	21. False
2. D	7. D	12. C	17. Home stack	22. False
3. C	8. C	13. D	18. Card	23. False
4. C	9. B	14. E	19. Browse	24. False
5. B	10. D	15. B	20. Background	25. True

26. A LEGO set is a toy similar to an erector set with many building blocks that can be assembled in different ways. Why is HyperCard considered the LEGO set for software?

HyperCard allows users to "build" personal application software. A piece of HyperCard information can be connected to any other piece, much like pieces in a LEGO set.

27. Why are programs like HyperCard becoming more necessary?

Computers are becoming more advanced and more complicated to program. HyperCard makes the programming much easier.

Chapter 14
Getting Started with HyperCard

MULTIPLE CHOICE		MATCHING	FILL IN THE BLANK	TRUE/FALSE
1. B	6. B	11. A	16. Button	21. True
2. D	7. C	12. B	17. Link	22. False
3. A	8. C	13. D	18. HyperCard	23. True
4. C	9. A	14. E	19. Home card	24. False
5. A	10. D	15. C	20. Foreground	25. False

26. Why does HyperCard have three different kinds of pointers? What does each one do?

Each of the three pointers is used for a different task. The I-Beam pointer is used for text. The arrow pointer allows you to select menus. The browse pointer is used for "browsing" or looking around.

27. How can you move a message box from one part of a screen to another?

First, place the pointer over the bar at the top. Then, hold down the mouse button. Next, use the mouse to drag the picture to the new location. Finally, let go of the button.

Chapter 15
Authoring with HyperCard

MULTIPLE CHOICE		MATCHING	FILL IN THE BLANK	TRUE/FALSE
1. D	6. B	11. B	16. Transparent	21. True
2. B	7. A	12. A	17. Rectangle	22. False
3. A	8. B	13. D	18. Authoring	23. True
4. C	9. D	14. C	19. Trait	24. False
5. C	10. A	15. E	20. Scrolling Field	25. False

26. List three things you need to do when planning a new stack.

(Any three of these:)

a. Planning the background and foreground.
b. Designing the fields.
c. Designing the buttons.
d. Determine a card size, a name for the card, and what folder to save the card in, essentially its characteristics or traits.

27. What is special about the readymade buttons?

These buttons come with HyperCard. They already have their own scripts and have been pre-programmed.

Chapter 15
Authoring with HyperCard

MULTIPLE CHOICE		MATCHING	FILL IN THE BLANK	TRUE/FALSE
1. B	6. A	11. B	16. Opaque	21. False
2. D	7. C	12. A	17. Shadow	22. True
3. A	8. D	13. E	18. Trait	23. False
4. D	9. B	14. C	19. Authoring	24. False
5. C	10. A	15. D	20. Rectangle	25. True

26. Why was authoring developed?

It was developed to make programming easier for today's more complicated computers.

27. List 4 of the 5 styles a field can have.

(Any 4 of these:)

Transparent, Opaque, Rectangle, Shadow, Scrolling

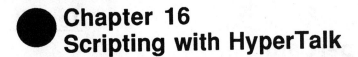

Chapter 16
Scripting with HyperTalk

MULTIPLE CHOICE		MATCHING	FILL IN THE BLANK	TRUE/FALSE
1. A	6. D	11. C	16. Idle	21. True
2. B	7. A	12. A	17. MouseUp	22. False
3. C	8. C	13. E	18. Syntax Error	23. False
4. C	9. B	14. D	19. System Message	24. True
5. A	10. A	15. B	20. Keyword	25. False

26. What is the difference between the messages *mouseDown* and *mouseStillDown?*

MouseDown means a system message is sent when the mouse button is pressed down. MouseStillDown means a system message is repeatedly sent while the button has been held down.

27. What is the purpose of HyperTalk comment statements?

These comments help document the program and make it easier to read.

Chapter 16
Scripting with HyperTalk

MULTIPLE CHOICE		MATCHING	FILL IN THE BLANK	TRUE/FALSE
1. B	6. C	11. E	16. MouseDown	21. True
2. A	7. A	12. D	17. System Error	22. False
3. C	8. B	13. C	18. Comment	23. True
4. B	9. D	14. A	19. Send	24. False
5. D	10. A	15. B	20. Handler	25. False

26. Which handlers are used in every HyperTalk script? Why?

On and End. All scripts begin with *on* and end with *end*. The Do keyword is used to execute any script, but it is not used IN the script.

27. What rules must you follow if you are creating a name in HyperCard? Give some examples of appropriate names.

a. They must begin with a letter.
b. They can contain more letters, numbers, and the underline character.
c. Should be meaningful to the programmer.
d. Should not contain negatives.
e. Can be any length.

Examples: NETPAY, INCOME1992, FOUND, TEAM1, TEAM2, HOME_TEAM

Appendix C

Answers to HyperCard

HyperCard Notes for the teacher.

These stacks are intended to be an extension of the teacher's talents and the *COMPUTER LITERACY SYSTEM.* They are not intended to be the sole source of student information. They can be used as introduction to a new topic, to be followed up on or reinforced by the teacher. They can also be used as follow-up for reinforcement to a teacher's introduction.

These stacks are very self-explanatory, and navigation through them is simple. However, knowledge of the buttons shown below will be necessary.

This button is used to return to the beginning of a particular section of a stack.

These buttons are used to simply move from one card in a stack to another.

If any other information is needed about navigating through these stacks, it will always be given on the screen.

It is suggested that the teacher become familiar with these stacks before they are given to students so that the teacher can provide assistance if needed.

Each stack ends with a summary of objectives and a chance to review any of the stack's sections by clicking on a button.

REQUIREMENTS AND INFORMATION

• Any Macintosh with two megs of RAM and HyperCard v.2.0 or later.
• The font Helvetica, in sizes 9 through 24, will be required for proper screen results.
• The stack protection password is Hornet (this is not case specific).

The Parts of a Computer System

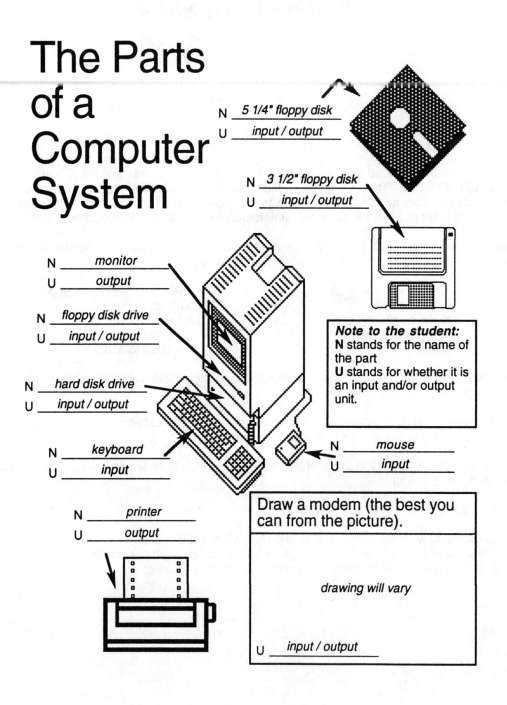

N _____ 5 1/4" floppy disk _____
U _____ input / output _____

N _____ 3 1/2" floppy disk _____
U _____ input / output _____

N _____ monitor _____
U _____ output _____

N _____ floppy disk drive _____
U _____ input / output _____

N _____ hard disk drive _____
U _____ input / output _____

N _____ keyboard _____
U _____ input _____

N _____ printer _____
U _____ output _____

Note to the student:
N stands for the name of the part
U stands for whether it is an input and/or output unit.

N _____ mouse _____
U _____ input _____

Draw a modem (the best you can from the picture).

drawing will vary

U _____ input / output _____

Anatomy of a 3.5" Disk

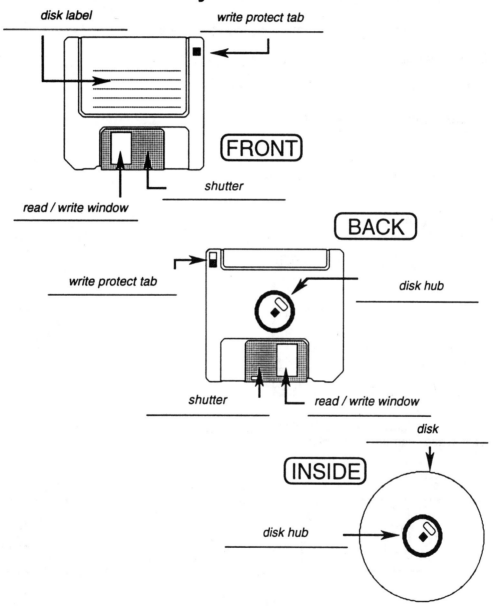

disk label

write protect tab

FRONT

shutter

read / write window

BACK

write protect tab

disk hub

shutter

read / write window

disk

INSIDE

disk hub

Answers to HyperCard Stacks Worksheets

Chapters 1 & 8   The Parts of a Computer System—Worksheets Answers

1. Used to display the title of the disk and/or a list of the disk contents.

2. Used to protect the area of the disk that the computer needs data from and writes data to.

3. An open area in the shutter that allows the disk drive's real/write head to get to the disk surface when the shutter is open.

4. Used to protect a disk from having something saved on it or erased from it.

5. Slide the tab all the way up so that a square hole is left in the disk.

6. Slide the tab all the way down so that the square hole is covered.

Chapter 2   The Macintosh: An Introduction—Worksheet Answers

1. desktop

2. It is on the desktop that you will place the things you will work with.

3. icons
display their contents
windows

4.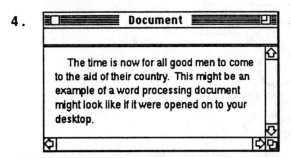

5. Pictures, on the screen, that are used to represent something. Clicking or double clicking ususaly makes something happen.

6. a. containers   b. application   c. documents

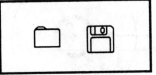      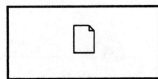

7. To push the mouse button down and let it go two times very quickly.

8. **a.** Causes that icon to open a window and show you its contents

b. The program will open and run itself in your computer.

c. It will first open the program that was used to create that document and then it will open the document in a window.

9. a. Point at the icon
   b. Press the mouse button
   c. Drag the icon to the new position

10. a. From one disk to another disk
    b. From one folder on a disk to another folder on the same disk.

11. Display menu titles

12. Selections "pull down" from that title

13. a. Point at the menu title
    b. Press the mouse button

14. A menu that is used when a menu command has a set of its own commands.

15. The menu command will be marked with a " ▶ ".

Chapter 2   Macintosh Windows—Worksheet Answers

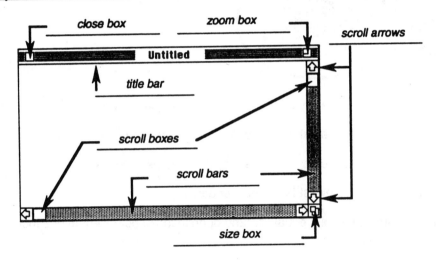

Title Bar: displays the title of the disk, folder, or document whose contents are shown in the window. You also can point, press, and drag on the title bar to move a window.

Close Box: used to close a window. Simply point and click on it to close the active window.

Zoom Box: used to quickly expand a window to its maximum size. Simply point and click on it to enlarge the window to its maximum size or reduce it to its original size.

Size Box: used to change the size or shape of a window. Simply point, press, and drag to change the window to the desired size or shape.

Scroll Arrows: used to slowly change the view inside a window. Simply point and click or press to change the view up and down (vertically) or left and right (horizontally).

Scroll Bars: used to more quickly change the view of the contents in a disk, folder, or document. Simply point and click inside a scroll bar to change the view in that window.

Scroll Boxes: used to quickly change the view of the disk, folder, or document's contents. Simply point, press, and drag the the scroll box up and down (vertically) or left and right (horizontally) to change the view in that direction.

Chapter 3   Desktop Publishing—Worksheet Answers

1. The use of a personal computer, special software, and a printer to produce professional-looking documents suitable for publication.

2. text; clip art

3. Deciding on how the pages of a document will look. In other words, where text and clip art will go in relation to one another.

4. Preparing text for printing by setting it in the selected type. This would include decisions about the size, style, and typeface of the text.

5. A representation of how a page will look when printed, with all the page elements in place.

6. The relationship between a block of text and a graphic image.

7.

8. The style or shape of letters; a family of type that has a common design.

9. A complete set of characters in a particular typeface, type size, and type style.

10. The size of a character, measured by a standard system that uses points.

11. The highest letter; ascender; lowest letter; descender.

12. A unit of type measure. One point equals 1/72nd of an inch; 72 points equal one inch.

13. 36
    1/4"

14. One of the small lines that decorate the edges of text.

15.

16. A typeface that does not use serifs to embellish the edges of text.

17.

![A in square and A in circle]

18. A variety of characters, usually symbols of some kind, that aren't shown on the keyboard. These characters are accessed by using the shift/option/control keys in combination with other keys.

19. The portion of a letter or character that extends above the X height.

20. Apple

21. The portion of a letter or character that extends below the X height.

22. Apple

23. The vertical distance between two lines of type, measured from baseline to baseline.

24. The invisible line upon which type rests.

25. Computers are a tool for the future.

26. Adjusting the space between a pair of letters.

Chapter 4   Database Introduction—Worksheet Answers

1. a. Information or facts
   b. A central location or home for storing something
   c. A central location for storing information or a collection of related facts or information

2. a. Manual: collection of information on a related subject where the information is searched and sorted by hand. Examples: telephone book, address book, mail order catalog, dictionary, cookbook, etc.
   b. Electronic: collections of information on related subjects where the information is searched and sorted by a computer.
   c. Database Management Program
   d. A program that allows you to do many different things to the data in a database.

3. a. Develop a format for the data
   b. Enter data into the database
   c. Retrieve data from a database
   d. Print information from a database
   e. Sort and search for data in a database

4. Sort and search for data in a database

5. a. File: all of the information stored on a related topic.
   b. Record: each set of related data that is in a file
   c. Field: each individual fact that is in a record

6.   Record   Field

```
        California                              Texas
State Flower:  Golden Poppy          State Flower:  Bluebonnet
  State Tree:  California Redwood       State Tree:  Pecan
  State Bird:  California Valley Quail   State Bird:  Mockingbird
  State Song:  I Love You, California    State Song:  Texas our Texas
 State Motto:  Eureka (I have found it!) State Motto:  Friendship
State Nickname:  Golden State      State Nickname:  Lone Star State

         New York                              Ohio
State Flower:  Rose                  State Flower:  Scarlet Carnation
  State Tree:  Sugar Maple             State Tree:  Buckeye
  State Bird:  Bluebird                State Bird:  Cardinal
  State Song:  I Love New York         State Song:  Beautiful Ohio
 State Motto:  Excelsior (Ever Upward) State Motto:  With God, all things are
State Nickname:  Empire State                        possible.
                                   State Nickname:  Buckeye State
```

Chapter 5   Telecommunications—Worksheet Answers

1.   **a.** nationwide
     b. worldwide
     c. cross town

2.   To talk (communicate) at a distance. When using a computer, telecommunications means to transmit signals (messages) from one computer to another.

3.   **a.** telephone
     b. computer
     c. modem
     d. telecommunications software

4.   A device that allows a computer to exchange (send and receive) information over telephone lines.

5.   Computers and phones send signals that are of different types.

6.   Analog; digital

7.   Translator

8.   The modem converts them into digital signals that the computer can understand.

9.   The modem converts them into analog signals that the phone can transmit.

10.   E-mail is short for electronic mail. It is a way of sending and receiving messages electronically through your computer.

11.   Electronic bulletin boards provide inexpensive software, places to find out information on particular subjects, e-mail, and many other services.

12.   **a.** news
     b. entertainment
     c. weather
     d. travel
     e. sports
     others: education, software, airline reservations, shopping, and technical & professional data

Chapter 6   Spreadsheet Introduction—Worksheet Answers

1.
```
    154
  + 104
    258
```
Answers will vary

2.   To make the problem easier to solve with less chance of error.

3.   **a.** Manual: calcuations are done by hand
      b. Electronic: calculations are made by the computer

4.   **a.** faster
      b. less chance of error
      c. neater

5.   Drawings will vary. However, all should show a series of intersecting columns and rows labeled with letters and numbers, respectively.

Chapter 8   Computer Memory—Worksheet Answers

1.   The place where a compuer stores data.

2.   Chemically; brain

3.   Electronically; computer chips; computer

4.   Instructions for your heart to beat, instructions for your lungs to breathe.

5.   Read Only Memory (ROM)

6.   When you get a textbook, you expect that the information is already in it and that it will be permanent.

7.   Random Access Memory (RAM)

8.   It is erased.

9.   When you get notebook paper, you expect that the paper will be blank and storage of data on this paper is temporary. It can be erased or thrown away.

10.   Bytes

11.   Nibbles; bits

12.   8; any combination of 8 zeros and ones
       4; any combination of 4 zeros and ones
       1; 1 or 0

13.   Kilobytes; megabytes

14.   All answers here will vary depending upon what random problems are generated by the stack.

Chapter 12   Programming Languages—Worksheet Answers

1. A set of instructions that can be understood both by people and computers.

2. Answers will vary but all should note differences in ease of use, speed, and user friendliness.

3. **a.** Machine
    b. Assembly

4. **a.** BASIC
    b. Pascal
    c. COBOL
    d. Logo
    e. Fortran

5. **a.** LISP
    b. Prolog

6. through 8. Answers will vary depending upon the language chosen.

Chapter 13   Problem Solving—Worksheet Answers

1. A modular approach to programming that emphasizes dividing a program into small logical sections. This makes the program easier to understand.

2. A way of designing programs where you begin with a big problem and then break it down into smaller more detailed steps.

3. The process of repeatedly refining or adding details to the steps in a top-down solution design. You are gradually breaking the steps down into smaller and smaller parts.

4. Set of steps, shown in logical order, that are needed to solve a particular problem.

5. Symbolic chart, drawing, or diagram showing the set of steps needed to solve a problem.

6. A description, in English, of a solution to a problem; written to aid in coding a problem.

7. through 9.   Answers will vary.

10.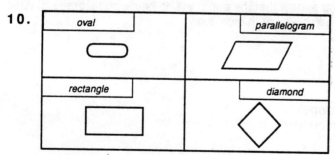

11. Open the jar—rectangle
    Is the pizza done yet?—diamond
    Begin—oval
    Add the cheese—parallelogram

12. Flowcharts will vary.

Chapter 14. Getting Started with HyperCard-Worksheet Answers

1. The browse tool.

2. Button.

3. HyperCard automatically saves all insertions and changes as they occur.

4. Field.

5. The background.

6. By choosing "New Card" from the Edit menu.

7. By choosing "Recent" from the Go menu.

Chapter 15. Authoring with HyperCard—Worksheet Answers

1. Transparent, opaque, rectangle, shadow, and scrolling.

2. Select "New Stack" from the File menu.

3. Select the button tool, double-click on a button, choose "icon" from the button dialog box.

4. By selecting the Auto Highlight in the button dialog box.

5. Stripes or slashes in the menu bar.

6. Text can be edited in a word processing fashion and it can be searched.

7. Select the field tool, double-click on a field, read the field name from the field dialog box.

Chapter 16. Scripting with HyperCard—Worksheet Answers

1. Scripting is the only level which allows programs to be written with HyperTalk.

2. Commands.

3. The next card in the stack is displayed.

4. A variable which can be used throughout HyperCard for any session.

5. A variable which can be used only in the handler in which it was created.

6. Messages.

7. Object.

Appendix D

Learning System

WEST'S COMPUTER LITERACY SYSTEM includes a dynamic new computer-based instructional program (the *Learning System*) that complements WEST'S COMPUTER LITERACY SYSTEM and assists computer teachers in effectively instructing students with varying abilities and interest levels.

Based on Rosenshine and Stevens' (1986) General Model of Effective Instruction, each computer-assisted lesson has five instructional components:
  (1) **Presentation** (e.g., proceed in small steps but at a rapid pace)
  (2) **Guided Practice** (e.g., high frequency of questions and overt student practice)
  (3) **Correctives and Feedback** (e.g., quick, firm, and correct, responses can be followed by another question or a short acknowledgment of correctness)
  (4) **Independent practice** (e.g., practice is directly relevant to skills/content taught)
  (5) **Periodic or "unit" review** (e.g., systematic review of previously learned material)

Effectively utilizing the capabilities of three common classroom computers (the Apple IIe/GS, Macintosh LC, and IBM 30 and above), each hands-on computer lesson features *learning objectives, instructional models, periodic learning checks, vocabulary, suggested enrichment activities,* and *skills application activities* that correspond to those listed in the Teaching Resources sections of the INTEGRATOR. Most importantly, each lesson is highlighted by ample use of still frames and full-motion vignettes as well as illuminating graphic art that brings computers and computer concepts to life. Within each chapter, students may click on highlighted items to see written and pictorial definitions of each new word or concept. Teachers may use the video library to review or choose both written definitions and full-screen, digitized illustrations.

As a classroom system, the system allows teachers to enliven their presentations, capturing the attention of the MTV general with animation, video narrations, and colorful, illustrative figures, easily issued from a single source: the computer screen. Teachers can also directly access the *Video Library* by clicking on descriptive buttons, and so expeditiously choose still and full-motion video for classroom display.

Students are guided through each lesson by clear and ample icons and control buttons which empower students without overwhelming them with choices. Flexibility is built into the system and allows for use control; students may proceed in a strictly linear flow, or may choose their own learning path through each lesson based on their interest and ability. Most system input is by computer mouse or joystick, and does not require typing proficiency. Teachers have a variety of options in directing the use of the system. Students may be individually guided through specific paths, or they may work together in cooperative learning groups utilizing the discovery method. Innovative teachers will surely create other methods which allow the *Learning System* to become part of their personal teaching style.

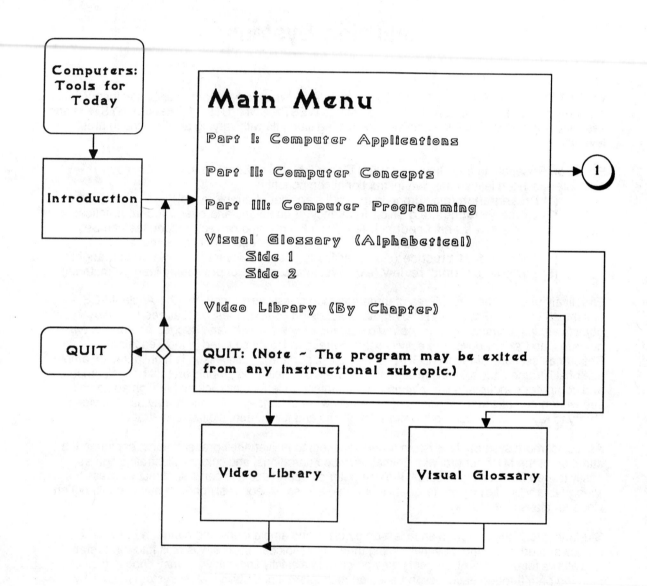

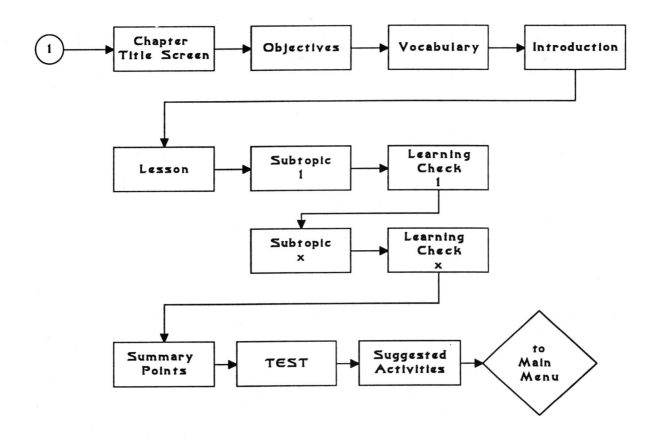